Co-Innovation Platforms

Tammy L. Madsen · David Cruickshank

Co-Innovation Platforms

A Playbook for Enabling Innovation and Ecosystem Growth

Tammy L. Madsen
Santa Clara University
Santa Clara, CA, USA

David Cruickshank
SAP
Palo Alto, CA, USA

ISBN 978-3-030-75976-6   ISBN 978-3-030-75977-3 (eBook)
https://doi.org/10.1007/978-3-030-75977-3

© The Editor(s) (if applicable) and The Author(s), under exclusive license to Springer Nature Switzerland AG 2022

This work is subject to copyright. All rights are solely and exclusively licensed by the Publisher, whether the whole or part of the material is concerned, specifically the rights of translation, reprinting, reuse of illustrations, recitation, broadcasting, reproduction on microfilms or in any other physical way, and transmission or information storage and retrieval, electronic adaptation, computer software, or by similar or dissimilar methodology now known or hereafter developed.

The use of general descriptive names, registered names, trademarks, service marks, etc. in this publication does not imply, even in the absence of a specific statement, that such names are exempt from the relevant protective laws and regulations and therefore free for general use.

The publisher, the authors and the editors are safe to assume that the advice and information in this book are believed to be true and accurate at the date of publication. Neither the publisher nor the authors or the editors give a warranty, expressed or implied, with respect to the material contained herein or for any errors or omissions that may have been made. The publisher remains neutral with regard to jurisdictional claims in published maps and institutional affiliations.

Cover credit: David Cruickshank

This Palgrave Macmillan imprint is published by the registered company Springer Nature Switzerland AG
The registered company address is: Gewerbestrasse 11, 6330 Cham, Switzerland

To Julie, Chelsea and Jaclyn Cruickshank, who without hesitation or failure, continuously support me with their love, time, empathy and endless encouragement. It was foundational to this entire endeavor for which I am forever grateful
—*David Cruickshank*

To Stephen Loy and James L. Madsen
—*Tammy L. Madsen*

To all the co-innovators who inspired this work…

Preface

It was a sunny afternoon in September of 2009 at the Leavey School of Business, Santa Clara University (SCU), when a colleague, Professor Manoochehr Ghiassi, stopped by Tammy's office to ask if she would serve as a thesis advisor for a student in SCU's Master of Science in Information Systems (MSIS) program. He mentioned the student was a Director at SAP and had a unique project proposal. Professor Ghiassi thought the thesis topic was at the intersection of strategy and IS, would I take a look? And that is where our, David and Tammy's, co-innovation began. The thesis, exploring the efficacy of SAP's first co-innovation enablement platform, was completed in 2010 and David graduated. Since that time, we have presented different parts of the project at the Academy of Management Conference, the Strategic Management Society Conference, the World Open Innovation Conference, the Druid Conference, and the Strategic Management Review's Conference on Open Innovation.

David continued to direct SAP's first co-innovation platform in Palo Alto, California, referenced as the Co-Innovation Lab or COIL. As COIL evolved, we iterated between practice and scholarship to develop the co-innovation platform model and how it contributed to ecosystem growth. In so doing, we were frustrated somewhat by the plethora of definitions that existed for ecosystems. We viewed this as the ecosystem soup effect—everything was beginning to be labeled as an ecosystem and a variety of studies and consulting firms offered different guidance regarding ecosystem strategy. The platform literature was more coherent but research tended to focus largely on transaction or hybrid platforms and this focus served as an anchor for theory as well. Where did the phenomena fit? If it was not like hybrid platforms such as Apple's iOS platform or Google's Android; it also was not similar to a transaction platform, such as those used by eBay, Airbnb, or Uber. It had some attributes in common with industry platforms discussed in early insightful work by Annabelle Gawer and Michael A. Cusumano but also differed dramatically in other ways. In our view, scholarly work lacked other innovation platform models that actively worked with complementors to create partnerships and provided resources and capabilities to help complementors *co-innovate*. The platform's degree of resource openness is one of its distinguishing characteristics—it plays a vital role in shaping innovation in an ecosystem and enabling a wide range of cross-industry co-innovation projects.

As we integrated ideas from work on open innovation, strategy, ecosystems, and platforms, we wondered what might be the best avenue for sharing the model. We also wanted to share the ideas with a broad audience. A book format allowed us to do so and gave us an opportunity to elaborate on the ideas, share multiple rich case studies, and devote attention to making the ideas actionable.

Fast forward 10 years: We continued to meet to discuss co-innovation and the platform model. By this time, SAP had established 14 more co-innovation platforms across the world; the additional locations were designed based on best practices from the first platform located in Palo Alto, California. We began to take a closer look at data on co-innovation projects, searching for patterns and trends. How were partners using the platform? What did they value? What value did they capture? Did complementors mostly pursue a single project or engage in serial co-innovation? If complementors engaged in more than one project, did they work with the same partners, other complementors affiliated with the platform, or firms external to the ecosystem? We observed a variety of patterns and recognized the need for more in depth analysis of multiple cases. We also wanted to spend more time speaking with co-innovation project participants. Additionally, David was struck by the number of companies and organizations that approached him about replicating the model. The interest and imitation reinforced the value of the model and motivated us to continue our pursuit.

During this period, our jobs also evolved. David moved from Director of SAP COIL Palo Alto to a new role as Vice President, SAP Multicloud Service and Operations (DevOps). Tammy was promoted to Full Professor, awarded the W. M. Keck Foundation Chair at SCU, and served as Associate Dean at the Leavey School of Business; she also was elected to, and served on, the Board Governors of the Academy of Management, and continues to serve on the Advisory Board of the Global Innovation Institute (GInI).

While our new roles were fairly consuming, we continued to meet to discuss co-innovation. Each meeting brought new ideas—it was the epitome of practice meets academic work. David would stop by Tammy's SCU office to chat about our evolving book proposal but the conversations always led to an increased understanding of what chronically contributes to successful co-innovation outcomes. While each meeting began with a focused agenda, the richness stemmed from David's stories of recent or past co-innovation project cases, from conversations with co-innovators, and from platform events. After these meetings, Tammy and David would step back and think about how lessons from the cases and insights from co-innovators shaped our understanding of the platform model. What new lessons were learned? Also, during this period, a burst of new studies on ecosystems and platforms emerged, advancing our understanding and informing our framing. As a result, the book benefits from a growing set of rich empirical and theoretical studies. As a preview, the book:

- Offers a novel approach for developing and maintaining a productive ecosystem—a co-innovation platform.
- Illustrates how to create and capture value from a co-innovation platform and how participating in projects with the platform can expose organizations to unexpected opportunities.
- Provides readers with strategies and practices to initiate, enable, and manage co-innovation and to advance ecosystem growth.

Santa Clara, USA Tammy L. Madsen
Palo Alto, USA David Cruickshank

Acknowledgements

The book is a result of over a decade of practice, research, and teaching in the areas of strategic innovation, platforms, and ecosystems. Over this period, various audiences—executives, SAP partners, Tammy's students, and colleagues in the academic community—helped us refine the ideas.

A huge thank you goes to Tammy's colleagues who provided detailed comments on multiple chapters and served as sounding boards for ideas, examples, figures, and concepts: Professors Michael Leiblein, Kumar Sarangee, Dara Szyliowicz, and Jennifer Woolley. We also are grateful to Anne Marie Knott and Melissa Schilling for advice and sharing their book proposals with us and to Ron Adner for insights on the book publishing process. Tammy is indebted to her support network who were always willing to hear another story about the book or the book's schedule: David Hoopes, Michael Janis, Shaohua Lu, Nydia MacGregor, Jo-Ellen Pozner, Barry Posner, Kumar Sarangee, Dara Szyliowicz, Jennifer Woolley, and Adele Xing. Classroom discussions with executives, Executive MBA students, and MBA students helped us ensure the ideas are actionable. Lastly, Tammy thanks the Leavey School of Business, the W. M. Keck Foundation, and Santa Clara University for research support.

The work of academics and business leaders studying ecosystems, platforms, open innovation, strategy, alliances & partnerships, and innovation management also sharpened and advanced our thinking: Ron Adner, Jay Barney, Carmelo Cennamo, John Carter, Michael A. Cusumano, Henry Chesbrough, Andre Delbecq, Pete DeLisi, Jeff Dyer, Raghu Garud, Annabelle

Gawer, Robert Grant, Andrei Hagui, Andy Hargadon, Connie Helfat, Prashant Kale, Rahul Kapoor, Anne Marie Knott, Michael G. Jacobides, Daniel Levinthal, Nilofer Merchant, Geoffrey Parker, Gary Pisano, Martin Reeves, Joost Rietveld, Melissa Schilling, Harbir Singh, Robert Sutton, David Teece, Marshall Van Alstyne, Andy Van de Ven, Gordon Walker, and Joel West.

David's co-innovation expertise was shaped by interactions with many people throughout his life and career. Those on the shortlist sincerely influenced the learning journey: Mildred Cruickshank, Carol Stewart, Anne Jameson, Charles Jameson I, Charles Jameson II, Dr. Landis Stewart, Joseph D. Stewart, John Harrison, Trudy McSorley, Alice Mott, Doug Miller, Jim Neal, Dr. Richard Mackinaw, Senator Donald Riegle, Don Burr, Chris Tholaug, Paul Van Gelder, Max Templeton, Thaddeus Bier, Don Bragg, Ken Tew, Pierre Saumande, Robert Thomas, Mark Yolton, and Dr. Tammy L. Madsen.

We are grateful to several executives who shared their insights and co-innovation experiences with us: Scott Allen, Kathy Barboza, Rudi Held, Sam Lakkundi, Christine Puccio, Roland Wartenberg, Tom Turchoie, and Andreas Schneider. David also thanks the entire SAP Co-Innovation Lab Team for their outstanding collaboration commitment and expertise over more than a decade to make co-innovation tangible: Axel H. Saleck, Kevin Liu, Stan Arnbrister, Roger Geddes, Manfred Pauli, Siva Gopal, Bjoern Ganzhorn, Shuuji Watanabe, Goran Stoiljkovski, Igor Pak, Rudi de Louw, Irakli Natsvlishnili, Dong Woo Lee, Vasanth Kumar, Pascal Hagerdorn, Jun Matsumoto, Peter Kulka, Hans-Joachim Odolonzski, Andrea Dellmuth, Winston Khoo, Ronildo Santos, Jurgen Opgenorth, Milau Pape, Martin Rosjat, Manjunath Chandrashekar, Sinan Tumer, Joachim Von Goetz, Peter Aeschlimann, Joerg Nalik, Igor Khrugin, and the team's always smart and supportive legal colleagues, Christoph Stieler, Andrew McDowell, and Michael Bascobet.

David also thanks those chronically supporting, advocating, and contributing to co-innovation and ecosystem innovation success: David Korn, Don Howe, Christine Brennan, Jeff Thurston, Bernd Harold, Luciano Rivera, David Hess, Sherry Yu, David Stump, Jay Thoden Van Velzen, James O'Donnell, Loraine Howell, Hardik Patel, Clark Masters, Denis Browne, Sam Yen, Larry Morgan, Alexandra Uhleherr-McGhee, Max Wessel, Rodolpho Cardenuto, Paul Hoffman, Keith Klemba, Wes Mukai, Prakash Darji, Steve Lucas, Dominick Coligliano, Stephen DeAngelis, Maria Simonians, Sven Brueckner, John Applby, Dinesh Sharma, Holly Castro-Sharp, Annie Mu Hayward, Peggy Scott, Heidi Johannsen, Raquel Fanucci, Debra

D'Armon, Zia Yusuf, Jagdish Bansiya, Sougatta Dutta, Gil Perez, Scott Leatherman, Jenny Lundberg, Chris Hallenbeck, Mike Brooks, Alex Bates, and Mark Pyatt.

We thank David's daughter, Jaclyn Cruickshank, for her creativity and graphic art skills. Jaclyn contributed to several figures in the book, including the main figure in Chapter 1.

We thank our Editors, Marcus Ballenger and Srishti Gupta, for their patience and generous assistance as we developed the manuscript for production. And of course, we thank Professor Manoochehr Ghiassi for introducing us.

Lastly, David is forever grateful for the immense and never-ending love and support of his wife Julie and daughters Chelsea and Jaclyn that without, would have made this much harder. Tammy thanks her partner, Stephen, for his enduring support. We also thank our families for their patience as our work chewed up weekends and evenings, crept into every conversation, and consumed our waking minutes…

Santa Clara, CA	Tammy L. Madsen
Palo Alto, CA	David Cruickshank
June 2021	

Praise for *Co-Innovation Platforms*

"Operational leaders working in the 21st century know the truth: the future is not created, the future is co-created. This book shows you how to use a co-innovation platform to advance innovation, scale, and growth. A refreshing read with clear, actionable insights – Co-Innovation Platforms provides that practical guidance for you to build what comes next."

—Nilofer Merchant, *An operational leader with companies like Apple, Adobe, and Autodesk, having driven 18 billion in revenues. One of the top 50 management thinkers, and top 10 HR thinkers. Author of three best selling books including the Harvard published 11 Rules for Creating Value in the Social Era*

"Tammy Madsen and David Cruickshank have developed a fresh perspective on platforms, built on both good theory and extensive practice. If you want to obtain more from your platform, get more involved with the participants in your ecosystem, and open up your resources to them – You'll get more collaborations, more innovations, and faster growth as a result!"

—Henry Chesbrough, *Professor at UC Berkeley's Haas School of Business, and Professor of Open Innovation at Luiss University, Rome*

"Innovation is seldom accomplished alone and it's high time the practice of co-innovation is laid out for organizations to build upon. David and Tammy establish the foundation for collaborative breakthroughs in their bold playbook."

—Steve Lucas, *CEO ICIMS, inc.*

"This playbook walks you through the essential, specific steps you need to take to develop an ecosystem. In the process, it gets you to think differently about what collaboration and innovation really mean, and why they are important. The book is essential reading for anyone interested in remaining relevant in business."

—Anita McGahan, *University Professor, Professor at the Munk School of Global Affairs & Public Policy, and a Professor of Strategic Management at the Rotman School of Management where she holds the George E. Connell Chair in Organizations & Society; author of* How Industries Evolve: Principles for Achieving and Sustaining Superior Performance

"David and Tammy have written an important and must-read guide for both large companies at the center of business and technological ecosystems as well as smaller firms who seek to co-innovate, enable and distribute their innovations in a scaled manner."

—Stephen F. DeAngelis, *President and CEO Enterra Solutions, LLC*

"Chock-full of practical insights and immensely useful, *Co-Innnovation Platforms* by experts Madsen and Cruickshank shares for the first time the successful method of SAP Co-Innovation Lab on stimulating innovation and ecosystem growth. Many books will tell you that ecosystems and open innovation matters: this one will show you how to make them work in practice."

—Annabelle Gawer, *Chaired Professor in Digital Economy, Surrey Business School, Director, Centre of Digital Economy (CoDE), University of Surrey, and co-author of* The Business of Platforms

"Co-innovation Platforms is a rich playbook for creating and managing ecosystem innovation. Recent case studies, involving thirty-five projects, helps the reader tangibly understand how to succeed. The authors deftly explain the important topic of value creation and capture – and show how it can be equitably shared by all."

—John Carter, *Founder and Principal, TCGen*

"Innovation increasingly requires the knowledge and creativity of multiple individuals and multiple organizations. The challenge is integrating these disparate contributions. Madsen and Cruickshank's *Co-Innovation Platforms* offers a practical and convincing solution to this challenge."

—Robert M. Grant, *Professor of Management (emeritus), Bocconi University, Milan, author of* Contemporary Strategy Analysis

"Tammy Madsen and David Cruickshank provide an excellent framing of the strategic benefits of a co-innovation platform for platform owners and co-innovation partners – from network effects to the next phase of co-innovation in the context of digital transformation using cloud and machine learning – an area I have been working on in Ag Tech for the past few years – spot on, and a cover to cover delightful read!"

—Phil Mora, *Head of Product, Vayda*

"Are you planning to create or considering whether to join a co-innovation environment? Read about a unique combination of "hands-on" platform, structured roles, and diverse interaction patterns similar to natural complex systems that creates a thriving ecosystem of diverse actors."

—Dr. Sven Brueckner, *Co-founder, CTO/Chief Scientist at ConvergentAI*

"Want to turbo-charge the scope, pace, and success rate of innovation in your organization? This playbook shows you how—through collaborative partnerships and enabling platforms, tested and proven under real-world conditions."

—Mark Yolton, *tech executive (Salesforce, Cisco, SAP, Oracle, PeopleSoft, Sun Microsystems, Unisys), board member, adjunct faculty*

"Co-innovation Platforms introduces us to an exciting "innovation in innovating" that seem to be crowd-sourcing 3.0. Whereas crowd-sourcing platforms like Innocentive seek innovations from any contributor using his/her own resources, co-innovation platforms curate access for particular innovators, and provide resources that facilitate collaboration among them. By hosting co-innovation platforms, companies have the potential to combine the best of both central R&D labs and open innovation. Better still, in the hands of University Technology Transfer Offices (TTOs), these platforms might be able to solve the "valley of death" problem that very few university inventions are commercialized."

—Anne Marie Knott, *Robert and Barbara Frick Professor in Business, Olin Business School, Washington University in St. Louis and author of* How Innovation Really Works *and Forbes contributor*

"Tammy and David's exceptional book describes the value of co-innovation platforms and shows how they can enable innovation and ecosystem growth. The book will resonate with any organization seeking to accelerate and advance its innovation capabilities."

—Michael Lynch, *CEO, Praxie.com*

"To stay ahead of the trend, companies must continually push the boundaries of their own knowledge. Often, the most disruptive solutions apply innovation from complementors to a company's existing technology. But going from ideation to application can be stymied when you don't have access to another company's technology and knowledge.

Madsen and Cruickshank show that the fastest way to fuel novel innovation and growth is through a new type of innovation platform: a co-innovation platform that takes the often-discussed theory of an innovation ecosystem and puts it into practice. This book is a must-read for anyone interested in how to collaborate to fuel innovation and growth."

—John Schneider, *Chief Marketing Officer, Betterworks*

"This book captures recipe for success on multiple fronts and offers tons of insights for entrepreneurs who are passionate about disruptive innovation and dream about fast tracking Uberization across all sectors in the age of Digital Transformation."

—Jasvir Gill, *CEO Alert Enterprise*

"Co-Innovation Platforms details the new business model for agile and breakaway innovation across a diverse ecosystem. I witnessed it in action at SAP and put simply, it works!"

—Margaret Breya, *Advisory Partner, JVP Ventures*

Contents

1	**Introduction: Co-Innovation Platforms**	1
	Ecosystems: Foundations	5
	Platform-based Ecosystems	7
	Strategy, Tactics, Questions: Where Do We Start?	9
	What are the Strategic and Organizational Benefits?	10
	Conclusion	14
	The Plan of the Book	14
2	**Platforms: Types, Governance, and Value Distribution**	21
	Platforms Types	22
	Transaction Platforms	22
	Innovation Platforms	23
	Co-Innovation Platforms	24
	Co-Innovation Platform Strategy: What, Who & How?	27
	Governing a Co-Innovation Platform	28
	Degree of Openness: Access and Resources	31
	Incentives: Mobilizing and Sustaining Participation	36
	Co-Innovation: Harnessing Complexity	39
	Harnessing Complexity via Platform Services	41
	Value Distribution	42
	Conclusion	45
	Key Takeaways	45
3	**Building a Co-Innovation Platform**	51
	Setting the Stage: Why a Co-Innovation Platform?	52

The Core Services	53
Co-Innovation Projects: From Origination to Demo & Showcase	55
Project Origination	55
Project Phases	56
Supply-Side Services	57
The Operations Management Team (Ops Team)	58
Protect and Manage	58
Information Technology (IT) System Landscape	60
Knowledge Broker Services	62
Operations Management Team: Additional Activities	67
Where Do We Collaborate?	72
The Zoo Effect	75
The Value of a Co-Innovation Platform	76
Key Takeaways	76

4 Co-Innovation Storytelling — 83

Storytelling and the Ops Team	84
Storytelling Sources and Opportunities	85
Demand-Side Services	88
Demos: Build, Run and Host	89
Documenting Project Activities and Results	93
Events	93
Marketing Content	96
Storytelling About the Platform	96
Key Takeaways	97

5 Enabling Co-Innovation as Behavior — 99

Simplify Contract Formation	100
Promote Productive and Generative Co-Innovation	102
Co-Develop a Shared Vision & Capitalize on Different Motivations	103
Foster a Climate that Promotes Knowledge Sharing	106
Encourage Iterative Learning	108
Is It All Good?	109
Fostering Buy-In	110
Co-Innovation Project Risk	110
Intellectual Property: Who Gets What?	111
Conclusion	113
Key Takeaways	113

6	**Bringing It All Together**	119
	Value Creation and Value Capture	122
	The Next Phase of Co-Innovation	124
	Digital and Cloud-based Business Transformation	125
	Final Thoughts	129
Appendix: Co-Innovation Project Case Briefs		135
Index		195

About the Authors

Tammy L. Madsen, Ph.D., is the *W. M. Keck Foundation Chair and Professor* of Strategic Management and Innovation at the Leavey School of Business, Santa Clara University (SCU). She teaches and consults in the areas of strategy, innovation, and business transformation.

Tammy's research examines topics such as temporary advantage and competitive heterogeneity, industry dynamics following a shock, and growth under uncertainty. Her work has received various awards from the Strategic Management Division, Academy of Management (AOM), including the Glueck Best Paper Award, and appears in outlets such as: *Strategic Management Journal, Organization Science, Journal of Management Studies, Industrial and Corporate Change, and Journal of Knowledge Management.* She also co-authored the fourth edition of *Modern Competitive Strategy* (2016, McGraw-Hill Press) with Gordon Walker.

Tammy is the Director of the Strategy Research Foundation's Dissertation Grant Program, Strategic Management Society, and serves on the Board of Advisors, Global Innovation Institute. She also has served on the Board of Governors of the Academy of Management and as an Associate Dean, Leavey School of Business, SCU, where she has received the University President's Special Recognition Award.

Tammy received her Ph.D. in strategy and organization (with distinction) from the UCLA Anderson Graduate School of Management. She also holds a B.S. in Mechanical Engineering (UC Santa Barbara) and an M.S. in Systems

Management (USC). She began her professional career as a test and evaluation engineer for the weapon control systems on the F14 aircraft and subsequently worked as a design engineer and program manager at Delco Electronics, General Motors. In her downtime, you'll find her surfing or ocean swimming.

David Cruickshank (MSIS, SCU) is vice president of SAP Multicloud devOps, responsible for enabling multiple lines of business to operate securely and resiliently over public cloud infrastructure from the top four public cloud providers. His teams oversee central account management, governance, security, and auditing for thousands of company cloud accounts harboring millions of virtual assets. The teams led by David originate and manage pioneering work in the migration to public cloud, and frequently share its knowledge across the company, the partner ecosystem and with customers.

Prior to leading SAP Multicloud, David spent more than a decade directing the SAP Co-Innovation Lab in Palo Alto, California. Here he remained at the forefront of leading co-innovated solutions for AI, ML, IoT, and big data for edge computing, developed with a multitude of partners from Silicon Valley and around the globe.

David's rich operational, engineering, and development skills cut across a wide range of topics ranging from cyber security product management to data center operations and edge computing.

As a recognized Industry thought leader, David has contributed to an array of articles and other publications on the topics of ecosystems-based co-innovation, AI and big data analytics, cloud platform and program development, as well as IoT edge computing for operational integrity.

David holds a B.S. in Political Science and English from Western Michigan University and an MSIS from Santa Clara University Leavey School of Business. His career spans three decades in Silicon Valley, working for a representation of high tech's best firms like Software Publishing Company, NetManage, SBE, Netscreen, Sun Microsystems, and SAP. When he's not problem solving at the edge of some cloud, David enjoys time with family and riding his longboard.

List of Figures

Fig. 1.1	Co-Innovation platform: enabling innovation and ecosystem growth	4
Fig. 1.2	The plan of the book	15
Fig. 2.1	Co-Innovation platform: network relationships	24
Fig. 2.2	Value distribution	25
Fig. 2.3	Interactions and novel intersections	25
Fig. 2.4	Continuum of resource openness	33
Fig. 2.5	Co-Innovation project: value creation and capture	43
Fig. 2.6	Co-Innovation platform: value creation and capture	44
Fig. 3.1	Co-Innovation platform: core services	53
Fig. 3.2	Co-Innovation projects: origins	55
Fig. 3.3	Co-Innovation project process	57
Fig. 4.1	Storytelling: sources and opportunities	85
Fig. A.1	Stellium Demo displayed at the SAP co-innovation platform	165
Fig. A.2	SAPNS2 HANA Intelligent Data Fusion (IDF) Platform	186
Fig. A.3	SAPNS2 HANA IDF process	186
Fig. A.4	SAPNS2 HANA IDF—data sources and flows	187

List of Images

Image 3.1	The zoo effect: a view from the lobby	75
Image 4.1	IoT and the mining industry: **a.** Co-Innovation project demo. **b.** Zoom in of co-innovation project demo	90
Image 4.2	Co-Innovation project demo recording IoT and the mining industry	91
Image 4.3	Co-Innovation project demo: simulator for IoT application in oil and gas industry	92
Image 4.4	Co-Innovation platform space: panel discussion setup with virtual participation	95

List of Tables

Table 1.1	Co-Innovation platforms: strategic and organizational benefits for partners	10
Table 1.2	Co-Innovation platforms: strategic and organizational benefits for the platform owner	13
Table 2.1	Platform governance: questions, activities, and examples	29
Table 3.1	SAP Co-innovation platform: mission and objectives	52
Table 3.2	Co-Innovation platform: core services	54
Table 3.3	Co-Innovation platform: knowledge broker activities	66
Table 4.1	Demand-side services supporting project storytelling	89
Table 5.1	Co-Innovation projects: examples of shared vision and a co-innovated solution	104
Table 6.1	Co-Innovation platforms: core tenets	120
Table 6.2	Strategic and organizational benefits for the platform owner	122
Table 6.3	Partner benefits and chapter examples	124
Table A.1	Co-Innovation project case briefs	136

1

Introduction: Co-Innovation Platforms

> A combination of things surprised me and delighted me. A group of people can accomplish something pretty cool, especially when things are uncertain.
> —Tom Turchoie, SAP CoE Spatial Expert; Co-innovation project partner while serving as CTO, Critigen

Whether you are a large or medium sized enterprise, a start-up, a partner in an ecosystem, or a platform organizer, sustaining productive innovation is not just about you. It depends on others as well as your willingness and ability to collaborate effectively. This book is about how to use, as well as develop, a co-innovation platform to accelerate innovation and sustain ecosystem growth. It will show how you, your team, and your organization can participate in, and foster, collaborative innovation among a variety of organizations that are located outside of your company's hierarchy.

Strategies and practices for building and growing ecosystems are becoming increasingly important in shaping and growing industries and markets. Value creation is no longer just about the knowledge your firm holds and the products or services it creates but is embedded in an ecosystem of firms with complementary capabilities and resources and spanning multiple sectors and technologies.[1] At its core, an ecosystem is comprised of "a set of actors with varying degrees of multilateral, non-generic complementarities that are not fully under hierarchical control."[2] The term "actors" encompasses a variety of participants operating in different industries, sectors, or institutions such as customers, competitors, complementors, entrepreneurs, and suppliers as well as public and non-profit organizations. Being multilateral and complementary, the system involves a variety of symbiotic interactions among actors with a focus on distinctive joint value creation. For instance, firms might belong to different industries, each contributing unique capabilities or knowhow to a partnership—filling resource or capability needs that other firms lack. These complementary collaborations may arise among firms that already have collaborated or among firms who have not previously collaborated. The interdependent nature of the interactions means that the collective value created by an ecosystem does not equate to the sum of its parts. Additionally, since ecosystem participants stem from different organizations and/or industries, they cannot be controlled through a classic hierarchy. As a result, the traditional strategy tools we employ at the product market or business level do not apply.

The ecosystem concept itself is not new to the business environment. Firms in a variety of sectors including automotive, banking, and retail have extended their strategic scope by coordinating value creation relationships among sets of firms for years. The digital wave and success of some of world's fastest growing companies such as Amazon, Google, Tencent, or Uber, however, has amplified awareness of the innovations and opportunities that may arise from an ecosystem strategy. It is not surprising that a rush to adopt, or perhaps the fear of missing out on unique value creation opportunities, has led to frequent use of the term. A 2019 analysis of annual reports by the Boston Consulting Group reveals that "the term ecosystem occurs 13 times more frequently now than it did a decade ago."[3] In a 2018 Accenture survey of business leaders, 50% of respondents indicated they would build ecosystems to fuel innovation and disrupt their industries and 63% viewed ecosystems as a way to participate in innovation.[4]

However, mentioning the term is easy; where firms struggle is understanding the actions needed to develop and orchestrate a robust ecosystem that supports ongoing innovation.

Using an ecosystems lens, we offer a new approach for developing and growing an ecosystem—a co-innovation platform. This model provides an environment where firms can combine or recombine ideas and/or products to generate a new solution and capture new value. A distinctive feature of a co-innovation platform is its resource-open and hands-on approach. For many firms, resource limitations, organizational obstacles, and/or time constraints often kill an idea before it takes shape. By providing access to supply-side services and demand-side services to facilitate co-innovation, the platform solves this problem. As a result, it gives firms the opportunity to explore an idea without the constraints of their own resource allocation processes and without having to deal with justifying the monetary value of the activity.

Figure 1.1 provides a preview of the model; *supply side services* are referenced as *Protect and Manage* (contract formation and management), *IT Systems Landscape, Knowledge Brokering*, and *Operations Management Team* and the *demand-side services* are referenced as *Demo and Showcase*. As one executive put it, using the platform to support a co-innovation project allows us to learn from others, combine our ideas, and in turn, develop distinctive solutions to a complex problem. As a result, his team was able to bring legitimacy and credibility to an early stage idea that served as a conversation starter in their organization—providing a foundation for next steps and informing the organization's roadmap. Before discussing the model in detail, we briefly describe the book's roots. We then highlight the ecosystem concept as a step in placing the co-innovation platform in context.

The book draws on our collective work in leading and shaping strategic innovation in organizations. Part of our journey began by experience with a platform that differs dramatically from other types of platforms. The differences motivated us to explore a host of questions: What differs? Why does it matter? How does it work? Under what conditions will it work? At the same time, the platform's approach was gaining attention not only from actors proposing co-innovation projects but also from other firms seeking to replicate it. SAP's Co-innovation Lab (COIL) is the co-innovation platform model that inspired our work; the first platform was developed in the 2007 to 2008 timeframe in Palo Alto, California, and spawned fourteen additional platform locations worldwide. Our initial model developed from David's experiences in leading the first co-innovation platform and our collective work in reviewing over two hundred and twenty-five co-innovation projects, spanning different technologies and industries, from a pool of more than 1500 projects that occurred between 2008 and 2020 across the fifteen locations. To gain a robust understanding of co-innovation work, we conducted a deep analysis of thirty-five co-innovation projects (using a random sample from the two hundred and twenty-five projects). Throughout the book we draw on these cases to illustrate the core ideas. Additionally, fifteen of the thirty-five projects are included as mini-cases or case briefs in the Appendix. Collectively, our work and case analysis is informed by project data and reports, including blogs, white papers, project images and videos, video interviews, company reports, articles, and press releases. Interviews with co-innovation project partners, Chief Technology Officers, innovation leaders, and SAP executives as well as experience in teaching the content to various audiences helped us further refine the ideas. The model also benefits from

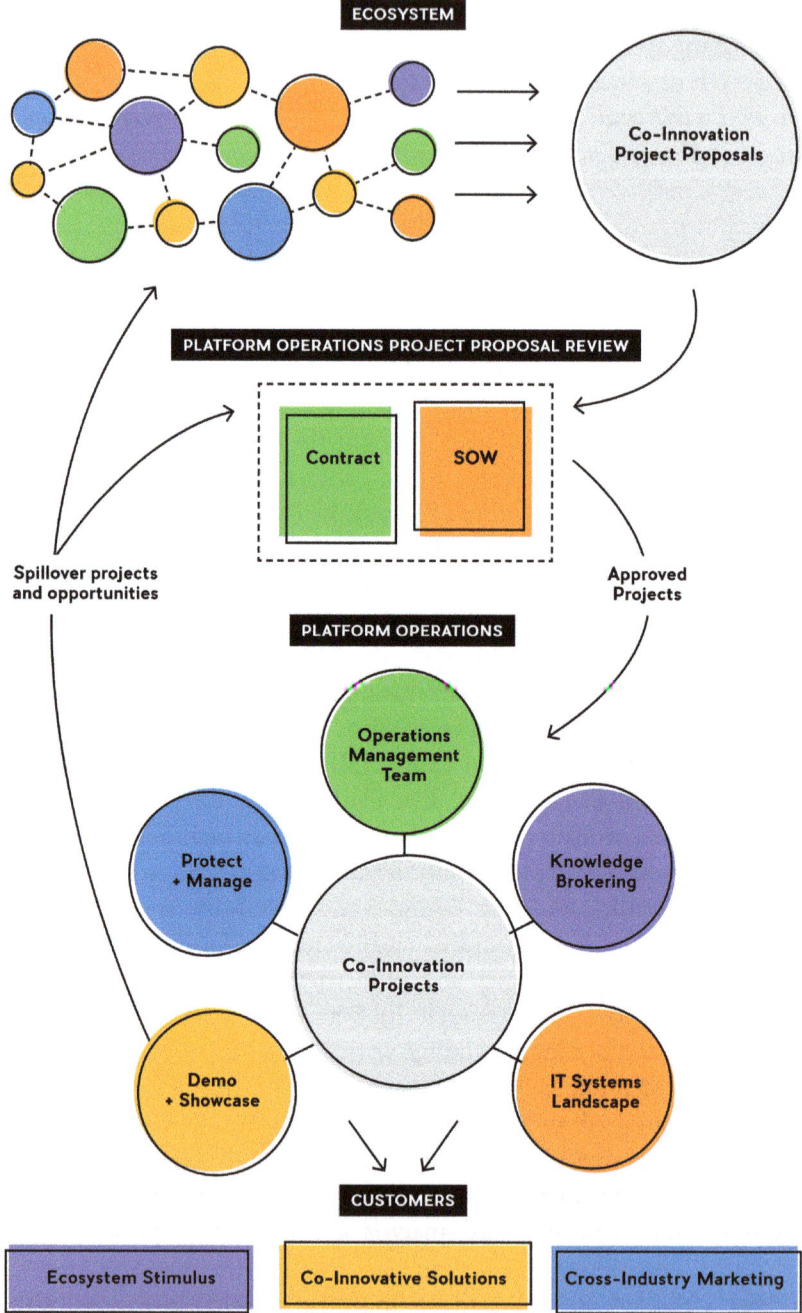

Fig. 1.1 Co-Innovation platform: enabling innovation and ecosystem growth

comparisons to other platform models. An additional set of insights stems from the rich academic work of colleagues in the areas of strategy, ecosystems, platforms, and innovation. In sum, the book provides tools and guidance for crafting a strategy to leverage this new path to ecosystem growth. Our intent is to assist readers in putting the ideas into action.

Ecosystems: Foundations

The emergence of new ecosystems, whether it be mobility, cloud, IoT, or smartphones, leads firms to wonder how they might create and capture value by participating in an ecosystem or adopting an ecosystem strategy. Building on insights from biological ecosystems, several attributes are critical to generating and sustaining an ecosystem's innovative capacity. For one, ecosystems thrive on the *engagement* of many different types of actors spanning different industries, sectors, and/or institutions (i.e., customers, complementors, competitors, entrepreneurs, suppliers, public and non-profit organizations). For example, today, the brains of cars and trucks require increasingly sophisticated software and hardware. As the sources of distinctive value shift, the traditional automotive ecosystem is transforming into a mobility ecosystem with a network of relationships among a variety of firms with different capabilities and knowledge stocks—global OEMs (Ford, GM, Nissan, Fiat-Chrysler, etc.), software and hardware providers (Apple, Google, Ericsson, Microsoft, Intel), and technology startups (Cruise, Waymo), as well as ridesharing companies (Lyft, Uber, Didi), government and regulatory bodies, and more. Many of these complementary organizations add value to the mobility ecosystem but reside outside of the traditional automotive industry. Adopting an ecosystem approach thus requires shifting one's mindset, or as Ron Adner advocates, "using a wide lens", to consider all relevant actors that exist outside the industry in which a firm competes.[5]

Next, *multiple direct and indirect interactions among diverse, loosely connected actors* in an ecosystem support the sharing, creation, and recombination of ideas and knowledge. These interactions fuel the ecosystem's scope of innovation. Coordinating interdependencies that arise among different actors improves the viability of resulting innovations. In the mobility ecosystem, a variety of software companies are partnering with traditional automobile manufacturers and/or other technology companies to explore opportunities. For example, in 2020, Fiat-Chrysler developed an exclusive partnership with Waymo to co-develop self-driving vehicles whereas, in 2019, the telecom firm, Vodafone, partnered with Ford on a digital parking guidance system.

Ford also has developed an agreement with Uber and Lyft to share data through a platform, Shared Street, and a partnership with Lyft for deployment of Ford's self-driving cars. The platform provides cities and mobility companies tools to manage congestion and reduce emissions. Microsoft, a firm one might consider as loosely connected to the auto industry, has partnered with Ericsson to provide an integrated connected vehicle solution, combining Microsoft's Azure cloud service with Ericsson's connected vehicle cloud platform.[7] Why should we care? Orchestrating collaborations that are not fully under hierarchical control requires firms rely on indirect influence and is a core function of an effective ecosystem strategy. Additionally, each collaboration involves different types of non-generic or unique complementarities that shape and extend the ecosystem.[8] By providing external actors access to services to facilitate innovation from ideation to launch, the co-innovation platform model directly enables these types of collaborations.

Lastly, the *reciprocal interactions* among firms with different knowledge and expertise promote the joint evolution of their capabilities. As the firms co-evolve, they learn about each other's capabilities, uncover unique, new opportunities that lie at their intersections, and develop productive mutual dependencies. If firms are not able to interact and learn from each other, value creation stalls and the health of the ecosystem is compromised. Employing an ecosystem approach thus requires developing activities that enable reciprocal interactions among firms and support the co-evolution of their capabilities. Through the co-evolution process, firms become immersed in an ongoing cycle of learning. The repeated innovation that arises from these activities extends the use value of the system's core products or services.

In sum, a strategy that fosters the engagement of many different types of firms, enables productive connections among complementary and distant knowledge bases, and facilitates joint capability evolution that is critical to shaping and extending the innovation trajectory of an ecosystem (the bullet points below summarize the 3 strategic activities).[9]

Building a Vibrant, Productive Ecosystem: 3 Strategic Activities

- **Mobilizing:** Engaging many different types of economic actors.
- **Enabling Interactions:** Adopting practices that enable multiple direct and indirect interactions among diverse, loosely connected actors to support the sharing, creation, and recombination of ideas and knowledge.
- **Facilitating Joint Learning:** Developing activities and processes that facilitate ongoing reciprocal interactions among firms with different knowledge and expertise to promote the joint evolution of their capabilities.

In platform-based ecosystems, the platform owner or sponsor coordinates or orchestrates these activities to advance the ecosystem.[10]

Platform-based Ecosystems

As the ecosystem concept has evolved, different forms have emerged. Our solution resides in a platform-based ecosystem where the value of a platform's core service, tool or technology is extended through innovations co-developed by complementors—actors external to the platform that provide products or services that strengthen the value of the platform's core.[11] For simplicity, hereafter we refer to actors as firms. Platforms facilitate connections between people and organizations so that they can pursue an array of unique complementary relationships that otherwise might not be feasible. These connections have the potential to exponentially increase the value created by the platform and the participating actors.[12] In this form of ecosystem, the focus is on advancing the use value of the platform's core (which, in turn, extends customer use value) as compared to an innovation ecosystem where the focus is on ensuring the end user can experience the full value of an innovative solution.[13]

Building on these ideas, we introduce the concept of a co-innovation platform. The platform provisions both supply-side and demand-side resources and capabilities to firms to enable and support collaborative innovation projects that advance the value of the platform's core (see Fig. 1.1). In this context, co-innovation involves two or more firms agreeing to invest in, and share, resources and capabilities to co-create products or services involving novel content. The platform is not simply an innovation hub or lab. Instead, it is an enablement service that actively facilitates the formation and execution of partnerships for co-innovation projects. The platform's "hands-on" or resource-open approach to innovation distinguishes it from traditional "hands-off" innovation or hybrid platforms, such as Google's Android platform or Apple's iOS platform. For example, Apple provides digital building blocks for app developers such as developer guides, app management tools, and a portal to the app developer community but not physical supply-side capabilities or resources that help firms navigate the co-innovation process, including assistance with forming and managing partnerships for innovation.[14] The services provided focus on helping complementors engage in business for the platform. In other words, the "hands-off" approach involves complementors building products or services *for* the platform as opposed to *with* the platform. In Chapter 2, *Platforms: Types, Governance, and Value*

Distribution, we discuss different types of platform models and platform strategy; in Chapter 5, *Enabling Co-innovation as Behavior*, we expand on the notion of co-innovation "with" the platform versus co-innovation "for" the platform.

Mapping the ecosystem features noted above to various approaches to ecosystem growth reveals that platform leaders tend to develop different types of dynamic capabilities.[15] A dynamic capability enables a firm to alter how it makes a living to support growth.[16] As noted, some platforms take a more hands-off approach, limiting resource access primarily to digital tools and/or documentation. Partner certification programs serve as an example. Once certified, partners typically gain access to a network of firms embedded in the certifying organization's ecosystem and in turn, exposure to new market opportunities. In many enterprises, once this type of arrangement is announced, it is presumed that participating companies are merely in contractual agreement to cross-license or resell products or services. This transactional or hands-off approach supports ecosystem scale but shaping and sustaining a productive and healthy ecosystem requires more than simply growing the number of participants. Additionally, partners' failures to collaborate contribute to partnership failure rates as high as 50–70%.[17]

The co-innovation platform solves the challenges associated with the hands-off approach in two ways. The co-innovation platform's hands-on approach to partnership formation and execution equips firms with processes and services, including legal services and contract guidance, designed to facilitate successful collaboration. Further, since supply-side resources and capabilities are the heart of how a firm creates products or services, they play a critical role in the co-innovation process. In this open innovation context, the platform is not exploiting the work of external parties but instead providing a nurturing environment where these firms can collaborate over complementary resources to explore opportunities for innovation and growth. The complementarity among partners increases the likelihood of success. Co-innovation partnerships typically involve complementors but also may include the focal firm or platform. By furnishing the resources and capabilities to support this exploration, the platform becomes increasingly attractive to firms over time. In sum, the platform's "hands-on" approach is a dynamic capability itself that enables the platform to continuously grow the set of firms contributing to the ecosystem while also co-creating and shaping the ecosystem's innovation trajectory.

Regardless of the type of ecosystem or platform, the strategies and tactics for building and sustaining vibrant ecosystems are somewhat fuzzy and distinct from a traditional business strategy. For instance, it is easy to say "grow the ecosystem" but *how do you do it*? And although many scholars offer insights regarding how to orchestrate platform-based ecosystems, approaches vary in their attention to enabling co-innovation. This observation leads to a set of questions:

- What actions can be taken to attract and retain complementary innovators?
- What practices support generative benefits—where self-reinforcing feedback loops among different firms are the norm and collaborative innovation proliferates?
- How do you create a co-innovation platform that enables novel and actionable intersections to arise among firms in an ongoing way?

In the chapters that follow, we answer these questions and offer additional guidance for successful co-innovation.

Strategy, Tactics, Questions: Where Do We Start?

A critical starting point is diagnosing the challenge or opportunity facing your firm. We frame this exercise using a series of questions:

1. What problem are you trying to solve? Alternatively, what opportunity are you pursuing? The diagnosis should help you address the next question.
2. What role do you want to play? In other words, where does your firm fit in the ecosystem? Are you seeking a partner for an innovation project and/or subject matter expertise to support activities such as experimentation, testing a novel idea, or developing a new solution? Do you have the necessary infrastructure resources, capabilities, and time to support investigating a new idea that will strengthen your firm's strategic position? Are you finding that many project ideas are killed due to a lack of resources, time, clogged innovation pipeline, and/or bureaucratic processes?
3. Shifting to a platform-view, does your firm offer a core product or service where the value of the core is extended by features, products, or services developed by complementors? Are you struggling with how to engage complementors in innovative activity that aligns with your firm's strategic objectives? Alternatively, is your firm seeking ways to kickstart innovation or considering developing an innovation lab?

Diagnosing your firm's role and needs will help you make the best strategic choices for value creation via co-innovation. The benefits provided by the platform, discussed in the next section, also will inform your approach.

What are the Strategic and Organizational Benefits?

From a strategic viewpoint, the platform helps firms interested in co-innovation expand their opportunity sets by (see Table 1.1): (1) providing a space for them to pursue projects that otherwise would not be feasible due to resource constraints, (2) facilitating the creation of new projects that are not on the firms' roadmaps, (3) developing novel intersections through connections with unfamiliar partners, and (4) exposing firms to a network of diverse actors and collaborators. The resources and capabilities provisioned by the platform also assist firms in accelerating solution development. For instance, the platform gives resource constrained firms the opportunity to flesh out new ideas in parallel with an established roadmap. Collectively, these activities promote value creation and capture from co-innovation for project partners as well as the platform.

Table 1.1 also identifies an array of organizational advantages that accompany the strategic gains realized by co-innovation project partners. In particular, partners benefit from exposure to different sources of knowledge and modes of learning as well as processes to support co-innovation. In any co-innovation project, partners obviously have an opportunity to learn directly from each other. However, a benefit unobservable to partners at the outset

Table 1.1 Co-Innovation platforms: strategic and organizational benefits for partners

Strategic Benefits for Partners	Organizational Benefits for Partners
Expanding the Opportunity Set • Enabling the pursuit of projects that otherwise would not be feasible • Exposure to project opportunities not on the roadmap • Developing novel intersections through connections with unfamiliar partners • Expanding the network of potential clients and partners • Advancing value creation and value capture through co-innovation	**Learning and Knowledge Acquisition** • Vicarious learning, Spillover exposure • Recombinatory learning • Knowledge sharing, Experiential learning and Iterative development
Accelerating Development and Launch • Developing projects in parallel with an established roadmap • Accessing supply-side resources and capabilities not readily available to the firm • Accessing demand-side resources and capabilities to demo and showcase project results	**Capability Development** • Partnership formation and execution • Co-innovation • Problem-solving • Project management

is the opportunity to learn *vicariously* from other firms operating in the platform's environment and ecosystem. Through informal and formal interactions, partners gain access to knowledge and information that is located outside of their local knowledge domain, dampening any self-reinforcing biases toward existing routines and ways of working. Additionally, connecting distant and local knowledge often yields new combinations of conceptual or physical elements and in turn, distinctive co-innovation.[18] By interacting with firms from different knowledge domains or with uncommon partners, firms can extend their understanding of what is feasible. Referencing a co-innovation project he pursued with the platform while serving as the Chief Technology Officer at Critigen, Tom Turchioe[19] framed it this way:

> Take a product and combine it in a different way to get a different result that someone has not done before. It could be around integration that had not existed before. The end result is a combination that did not exist that adds value. And we did this probably 2-3 times.

Scott Allen's (Strategic Relationship Manager, Intel) experience reinforces the benefits of learning from recombination:

> The first three phases to your engagement are: technology pathfinding involving looking ahead 2-3 years, technology enablement such as enabling s/w code to take advantage of certain technologies, and solution development where we take the enabled products from technologies found 2-3 years ago, and blend them together into a solution a customer can use. There was not a venue for this type of solutions development– this is the problem that COIL (SAP's Co-Innovation platform) fixed. Without this pillar, there is a loss of value creation and capture.

Many partners in the co-innovation projects we studied viewed these vicarious and recombinatory learning opportunities as transformative. We spoke with Sam Lakkundi, Vice President, Innovation and Head of BMC Innovation Labs, BMC Software, about his initial experience tapping into SAP's co-innovation platform. At the time, Sam was the SVP and CIO at Kore.ai, a startup with an enterprise conversational bots platform. His team's co-innovation project focused on developing and integrating bots with SAP applications and platforms. Sam shared:

> What helped us was making the connections to the other partners; they helped shed light on what we should be doing and not be doing. The connections helped tremendously; as a result, we were able to expedite a lot of what we needed.

As an enablement service for co-innovation, the platform also exposes partners to a variety of processes necessary for successful co-innovation behavior. As noted above, this includes contract formation and management. For instance, if your firm seeks a partner with specialized domain expertise, the platform can broker connections to a relevant complementary firm in the ecosystem. If your firm needs to fine tune its skills in working with partners, the platform provides resources and guidance for collaboration and project execution. Design thinking and experimentation processes support co-innovation project work, providing opportunities for firms to strengthen their problem solving skills and innovation capabilities. For Sam Lakkundi's Kore team, the platform made innovation tangible. He voiced that his team walked away with lessons that expanded their innovation capabilities:

> We learned how to innovate with partners, how to innovate with software vendors and how to innovate with hardware vendors.

One multi-project participant, Kathy Barboza,[20] Head of Google Cloud Sales-NetApp, and recipient of the 2016 Top 50 IoT Specialist and Innovators Award, emphasized:

> I could throw anything in the lab and I didn't have to worry about security requirements or infrastructure requirements; they get you up and running and provide critical resources that complement our expertise.

On the platform side, strategic and organizational advantages arise from the ability to accelerate and sustain innovation and ecosystem growth in a nontraditional way (See Table 1.2). Successful innovative collaboration involves more than holding or provisioning the relevant structural antecedents to innovative activity (e.g., R&D capabilities, product innovation capabilities). A key mechanism for sustaining value creation from co-innovation in a platform-based ecosystem involves establishing a governance model that facilitates problem solving. The co-innovation platform provides the problem-setting context as well as the services, resources, and capabilities necessary to orchestrate collaborative problem solving among diverse firms spanning different industries and knowledge domains. As mentioned above, essential capabilities include processes and practices for forming and governing partnerships focused on innovation. These factors ease the process of contract formation and implementation, increasing the platform's attractiveness to external parties or complementors.

Further, growth in an ecosystem's partner network also is fueled by the platform's ability to foster relationships and new projects among unconnected

Table 1.2 Co-Innovation platforms: strategic and organizational benefits for the platform owner

Strategic Benefits for Co-Innovation Platforms	Organizational Benefits for Co-Innovation Platforms
Ecosystem Growth – Beyond tradition • Extending the network of ecosystem participants • Expanding strategic scope via co-innovation projects spanning different technologies, industries, and sectors • Seeding new growth paths • Identifying and capitalizing on unique intersections • Advancing the platform's reputation • Promoting ongoing value creation, capture and distribution	**Learning from Co-Innovation Enablement** • Partner identification and selection • Multi-lateral contract formation • Partnership governance and execution • Building Organizational Memory
Shaping and Accelerating Innovation • Enabling co-innovation • Developing and managing a co-innovation project portfolio • Extending the use value of the platform's technological system • Showcasing co-innovation outcomes and the platform's portfolio	**Capability Development** • Orchestration • Fostering generativity • Platform governance and management • Relational governance • Knowledge brokering • Co-innovation

and varied firms. A byproduct of mobilizing different partners, each who brings a different set of resources and capabilities to a co-innovation project, is sustained variety in the co-innovation project portfolio. The unique intersections (referred to as intersects) that arise between previously unconnected firms enable the platform and participating firms to develop and capitalize on distinct opportunities that are not on any one firm's roadmap. In this way, the co-innovation platform's activities seed new growth paths for the platform as well as for its partners. With this growth, the platform gains expertise in partner identification and selection, multi-lateral contract formation and partnership governance. In combination, the activities underlie the system's generativity[21]—its capacity to produce new output from a wide range of different actors. Continuously advancing the scope and content of co-innovation extends the use value of the platform's technological system or core and in turn, end customer value. Studies of innovation-focused platforms often overlook how generativity occurs, especially in contexts where the platform curates access or filter's complementor participation. A distinctive feature of the co-innovation platform model is its ability to advance generativity by providing supply-side and demand-side services to support collaboration for innovation. By engaging in a set of activities over time, the platform develops a repeatable capability for ongoing co-innovation and ecosystem growth.

Conclusion

How can platform owners (or sponsors) and co-innovation partners create, capture, and distribute value from a co-innovation platform model? Informed by lessons learned from studying innovation projects spanning multiple industries and co-innovation platforms across the globe, the chapters that follow discuss the strategies and practices underlying a successful co-innovation platform. We also offer guidance regarding the dos and don'ts of productive co-innovation. Our goal is to provide a comprehensive playbook for co-innovation and its contribution to ecosystem growth. Each chapter offers insights and tools for acting on the ideas.

The Plan of the Book

The book provides a playbook for successful co-innovation using a co-innovation platform model. Chapter 2, *Platforms: Types, Governance & Value Distribution*, expands on the platform concept, highlights the differences between a platform strategy and a product strategy, and provides background on different types of platforms. We identify the governance mechanisms critical to developing and maintaining a successful co-innovation platform. As part of this discussion, we apply a strategic positioning framework to illustrate the paths of value creation and capture for a co-innovation platform and for its partners.

If you want to build a co-innovation platform, where do you start? What problem are you trying to solve? What resources, capabilities, activities, and practices make up a co-innovation platform? Chapter 3, *Building a Co-Innovation Platform*, specifies the what and how of a co-innovation platform, beginning with the platform's objectives. We provide a detailed view of the platform's supply-side services and how they operate together to generate a robust co-innovation system. Chapter 4, *Co-Innovation Storytelling*, shifts attention to the platform's demand-side services designed to generate awareness and demand through storytelling. Each co-innovation project provides various sources and opportunities for storytelling—from initial project proposal development to demos and live events. The chapter offers guidance regarding different modes of storytelling including demo development, storytelling documents (white papers, solution briefs, etc.), showcase events, and digital content.

Chapter 5, *Enabling Co-innovation as Behavior*, elaborates on the behaviors and actions that promote productive collaboration for innovation. Complementing Chapters 2 and 3, we first expand on the platform's simplified contract formation process and illustrate the operations team's role as coach in facilitating contract formation. Next, we offer guidance on how to create a platform environment that fosters mutual understanding, trust-building, and relational attachment. We conclude by considering frictions that may arise in co-innovation work and offer guidance to inform your thinking around intellectual property management in the co-innovation platform context. The practices and guidance discussed in this chapter work in combination with the co-innovation platform's equitable value distribution—reinforcing the mindset that partners are working "with the platform" vs. "for the platform."

Chapter 6, *Bringing it All Together*, recaps the core tenets and benefits of a co-innovation platform. We conclude by identifying some future directions for co-innovation with a spotlight on digital-based business transformation, cloud-based business transformation and enterprise co-innovation strategy (Fig. 1.2).

As we developed the book, we recognized that readers might explore the book in different ways. For those whose work plates are overflowing and attention spans are taxed, a quick look approach may be preferred. While

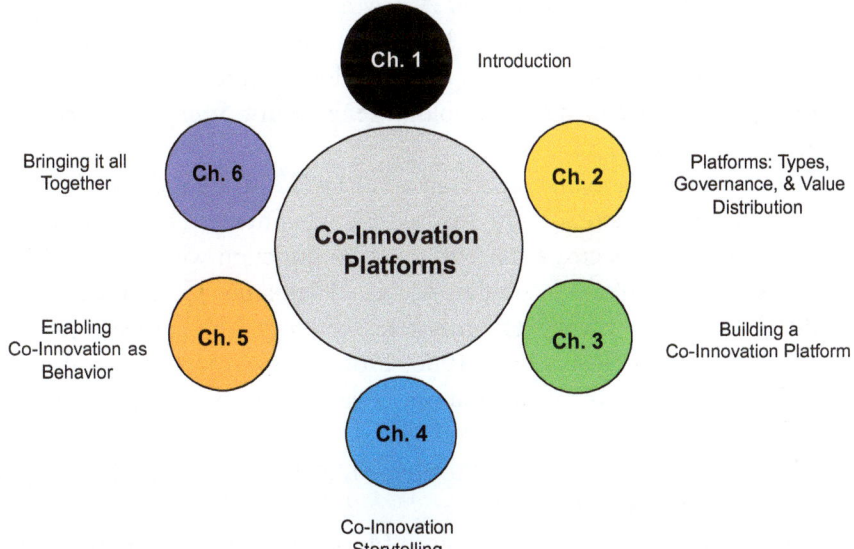

Fig. 1.2 The plan of the book

we value a reader who is inspired to trek through and soak up the chapters in order, we offer additional guidance for those seeking a quick look at one or more ideas.

- If you want to understand the model and how it works, Chapters 1 and 2 layout the foundations and Chapters 3 and 4 detail how to put the ideas into action.
- For those interested in different types of platforms, platform strategy and ecosystem strategy, Chapter 2 provides the "what, who and how" of co-innovation platform strategy and complements Chapter 1's ecosystem strategy discussion.
- "I don't care about platforms, I only am interested in co-innovation!" Chapters 1, 5, and 6 are for you.
- Lastly, for those you just want the high-level takeaways, each chapter concludes with key takeaways.

Questions, quibbles, comments? Regardless of how you approach the book, please share your thoughts and ideas. We would value hearing your co-innovation story. You can reach us at: coinnovationstrategy@gmail.com.

Notes

1. Adner, R., 2012. *The wide lens: A new strategy for innovation.* Penguin, UK; Adner, R., and Kapoor, R. 2010. Value creation in innovation ecosystems: How the structure of technological interdependence affects firm performance in new technology generations. *Strategic Management Journal, 31*: 306–333.
2. See Jacobides, Cennamo, and Gawer (2019: 2264) for a detailed discussion of complementarity in the ecosystem context. The basic idea is that a firm's assets create more value in conjunction with another firm's assets (Teece, 1986). Jacobides, M. G., Cennamo, C. and Gawer, A. 2016. Toward a theory of ecosystems. *Strategic Management Journal, 39*: 2255–2276; Teece, D.J., 1986. Profiting from technological innovation: Implications for integration, collaboration, licensing and public policy. *Research Policy, 15*(6): 285–305.
3. Pidun, U., Reeves, M., and Schussler, M. 2019. Do you need a business ecosystem? BCG Institute.
4. Lyman, M., Ref R., and Wright, O. 2018. Cornerstone of Future Growth: Ecosystems. *Accenture Strategy*, pages 1–14.

5. Adner, R., 2012. *The Wide Lens: A New Strategy for Innovation*. UK: Penguin Press.
6. Ford Media Center, September 26, 2018. Ford, Uber, Lyft announce agreement to share data through new platform that gives cities and companies new tools to manage congestion, cut greenhouse cases and reduce crashes. https://media.ford.com/content/fordmedia/fna/us/en/news/2018/09/26/ford-uber-and-lyft-agreement-data.html, accessed May 3, 2021.
7. www.ericsson.com/en/internet-of-things/automotive/partners/microsoft; https://www.eenewsautomotive.com/news/vodafone-and-ford-test-digital-parking-guidance-system, accessed May 3, 2021.
8. Teece, D.J., 1986. Profiting from technological innovation: Implications for integration, collaboration, licensing and public policy. *Research Policy*, 15(6): 285–305. For a recent discussion, see Jacobides, M. G., Cennamo, C. and Gawer, A. 2016. Toward a theory of ecosystems. *Strategic Management Journal*, 39: 2255–2276.
9. Reeves, Love, and Tillmans (2012) introduce the notion of a shaping strategy as an alternative approach when environments are unpredictable yet malleable to a firm's advantage. Fuller, Jacobides and Reeves (2019: 6) extend the idea to the contexts of ecosystems and define a shaping strategy as "collaborating with others using indirect influence (including being influenced by others), being responsive to unpredictable changes, and evolving the ecosystem for mutual benefit." Our approach is similar but expressed through three core strategic activities necessary for shaping and extending an ecosystem: mobilizing, enabling interactions (direct and indirect influence), and facilitating joint learning. Reeves, M., Love, C., and Tillmanns, P., 2012. Your strategy needs a strategy. *Harvard Business Review*, 90(9): 76–83. Fuller, J., Jacobides, M.G., and Reeves, M., 2019. The myths and realities of business ecosystems. *MIT Sloan Management Review*, 60(3): 1–9. Also see, Williamson P.J., and , De Meyer A. 2012. Ecosystem advantage: How to successfully harness the power of partners. *California Management Review*, 55(1): 24–46.
10. See Gawer, A., and Cusumano, M. 2002. *Platform Leadership: How Intel, Microsoft and Cisco Drive Industry Innovation*. MA: Harvard Business School Press; Iansiti, M. , and Levien, R. 2004. *The Keystone Advantage: What the New Dynamics of Business Ecosystems Mean for Strategy, Innovation and Sustainability*. MA: Harvard Business School Press; Teece, D.J. 2007. Explicating dynamic capabilities: the nature and microfoundations of (sustainable) enterprise performance. *Strategic Management Journal*, 28(13): 1319–1350; Teece, D.J. 2018. Profiting from innovation in the

digital economy: Enabling technologies, standards, and licensing models in the wireless world. *Research Policy, 47*(8): 1367–1387.
11. See Shiplov, A. and Gawer, A. 2020. Integrating Research on Interorganizational Networks and Ecosystems, *Academy of Management Annals, 14*(1): 92–121; Kapoor, R. 2018. Ecosystems: Broadening the locus of value creation. *Journal of Organization Design, 7*: 1–16.
12. Gawer, A., and Cusumano, M.A. 2002. *Platform Leadership: How Intel, Microsoft, and Cisco Drive Industry Innovation.* Boston, MA: Harvard Business School Press; Cusumano, M.A., Gawer, A., and Yoffie, D.B. 2019. *The Business of Platforms: Strategy in the Age of Digital Competition, Innovation and Power.* HarperCollins Publishers.
13. As a simplistic example, a smartphone ecosystem relies on complementors to create innovative apps that enhance the use value of a smartphone. In an alternative view, coordinating interdependencies among complementary organizations is necessary in order for a customer to experience the full value of a firm's innovation. Ron Adner, author of *The Wide Lens*, uses the Michelin's PAX run-flat tire innovation case as an example. Although tire and auto producers were on board, they overlooked a critical blindspot—traditional auto-repair or tire shops lacked the capabilities to repair run-flat tires. The lack of service resulted in customers replacing run-flats with traditional tires. The case illustrates why coordinating interdependencies among actors in an ecosystem is necessary to ensure a coherent customer offering. Adner, R.. 2012.*The Wide Lens: A New Strategy for Innovation.* Penguin UK.
14. https://developer.apple.com/support/, date of access November 13, 2020.
15. See Helfat, C.E., Finkelstein, S., Mitchell, W., Peteraf, M., Singh, H., Teece, D.J., and Winter, S. G. 2007. *Dynamic Capabilities: Understanding Strategic Change in Organizations.* MA: Blackwell Publishing; Helfat, C.E. and Winter, S.G., 2011. Untangling dynamic and operational capabilities: Strategy for the (N) ever-changing world. *Strategic management journal, 32*(11): 1243–1250; Helfat, C. E., Raubitschek, R.S. 2018. Dynamic and integrative capabilities for profiting from innovation in digital platform-based ecosystems. *Research Policy*, 47: 1391–1399; Teece, D.J., Pisano, G., and Shuen, A.. 1997. Dynamic capabilities and strategic management. *Strategic management journal*, *18*(7): 509–533.
16. Winter, S.G., 2003. Understanding dynamic capabilities. *Strategic Management Journal*, *24*(10): 991–995; Helfat, C.E., Finkelstein, S., Mitchell, W., Peteraf, M., Singh, H., Teece, D., and Winter, S.G.

2009. *Dynamic Capabilities: Understanding Strategic Change in Organizations.* Wiley.
17. Association Overview report, 2020. Association of Strategic Alliance Professionals, April; Hughes, J., and Weiss, J. 2007. Simple rules for making alliances work. *Harvard Business Review,* November issue; Kale, P., Dyer, J.H., and Singh, H. 2002. Alliance capability, stock market response, and long-term alliance success: The role of the alliance function. *Strategic Management Journal, 23*(8): 747–767. Other studies identify suggest a failure rate of 30–70% (Bamford, Gomes-Casseres, & Robinson, 2004). Bamford, J., Gomes-Casseres, B., and Robinson, M. 2004. *Envisioning Collaboration: Mastering Alliance Strategies.* San Francisco: Jossey-Bass.
18. See Schumpeter, J. 1939. *Business Cycles.* McGraw-Hill Book Company, Inc., New York; Fleming, L., 2001. Recombinant uncertainty in technological search. *Management Science,* 47(1): 117–132; Nelson, R., and Winter, S. 1982. *An Evolutionary Theory of Economic Change.* Cambridge, MA: Belknap Press.
19. Tom Tuchoi currently is at SAP where he serves as a CoE Spatial Expert.
20. Kathy Barboza was the Director of Software Alliances at Intel when she participated in multiple co-innovation projects at SAP's co-innovation platform in Palo Alto, California.
21. Generativity requires that platforms actively promote the participation of heterogeneous complementors (for example, see Cennamo and Santalo, 2019; Wareham, Fox and Giner, 2014). The literature explores generativity from different angles. In the simplest form, the focus is on fostering the next generation of heterogeneous complementors and in turn, supporting the creation of new products or services. Zittrain (2008: 70) applied the concept to technology where generative technologies contribute to "unanticipated change through unfiltered contribution from broad and varied audiences." Cennamo, C., and Santalo, J. 2019. Generativity tension and value creation in platform ecosystems. *Organization Science, 30*(3): 617–641; Wareham, J., Fox, P.B., and Giner, J. 2014. Technology ecosystem governance. *Organization Science, 25*: 1195–1215; Zittrain, J., 2008. *The Future of the Internet–and How to Stop It.* Yale University Press.

2

Platforms: Types, Governance, and Value Distribution

> What counts is making the most of an idea – together. Technological change has become so rapid and today's tech scene is so diverse and specialized that it would be neglectful not to join forces to bring the greatest possible value to a customer.
>
> —Rudi Held, Global Head of SAP's Co-Innovation Platforms

Platforms facilitate connections between people and organizations so that they can pursue an array of unique complementary relationships that otherwise might not be feasible. By enabling connections such as supply–demand side matching or partnerships for innovation, platforms have the potential to generate "nonlinear increases in utility and value."[1] While the platform concept has a rich history, two prominent types of platforms have emerged, transaction platforms and innovation platforms. We introduce one type of innovation platform, a co-innovation platform, where the primary strategic objective is facilitating innovation via collaborative arrangements among external actors as well as with the platform. All three platform types operate at the industry or ecosystem level and leverage digital technologies to facilitate interactions among a platform's users. Each type however has distinct strategic objectives, involves different resources and capabilities, and attracts a different mix of participants, each playing different roles. For example, Google's Android platform can be characterized as a five-sided network engaging industry verticals (advertising), telecom service operators, users, handset OEMs, app developers, and media publishers. The platform types

© The Author(s), under exclusive license to Springer Nature Switzerland AG 2022
T. L. Madsen and D. Cruickshank, *Co-Innovation Platforms*,
https://doi.org/10.1007/978-3-030-75977-3_2

also vary in how interactions are enabled and in how value is created and distributed. The chapter focuses on four key questions:

- What are the prominent types of platforms and how do they differ?
- How does a co-innovation platform create and distribute value?
- What factors underlie an effective co-innovation platform strategy?
- What governance mechanisms are critical to developing and maintaining a successful co-innovation platform?

Platforms Types

Transaction Platforms

Most people are familiar with transaction platforms, where the platform operates as an intermediary of a two-sided network, facilitating exchange among users whose interactions are subject to direct and/or indirect network effects. Classic examples of these "matchmaker" type platforms (often referenced as multi-sided markets)[2] include eBay, Airbnb, Didi Chuxing, and Uber where providers on the platform's supply-side offer products or services to buyers or end users on the demand-side. In this type of arrangement, all parties create and capture value: the supply-side of the network creates and captures value from transactions with buyers and the demand side of the network captures value from the products or services acquired in a transaction. As a network mediator, the platform creates and captures value by enabling transactions and typically, not by owning the assets used to create and deliver products or services.

Each side of the platform benefits from indirect network effects or cross-side effects, where the incremental value of the platform increases for one side when a new actor joins on the other side of the platform. The larger the number of suppliers of goods or services operating with the platform, the more attractive and valuable the platform is to buyers and vice versa. Buyers on the demand side thus seek a large number of sellers on the supply side; similarly, suppliers have a preference for continuous growth in buyers. Using Airbnb as an example, the more renters (demand-side users or buyers) that join the platform, the more valuable it is to the suppliers of Airbnb rentals—they have a larger audience to provide their offerings. Similarly, an increase in the number of suppliers of rentals yields benefits for buyers as they have more rental options. Thus, the platform grows by adding participants. However, as the number of suppliers increases, so too does competition among suppliers creating a negative (direct) same side network effect. And while one more buyer on the demand size benefits the supply side, there is limited additional value created for the existing buyers. Further, in platforms such as Airbnb, Uber, and Lyft, differences in the platform's design and governance affect the attractiveness of participating as a supplier, user or investor, and in turn, the size and distribution of gains.[3]

Innovation Platforms

Innovation platforms, such as Apple iOS, Google Android, SAP HANA, and Amazon Web Services (AWS), revolve around a core offering—a product, service, tool, or technology. Third-party innovators or complementors create products or services that enhance the functionality of the platform's core and extend its use value to customers or end users. As such, complementors make up one side of the platform and end users reside on the other side. For instance, independent software vendors create a variety of products that complement the functionality of AWS for business users. App developers and media publishers contribute apps and services to Google's Android platform. Similar to transaction platforms, the overall value of the platform increases for one side of the platform when new participants join the other side. For example, increases in the number of innovative complementors affiliated with a platform spurs demand-side interest. Similarly, platforms with the most users are more attractive to complementors.

Facilitating innovative activity with and among third-parties requires designing a core offering that is easy to access and has sufficient modularity to enable innovative development. The platform must decide how open its system, architecture, IT landscape, or technology will be to third parties. But accessing a platform's system is not the same as accessing the platform's bundle of resources and capabilities. Complementors often seek resources to support their innovations that extend the use value of the platform's core offering. As a result, an additional critical choice for innovation platform owners or sponsors resides with how much they should open-up their resource base to external parties. Innovation platforms typically offer baseline resources, such as digital toolkits, s/w integration tools, or application programming interfaces, that help complementors connect to the core's functionality. While these resources attract complementors, the platform also needs to think carefully about how to entice complementors that generate high quality, relevant, non-generic complements. These types of complementary products or services increase an end user's willingness to pay for the platform's offerings and in turn, provide value capture opportunities for the complementor and the platform. As such, some platforms in this category are hybrids—involving both transaction and innovation platform features.

Co-Innovation Platforms

We introduce a co-innovation platform where the primary strategic objective is facilitating innovation via collaborative arrangements among developers of complementary products or services as well as with the platform. One distinctive characteristic is the platform's degree of resource openness—the platform provides complementors access to supply-side services to support the formation and execution of co-innovation projects *and* demand-side services to demo and showcase project results.

Figure 2.1 illustrates the relationships among the platform's value creation and value distribution activities. Developers of complementary products or services leverage the platform's services to co-create products or services that extend the use value of the platform's core offering. However, value is not only captured by the platform; collaborators also capture value directly from their project activities and outcomes (see Fig. 2.2). This equitable approach to value distribution attracts additional developers of complementary offerings. The platform then curates or screens complementors to ensure high quality and diversity in participants as well as project alignment with the platform organization's objectives.

Additional utility arises from the informal interactions among co-innovation project teams working concurrently. These same-side network

Fig. 2.1 Co-Innovation platform: network relationships

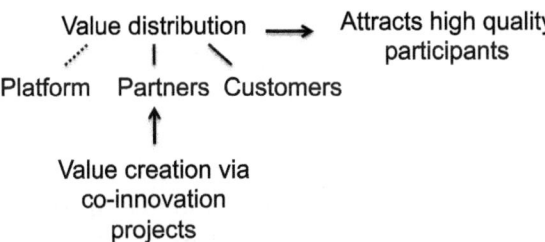

Fig. 2.2 Value distribution

benefits are enabled by the platform's integrated services and environment. The platform's physical environment is designed to promote knowledge sharing, spillovers and informal interactions among firms working on different co-innovation projects (see Chapter 3, *Building a Co-Innovation Platform*). The focus is less on efficiency and more on building and leveraging economies of innovation. The interactions among co-innovation project teams facilitate learning and knowledge acquisition, but also spawn new project ideas or novel intersections among previously unconnected partners (Fig. 2.3).

Similar to transaction platforms, a cross-side network effect exists where the platform's customers value growth in the number of complementors engaging with the platform and complementors benefit from growth in the size of the platform's customer base. The co-innovation platform's primary role, however, is not as a transaction-oriented matchmaker, facilitating a transaction between co-innovators and customers. Instead, the platform's focal task is to enable and support the development of co-innovation projects with and among diverse actors. This includes activities connecting actors with

Fig. 2.3 Interactions and novel intersections

complementary resources and capabilities as well as providing services that address a project's resource and schedule needs.

For example, GS1, a global, nonprofit, standards setting organization represented in 150 countries collaborated with SAP's co-innovation platform to solve a problem related to highway safety and truck tires. The project's objective was to digitize tire retread activities so that the tires could be monitored and repaired prior to causing an accident (regulations governing truck tire renewal vary by region). Tire treads could be renewed multiple times; however, it was difficult to track the number of retreads on a tire. Further, a tire that was banned in one country might be sent to another country and subsequently, returned to the original country for use. Visual inspection does not reveal the number of times a tire's treads have been renewed. As a result, manufacturers or warranters of the tires lack trusted information on a tire's history—making it difficult to provide warranties. Solving these problems required a technology that could provide reliable data on a tire's lifecycle management.

Collaborating with the platform provided GS1 with access to subject matter experts in the relevant technology domains. With support from the platform's operations management team (ops team), GS1 developed a tire lifecycle management prototype using blockchain and RFID technology. Nicolaus Pauvre, Project Manager, GS1 summarized the solution: "Each tire is equipped with an RFID device that uniquely identifies the tire, while blockchain records the tire mileage and service activities." "The carrier or repairer can scan the RFID tag, and read the individual tire's complete history of usage in the blockchain."[4] The history included information about any repair or retread. Given the decentralized aspect of blockchain technology, no individual participant could edit the stored data; this feature addressed the warrantor's concerns. The platform's demand-side services contributed to building awareness of the solution, and GS1 benefitted from feedback gained during live demonstrations. Subsequently, GS1 showcased the solution at various industry and supply chain events and received positive feedback and interest from managers in the automotive, rail, transport, and logistics areas. The collaboration with the platform helped GS1 increase their understanding of how different technologies could be used and implemented. Pauvre viewed the platform's services and mix of expertise as key to the partnership and valued the platform's "pleasant atmosphere of openness and trust among teams."

Given the platform's strategic objective, does a co-innovation platform yield nonlinear increases in utility over time? In *The Business of Platforms*, Michael Cusumano, Annabelle Gawer, and David Yoffie explain that an industry platform's utility strengthens as its network advances—in other words, an additional user benefits by access to other users and to innovations made available through the platform.[5] While adding a co-innovation project to the platform is beneficial, the utility created and captured by a co-innovation platform and its participants is not isolated to the project outcomes alone. As such, the benefits of co-innovation platforms are multiplicative. Engagement with the platform's integrated services exposes complementary innovators to opportunities for learning by doing, learning from others (via spillovers or direct interactions), building innovation and collaboration capabilities, accelerating innovation, and expanding their opportunity sets. For example, the results from a past project may help to solve a problem identified in a new project. An oil and gas company working on a co-innovation project observed and learned about another co-innovation project focused on augmented reality technology. The oil and gas company thought it might be able to apply the technology to maintain and repair oil rigs but lacked a partner with experience in augmented reality (AR). The platform's knowledge brokers, part of the platform's supply-side services, worked with the oil and gas company to distill their needs, identify a partner with the appropriate AR expertise, and develop a statement of work for a new co-innovation project. The platform's services helped the oil and gas company reduce uncertainty, accelerate learning, and lower project costs.

As a result, and consistent with a robust ecosystem strategy, the platform's utility strengthens with increases in the combination of different actors and activities engaged in co-innovation with the platform. By mobilizing actors, facilitating unique combinations of actors and activities, and enabling joint learning, the platform shapes the scope and content of an ecosystem's innovation activities. Co-innovation projects contribute to the growth of the platform's and complementors' existing businesses, but also spawn new business activity by giving actors resources to explore an early stage idea in an emerging business area.

Co-Innovation Platform Strategy: What, Who & How?

As mentioned in Chapter 1, the strategy development process begins with diagnosing the challenge or opportunity facing a firm: What problem is your firm trying to solve? Diagnosing a product market opportunity is very different than diagnosing a platform-based ecosystem opportunity.[6] When considering developing a co-innovation platform, the questions that need to be asked are: (1) What innovation topics/areas play a strategic role in the parent organization's future?; (2) Are there opportunities to collaborate with external organizations to accelerate innovation?; and (3) Can greater economies of innovation and complementarity be achieved through co-innovation with external organizations than by going it alone? For instance, one goal is to increase upside potential while managing downside risk.

The answers to the above questions lead to the next set of strategic choices—who and how—and flow directly from the diagnosis. Regarding scope, who are the relevant actors? A platform strategy requires shifting from a traditional product-market focus to an ecosystem focus. To ensure ecosystem generativity, scope choices must promote a diversity of actors and activities. This means that the relevant actors include unfamiliar firms as well as firms from a variety of industries or sectors. As a result, this activity requires creative thinking as the usual actors will not create sufficient diversity. Scope choices also might encompass a range of emerging technologies or a variety of verticals. For instance, the co-innovation projects in SAP's fifteen co-innovation platforms spanned twenty-six different industries (such as Aerospace & Defense, Retail, Industrial Machinery and Components, Healthcare, etc.), nine technology areas (such as Cloud, Tech Trends—Machine Learning, Analytics, IoT), and nine functional or phenomenon driven areas (such as manufacturing, services, sustainability and information security).

The next issue is about how the platform should be governed to create, capture, and distribute value via co-innovation. The subsequent section focuses on four key areas of platform governance. In Chapter 3, *Building a Co-innovation Platform*, we detail how to build and operate a co-innovation platform and expand on the activities underlying each area of platform governance.

Governing a Co-Innovation Platform

The value created in co-innovation platforms relies on collaboration with, and among, firms external to the platform and that the platform owner or sponsor (hereafter, we refer use the term 'owner' for simplicity) does not control. Given the limited formal authority over these actors, a platform owner governs the platform-based ecosystem by playing the role of orchestrator rather than director.[7] Effective orchestration requires that the platform owner recognize its role is to shape, enable, and influence distributed innovation and to integrate complementary innovations into the ecosystem.[8]

Ensuring wealth is equitably distributed among ecosystem participants that create value also is vital to maintaining quality participation and ecosystem growth. Addressing these needs and achieving the partner and platform benefits discussed in Chapter 1 requires a governance system that specifies how the platform will design and manage 5 key mechanisms summarized in Table 2.1. As a preview of each mechanism, Table 2.1 offers relevant questions, platform-specific activities, and examples; the subsequent sections discuss the activities associated with each mechanism.

Table 2.1 Platform governance: questions, activities, and examples

Governance Mechanism	Relevant Questions	Co-Innovation Platform Activity	Examples
Degree of Openness: Access	Given strategic objectives, how much should the platform open up its system (such as its architecture, s/w landscape, technology) to external actors?	• Establish rules to guide project selection. • Provide services to support contract formation.	• Executive sponsorship of a complementor's project proposal. • Simple contract templates—statement of work and frame agreements—clarify a project's access needs.
Degree of Openness: Resources	Given strategic objectives, what is the appropriate degree of resource openness? What resources and capabilities should the platform make available to external actors?	• Define the scope of supply-side & demand-side services to make available to external actors.	• Knowledge broker services providing connections to subject matter experts to support a project's needs. • Operations team assisting with demo development.
Incentives: Mobilizing and Sustaining Participation	What incentives will attract and sustain participation?	• Create services that fulfill co-innovation project needs. • Provide external actors opportunities for interaction, learning, and joint capability development.	• Knowledge broker services connecting firms with complementary resources to support a project. • Operations team identifying hidden project opportunities among unconnected partners.
Co-innovation: Harnessing Complexity	What forms of complexity are present?	• Create services that help co-innovation teams manage temporal and relational complexity. • Develop practices to guide, manage and advance the scope and scale of the co-innovation project portfolio.	• Use structures and processes that assist with project and contract formation. • Provide timely access to services (resources & capabilities) that address evolving project needs. • Use portfolio development and management tools such as Aggregate Project Planning.
Value Distribution	How should value be distributed?	Emphasize value distribution over platform value capture: • Co-innovation project partners capture value from their co-innovation projects and from active engagement with the platform. • The platform captures value from co-innovation projects that extend the use value of the platform's core offering and from active engagement with a variety of external actors.	• Emphasize co-innovation "with" the platform vs. "for" the platform.

The governance choices for a platform environment differ from those used to manage product or service innovation activities within an organizational hierarchy. First, since complementors operate outside of the platform organization's hierarchy, the platform lacks authority over them. As a result, platform leaders must incentivize complementors to participate with the platform. A counter example is product innovation occurring within an organizational hierarchy where managers have authority over project teams. Additionally, co-innovation platform owners need to identify the extent to which they should open up their resources and capabilities to complementary organizations to support innovation. On the other hand, product developers within an organization are charged with protecting their resources and capabilities from imitation. Sustaining ecosystem growth via a co-innovation platform requires encouraging actors outside of an organization's hierarchy to collaborate to generate non-generic innovations that extend the use value of the platform's core offering. This outside-in approach to innovation contrasts with traditional approaches where the locus of innovation resides within an organization's boundaries.

A co-innovation project focused on sustainability illustrates how the platform and a project's partners open up and share their resources to achieve a project's objectives. Gerolsteiner Brunnen GmGH & Co., a mineral water provider, and INTENSE AG, a software and IT consultancy, collaborated to optimize the volume of mineral water extracted from springs for 125 products containing different types of mineral water. The project team sought the best way to get the right type of mineral water to the right bottling line, in the right quantity, at the right time. The platform provided access to SAP's cloud platform (SAP HANA) where the partners shared development methods; INTENSE AG wrote the code for the solution and retained intellectual property (IP) rights for the code; SAP's team in Johannesberg, South Africa, provided architecture consulting as well as development support. Matthias Orth, INTENSE AG, stated that collaborating with SAP's subject matter experts was "an ideal situation for us, because it meant we could address specific questions to them while we were working on the proof of concept at the customer. We held weekly touchdowns that really helped us build up our knowledge, which drastically reduced development time."[9] The project yielded an IoT-based solution that allowed Gerolsteiner to optimize the volume of mineral water it draws from springs. Real-time sensing and usage data collected on bottling lines allow for monitoring water usage during production. The solution provided Gerolsteiner a path to more precise forecasting, reducing costs and waste.[10] Capitalizing on the success of the project, collaboration continued: INTENSE began developing and implementing extended solutions on SAP's cloud platform including an Intelligent Efficiency Solution (IRES), which is partially deployed by Gerolsteiner.

As noted in Fig. 2.1, a fourth point of distinction relates to how value is distributed. When firms invest in creating a new product or service, they seek to appropriate as much value as possible from the investment. However, when a platform uses the same approach, complementors might balk and over time, the platform will become less attractive. For instance, Apple's 30% commission rate on app sales has drawn criticism from complementors (in this case, app developers) and motivated some revisions to Apple's service fee policies. Resistance to the so-called "Apple-tax" also has contributed to the agenda of the Coalition for App Fairness, an organization focused on fair treatment of app developers.[11] Co-innovation platform governance thus requires designing a value distribution approach where complementors create and capture more value by working with the platform than they would achieve independent of the platform. Recall that INTENSE AG retained the code IP developed for the mineral water project. A successful governance system embodies a mindset where complementors are "working with" the platform as opposed to "working for" the platform. In sum, the platform's governance mechanisms determine who co-innovates with the platform, the structure of interactions among actors, and how value is distributed.

Degree of Openness: Access and Resources

A critical concern for managers is how open the platform should be to external actors or participants. Choices about a platform's degree of openness are informed by its strategic objectives and invoke tradeoffs of growing participation while managing appropriability concerns.[12] Two dimensions of platform openness, the degree of access and the degree of resource openness, are relevant to co-innovation platforms.

Degree of Access. Open access characterizes a platform which places few restrictions on external participation. Granting external firms access to a platform's system (via information about the platform's core architecture, technology, and/or landscape) promotes a vibrant microeconomy of participation but it also involves giving up some control over the platform's usage. In this context, control refers to the rules guiding usage of the platform. Platform owners regulate access and usage by adopting standards, rules, and/or policies that govern the interface between the platform and external participants. Some scholars discuss access as independent of control whereas others consider access and control as part of a broad discussion of openness.

In general, open access promotes complementary innovation whereas tight control rules tend to dampen complementary innovation.[13] In our view and in the context of co-innovation platforms, access and control are part of an integrated set of decisions informing platform governance.

Access policies are informed by the platform's strategic objectives and often vary by platform type. For example, Apple's mobile platform supporting the iPhone and iPad is an integrated model combining both transaction and innovation platform functions. The platform encourages innovation by app developers (complementors or supply-side participants) and operates as an intermediary, facilitating the sale of apps to consumers or demand-side participants. App developers must agree to a set of policies but Apple places few limitations on app consumers. Even with some controls over supply-side access, diseconomies of scope emerge. For instance, beyond some point, do we need another productivity app? Considering a transaction platform example: Uber's initial growth partly is attributed to limited restrictions on the platform's supply-side participants or drivers. Growing the driver supply makes the platform more attractive to users or the demand-side participants. These conditions, however, also raise questions as to who is appropriating value created by the platform and whether a platform is exploiting complementors.

In the co-innovation platform model, access policies are informed by the platform's strategic objectives. For instance, policies may differ when the focus is on growing existing businesses as compared to incubating early stage ideas to keep pace with an emerging business area. In this context, access policies center on curating an inflow of co-innovation project proposals. The platform's ops team supports this effort by developing routines for scanning, sensing, and seizing co-innovation opportunities.[14] Since the platform is all about advancing co-innovation, attention is on developing a symbiotic co-innovation project portfolio that yields economies of innovation rather than pure growth in the number of participants. Why does this process matter? Strategically managing the portfolio of co-innovation project proposals helps the platform cultivate variety and, as a result, enriches the platform's value and relevance (see Chapter 3, *Building a Co-Innovation Platform*, for guidance on portfolio development and management).[15] The process also a dampens the risk of generating diseconomies of scope and a fragmented ecosystem.

Aligning policies with strategic objectives is critical and may be achieved in different ways. For example, when the platform is part of a large, multi-business organization, the platform or its parent organization might require that co-innovators gain the sponsorship of executives or business unit leaders within the parent organization for a proposed project. Such sponsorship ensures that a proposed project complements the organization's strategic direction. In the co-innovation platform we studied, executives in the platform's parent organization sought projects exploring a variety of growth areas such IoT, sustainability, big data, machine learning, and artificial intelligence. Executives also encouraged the platform to nurture projects in industries new to the organization such as sports and entertainment. The ops team would decline projects that reinforced legacy technologies or initiatives. Alternatively, when a co-innovation platform is a standalone organization, a similar selection process may be employed but is defined by the platform director or the platform's leadership team. As an additional tactic to ensure a partner's commitment to a co-innovation project, the platform may require the partner to contribute a nominal fee to access the platform (or resources might substitute for the fee).

Once sponsorship is locked in, a project's proposal is used to develop the project's contract elements—a statement of work (SOW) and simple frame agreement—the documents specify a project's degree of access to the platform's services as well as each partner's contributions to the project. Typically, once contracts are in place, teams have access to the platform's full range of supply-side and demand-side services (including basics such as remote VPN connectivity to a project landscape); in some instances, additional approval is warranted for unique project needs (such as computing capacity, etc.). Chapters 3 and 5 offer additional guidance on the partnership formation process and the contract approach.

Degree of Resource Openness. As illustrated in Fig. 2.4, platforms vary in the scope of resources that they open up to complementary organizations. Most platforms employ a hands-off approach, offering a relatively streamlined set of digital resources to complementors to support their value creation activities. For example, some platforms adopt partner certification programs. We view certification programs as hands-off because they typically do not

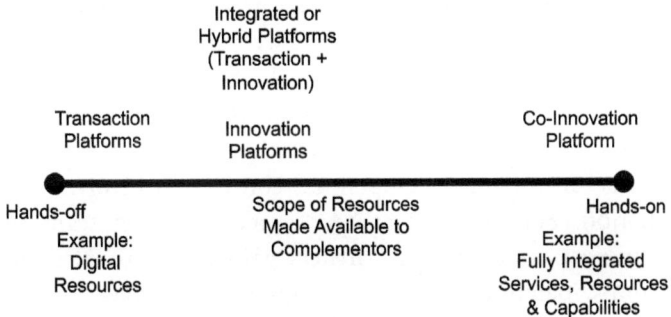

Fig. 2.4 Continuum of resource openness

provide external parties access to a platform's supply-side resources and capabilities that support the physical creation of a new product or service. Instead, the focus is on promoting alignment with the platform organization's objectives, signaling the legitimacy and value-add of the partner's offering to the ecosystem, and providing pathways for market exposure.[16] For example, Cisco offers a variety of digital services to potential partners including an online hub for finding a partner, a formal certification process, and a pathway for benefitting from Cisco's market access. Apple's App Developer program offers a second example, albeit with a bit more resources. The program equips developers with digital guides and documentation for app development, management and launch, and access to developer forums.[17] In this hands-off approach, complementors develop apps without access to Apple's software capabilities to support app creation; however, the developer program offers some limited technical support capabilities or technical support for a fee. As a result, we locate Apple's platform slightly to the right of hands-off end of the resource-openness continuum in Fig. 2.4.

The co-innovation platform presents an alternative model where the platform opens up both its supply-side and demand-side services, resources, and capabilities to external firms. We refer to this approach as hands-on since the supply-side services assist firms in the actual work of co-creating products or services. As mentioned in Chapter 1, supply-side services include Protect and Manage (contract formation and management), IT Systems Landscape, Knowledge Brokering, and Operations Management Team. The platform's demand-side services also involve hands-on capabilities such as support for creating demos and publications as well as showcasing co-innovation project outcomes to the ecosystem. These demand-side activities are found to increase the rate of new product development.[18] Chapter 3 discusses each supply-side service and Chapter 4 details the demand-side services.

While the platform employs a resource-open approach, the services provisioned to any one project also involve some degree of curation. In some instances, project teams might ask for the limo or supreme version of the platform's compute, network, and storage services when the project, and its systems architecture, suggests a sedan level of service would be sufficient. This means that the ops team must work with each project team early on to set expectations and clarify each project's service needs. As such, figuring out where to be on the resource-openness continuum involves some project specific variation. For instance, at SAP, once a partner team signs a co-innovation project contract, the partners gain access to platform services (resources and capabilities) needed to support the project's objectives, up to and including future releases of SAP products. Consider a project where a team is building a solution for a future generation (version 7.0) of an SAP technology. However, the team knows that its customers have access to version 6.0 but lack access to version 7.0. As a result, the project scope might require that the platform provide access to, and support for, developing the solution on both versions of the technology. In cases involving testing across releases, the platform typically would accommodate the request.

Using a managed approach to co-innovation project selection—access via sponsorship—combined with a high degree of resource openness enables the co-innovation platform to continuously engage a diverse set of participants in relevant and valuable co-innovation. Both features are essential to the co-innovation platform's health and its generative capacity.

A co-innovation project with Kore.ai, an enterprise virtual assistant platform and solutions company, illustrates the platform's hands-on approach. In 2016, Kore sought a partnership with SAP to develop and integrate enterprise bots with SAP's applications and platforms. Kore wanted to demonstrate how enterprise bots could create value in different industry applications. Bots, using natural language, allow users to receive alerts, get reports, execute direct actions, and complete workflow tasks. The project explored several customer use case scenarios including using bots with IoT applications in different industries, such as oil and gas, mining and construction, and energy. Sam Lakkundi, who was Kore's project lead at the time, indicated that Kore wanted to partner directly with product teams at SAP but the product teams were reluctant. Sam stated: "It was a struggle to convince them to co-create with Kore whereas in COIL [the co-innovation platform], we could easily co-innovate and as a byproduct of working with COIL, we had access to lots of connections at SAP." In addition to resources, Sam emphasized that the platform's understanding of partner needs and customer needs as well as its knowledge of similar projects and technologies advanced Kore's learning.

To execute the project, the platform provided the co-innovation project team supply-side resources including an Enterprise Resource Planning (ERP, SAP ECC) landscape and access to SAP's HANA system. The platform's ops team also worked with Kore on the initial technology integration. The platform's supply-side resources and capabilities allowed Kore to focus on how its bots functioned as part of an SAP cloud. Kore installed its Enterprise BoT messaging platform on SAP's HANA system and designed bots to follow commands as well as make predictions. Using the provisioned landscape, Kore created various demos featuring API integration, illustrating how the technology could be deployed. Demos blended software experts with operational experts to show how the integration of enterprise bot's capabilities production systems could create value for the customer. For example, one use case demonstrated how a maintenance or facilities engineer could easily chat with a building's HVAC system to gain status and insight into potential problems. In combination, the case illustrated how the solution could lower costs while also enhancing customer value.

The project also involved extensive testing and documentation. Kore tapped the platform's demand-side services to showcase and distribute the results. For instance, in collaboration with the platform, the project team recorded demos and participated in a variety of live events produced by the platform. Additionally, the project served as a stepping stone to Kore's completion of solution qualification and certification from SAP's Integration and Certification center (an entity that is independent of the platform). The repeated public exposure to Kore's technology yielded a variety of articles and press releases across industry news outlets, strengthening their reputation and visibility within the ecosystem.

Incentives: Mobilizing and Sustaining Participation

How can a co-innovation platform attract and mobilize a variety of complementors? In the co-innovation platform context, direct and indirect incentives work in combination to catalyze a self-reinforcing cycle of collaborative interactions.

The most obvious incentive for participants is access to the platform's services to support partnership formation and project co-innovation work. Organizations often lack resources to explore a new project idea, experience in forming partnerships, or partnership options. As a result, projects are set aside, delayed or abandoned, compromising a firm's future growth value, especially in a rapidly shifting environment. Alternatively, an organization may hold the necessary resources and capabilities but, due to strategic priorities, is not able to allocate resources to a project in a timely fashion or simply cannot pivot fast enough to capitalize on a project opportunity. Sound familiar? The co-innovation platform's supply-side services solve these resource and time-to-market needs. Project teams love using someone else's resources, whether they are compute, storage or network resources, especially when significant hardware resources are needed. And when a firm seeks a project partner and/or lacks a pathway to finding a partner, the platform's ops team can reach out to their networks to identify a partner with the appropriate complementary resources. Alternatively, if a co-innovation project requires additional subject matter expertise, the platform's ops team will work to find the appropriate expert to support the project. In other words, the platform enables co-innovation by matching actors holding relevant knowledge with those in need. In this relational, rather than transactional, approach to governance, the platform not only supports projects by connecting actors but also by coordinating contributions and promoting effective collaboration practices (see Chapters 3 and 5 for additional discussion).

As we mentioned in Chapter 1, indirect incentives also attract participants and originate from learning opportunities that emerge through engagement with the platform. The most obvious benefits stem from learning that occurs during a co-innovation project. Innovation does not evolve in an orderly fashion but instead, is characterized by cycles of divergence and convergence. Through joint work involving experimentation and tacit knowledge exchange, partners gain insights into other co-innovators' resources and skills. Learning from others combined with experiential learning provides opportunities for partners to evolve their capabilities, including enhancing their problem solving skills. This is especially crucial in contexts that are rapidly changing, as joint development is critical to building capabilities for the future and producing new output for the ecosystem.

By participating in co-innovation projects with the platform, organizations also gain insights into the co-innovation process. This exposure yields several benefits. For one, project partners improve their understandings of customer needs and their abilities to demonstrate customer value. One Global Vice President summarized his company's activity with SAP's co-innovation platform: "The COIL [co-innovation platform] gave us a framework for drawing out customer needs; helping us learn from our customers." Another Vice President noted: "Through our work at the Co-Innovation Lab we have been able to demonstrate customer benefits that extend beyond the recognized project acceleration and hardware cost savings." Experience with the platform's co-innovation approach also assisted firms in developing and refining their own innovation capabilities. One co-innovation project executive in our study remarked that co-innovation work with the platform helped his team "learn a lot about our assumptions that will help us in our product development." In fact, project partners indicated that several assumptions might not have been unearthed and discussed in their traditional approaches to product development.

Exposure to other co-innovation projects running concurrently with the platform provides additional opportunities for information and knowledge spillovers among unconnected complementors. Such vicarious learning inspires idea generation and stimulates new project development. For example, a co-innovation project emerged at the intersection of two projects running concurrently with the platform. Telit, an IoT solutions provider, was collaborating with an SAP analytics product team to provide a managed IoT sensor data flow service for SAP's HANA analytics applications. Concurrently, another product team supporting SAP's data warehouse and digital supply chain solutions was pursuing a co-innovation project with Stellium, a company providing services to support excellence in supply chain management, manufacturing, and industrial IoT. The purpose of the project was to illustrate how to use IoT data and machine learning in SAP systems to create a smart, lights out manufacturing environment. The two project teams met in the platform's collaboration space, observed each other's project demos, and learned about their complementary capabilities. The teams also realized that they served many of the same customers, addressing different dimensions of the customers' needs. Through these interactions, the teams began to form ideas about a new co-innovation project, expanding their opportunity sets. The new project was shared in an IoT symposium at SAP focused on unique intersections that emerge among co-innovation project teams. Telit and Stellium subsequently funded a booth at SAP's SAPPHIRE NOW event and collaborated to engage SAP customers.

Indirect incentives extend beyond interactions with partners or potential partners in the ecosystem. A host of externalities arise from affiliation with the platform. Participating in co-innovation projects with the platform bolsters a firm's visibility within the platform owner's organization and, as a result, boosts the firm's legitimacy in the eyes of the platform owner's customers. In fact, in SAP's co-innovation platforms, potential partners often think that if they can demonstrate that they are an effective partner, they will be able to tap into a lot of extra revenue given the breadth and depth of SAP's reach. These types of project participants are eager to capitalize on every opportunity for exposure. For instance, they will seek to join every event the platform hosts—they want to participate in any events where actual SAP customers are present. They also encourage the platform to showcase their company's logo and to share their co-innovation journey using all demand-side channels. In general, it is not unusual for a project participant to be persistent in their pursuits, asking—can we be on SAP's TechEd live TV broadcast? Can we present at SAP virtualization week? Can we run our demo at your booth at SAP SAPPHIRE NOW? Can our machine logo face the glass of the platform's compute center so people walking up to the building's Exec Briefing center will see it [in reference to the Palo Alto, CA location]? Can you get us a meeting with customer X? One SAP executive stated that one firm "…nearly begged me to help them attract SAP execs to their customer event at Giants stadium one year."

Gaining legitimacy is especially important for young, small organizations or startups. The co-innovation platform provides these organizations an opportunity to demonstrate their ability to execute successful co-innovation projects with an established member of the ecosystem (the platform owner) and other actors in the ecosystem. For example, Bluecoat Systems, a WAN acceleration solution provider, completed a co-innovation proof of concept (POC) project and wrote a whitepaper documenting the process and results. A potential customer of Bluecoat, Mapleleaf Foods in Toronto, Canada, typically required providers to complete Mapleleaf's POC process prior to developing a contract. Instead, Mapleleaf accepted the whitepaper as POC evidence and allowed Bluecoat to avoid a lengthier POC process, accelerating Bluecoat's sales cycle with the customer.

Further, co-innovation project partners also can benefit from interacting with different parts of the platform owner's organization at sponsored events such as innovation symposia. For example, Kore attended SAP's annual industry event, SAPPHIRE NOW, and presented their project as part of SAP's co-innovation platform group. SAP sponsors the event in cooperation with Americas SAP User Group (ASUG); the event is viewed as the definitive place to learn everything about SAP products, services, innovation, and ecosystem.[19] Sam Lakkundi, Kore's project lead, stated: "This was huge for us. The experience made us feel like an SAP partner versus just a project participant."

Lastly, you might be wondering how the platform develops its initial cohort of projects. After all, fruitful projects don't fall from the sky. One approach is to seek sponsorship from a variety of organizations operating in different industries and with an interest in emerging technologies and their applications. Each sponsor's strategic agenda should be symbiotic with the platform's purpose. While sponsors are not a requirement, they enhance the platform's legitimacy, signal the platform's commitment to collaboration, and can help build project momentum for the platform in its early stages of development.

Co-Innovation: Harnessing Complexity

Direct and indirect incentives are vital to attracting participants to the platform and work in combination with the platform's curation mechanisms to advance the quality of co-innovated offerings. Adding to this system are platform services that manage the complexity of co-innovation and enable the development of non-generic or unique complementary relationships. For instance, as part of the platform's protect and manage services, the ops team works with a project's partners to support contract formation including establishing a statement of work (SOW), ensuring goal alignment, clarifying resource needs, and identifying knowledge voids. Ongoing, productive co-innovation is feasible when organizations harness, rather than reduce, complexity. We highlight two forms of complexity relevant to co-innovation project teams, temporal and relational, and discuss how the co-innovation platform's services operate to harness this complexity. We conclude by discussing how complexity emerges at the platform level.

Temporal. Temporal complexity arises from the characteristics of the innovation process—non-linear and varying in pace or tempo. In any given project, some activities will require more time and attention whereas other activities will align with the project's original schedule. In other words, not every aspect of a project will be in synch. Roadblocks emerge when relevant technologies evolve at different rates and these technologies are needed to advance a project's progress. Alternatively, a project might be on schedule when an experiment reveals the need for new subject matter expertise or an additional partner. A lack of access to necessary infrastructure also may delay or halt progress. Of course, partners also bring different experiences and ways of working to a project and may vary in their orientations toward the past, present, and future.[20] Tom Turchoie, SAP CoE Spatial Expert and Co-innovation project partner while serving as CTO, Critigen, described these issues: "Not everything you want to happen will. The combination of people is a multiplicative effect. You think you have thought of everything and then realize how little you considered. You found out the space is expanding. Of course, you are trying to fight it because you want to keep your narrow project focus but you need to know how big the space is because this informs future directions."

Relational. Co-innovation occurs through relational engagement, rather than transactional interactions, among firms and the environment in which projects are situated. Projects seek to capitalize on unique complementarities among two or more firms typically from different industries, such as a dairy cooperative and a digital consultancy; a standard-setting nonprofit organization, tire repair technology, and a blockchain provider; or a bot company and an industrial equipment producer. Given the focus on developing unique complementarities, each co-innovation project involves investments in relationship-specific assets. The investment of time and energy in developing mutual trust among partners is critical to successful co-innovation and augments the limits of formal contracts (*see* Chapter 5, *Enabling Co-Innovation as Behavior*). However, even when project participants act in good faith, and commit to fulfill their promises and to not exploit one another's vulnerabilities, ongoing interactions combined with the non-linear nature of co-innovation can contribute to relational complexity.

Harnessing Complexity via Platform Services

Harnessing complexity requires structures and processes that help teams execute their projects, facilitate the sharing of co-innovation journeys, and support the platform's organizational memory—through the development and retention of co-innovation narratives. However, too much structure is likely to kill a project at the first iterative hiccup. How does the platform harness the temporal and relational complexity associated with co-innovation? The platform's services are designed with simple, agile processes in mind.

The effort begins with a project's proposal and the development of a project's contract. Simple, adaptable templates are provided for the primary contract elements—a project proposal form or document, a statement of work (SOW), and frame agreement (Chapters 3 and 5 provide additional details). At this stage, the ops team works with all project partners to set expectations and to converge on goals, resource commitments, schedule, and milestones. Clarifying expectations is a critical part of the project formation process. Often project partners become distracted by access to the platform's variety of services. The ops team helps to keep the discussion focused on the problem the project is trying to solve. These initial discussions help to harness complexity by clarifying the project's scope and activities. As a result, they set the stage for building mutual trust among partners. Teams also are provided project management tools for managing iterative development and change.

Additionally, the platform's deliberate investments in supply-side and demand-side services ease the co-innovation process for participants. For one, the services fill resource needs that emerge, dampening the likelihood of project delays. For instance, as described in more detail in Chapter 3, the platform's knowledge broker facilitates collaboration among partners, provides connections to subject matter experts or other partners to support project needs, and shares lessons learned from past or concurrent projects. Second, the platform provides a context that encourages experimentation and knowledge recombination, including a change management process to address project shifts. The latter helps teams navigate the non-linear and iterative development process.

Platform-specific Complexity. An additional layer of complexity is associated with the platform's evolving ecosystem as new actors, ways of working and technologies emerge. How can a platform leader keep pace with the ecosystem's interacting parts? The co-innovation platform model, as illustrated Fig. 1.1 in Chapter 1, addresses this complexity by developing a co-innovation portfolio that explores a variety of technologies and cross-industry collaborations. Activities that inform and shape the portfolio include technological pathfinding, recombination (blending past and present), and solution enablement. All three activities are vital the platform's generative capacity—its ability to enable ongoing innovation in support of ecosystem growth. Lacking activities that support variety, the platform will be unresponsive to shifts in technology or market conditions. Chapter 3 offers guidance and practices for developing and managing the platform's portfolio of co-innovation projects.

Value Distribution

Promoting collaboration and open innovation requires a system that provides equity in the distribution of the value created in co-innovation projects. When most of the value created by complementors or 3rd party participants is captured by a platform, complementors feel exploited and consequently, less motivated to engage with the platform. In contrast, creating an environment where both the project participants and the platform owner create and capture more value by working together as compared to what the participants would achieve independent of the platform fosters trust among participants and the platform. These conditions contribute to enduring relationships and increase the platform's attractiveness. They also have contributed to the emergence of serial co-innovators.

We apply a strategic positioning framework, the value minus cost approach, to illustrate value creation and value capture at the project level and the platform level.[21] Our focus is on how value is distributed by the platform rather than on demand-side factors that may affect adoption of an innovation (such as the role of intermediaries, customer preferences, etc.).[22] Figure 2.5 illustrates the relationships at the project level: co-innovation projects target creating something new or novel that increases a customer's value or willingness to pay; and the platform's services, in combination with each partners' resources and capabilities, lower the costs of creating that value. The gap between value and cost reflects the total value created by a project in a transaction with a customer; a firm that creates the largest gap between value and cost as compared to that achieved by close competitors has an advantage. Each partner captures value from the project (represented as the delta between price and cost in Fig. 2.5) and customers gain some utility from the offering

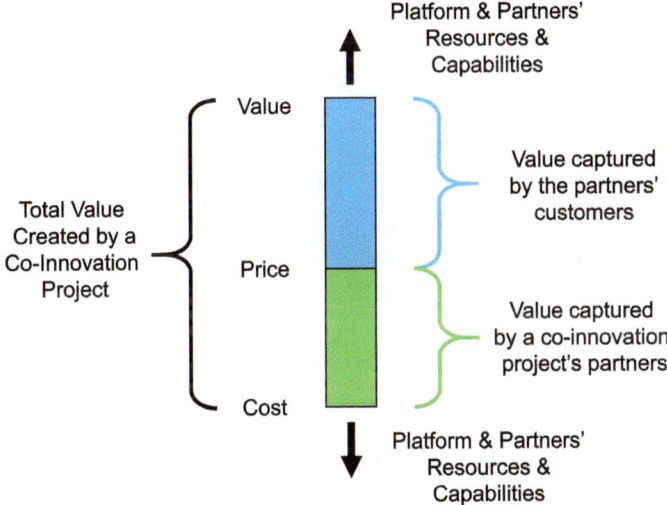

Fig. 2.5 Co-Innovation project: value creation and capture

(the delta between value and price).[23] The platform also provides an additional, unobserved benefit to firms—an opportunity to pursue a project that they otherwise might not have been able to act on due to resource or timing constraints within their organizations.

While projects vary in activity and focus (e.g. testing of an idea, early stage experimentation, solution development or part of a larger system of exploration) all aim at enhancing the value provided to the customer and contributing to a go-to-market solution. Value can be achieved in a variety of ways. Bluecoat Systems proof of concept project results contributed to its offerings in relationship with a new customer, Mapleleaf Foods. Kore's enterprise bot project, described above, contributed to its solution qualification and certification from SAP's Integration and Certification center and activities with the platform expanded awareness of Kore's offerings across SAP's ecosystem.[24] A collaboration between a dairy cooperative and a digital consultancy yielded a food transparency solution, QR codes on milk containers to access digital information about the product's journey. The dairy cooperative eagerly implemented the solution and received rave reviews from customers. As a result, the solution was subsequently applied to another product offered by the dairy cooperative. The digital consultancy used lessons learned from the dairy project to expand their offerings and began to apply the digital solution to other industries.

Although the platform creates value for each co-innovation project, it benefits when projects extend the use value of the platform's core offering.

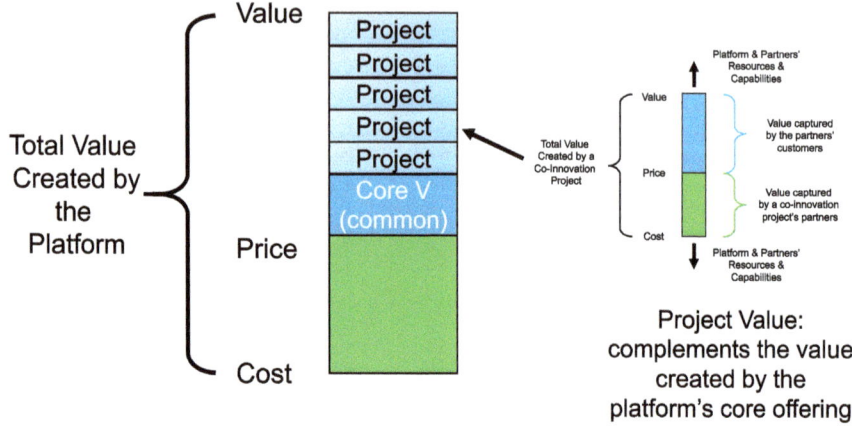

Fig. 2.6 Co-Innovation platform: value creation and capture

When a complementary service or product enhances the core offering's use value, customers are attracted to the platform's core as well as to the complementary offering. In this way, both the platform and the partners create and capture more value in combination than they would achieve independently. Figure 2.6 illustrates the value minus cost framework at the platform level: The platform has a core offering that creates value for its customers and each co-innovation project has the potential to add complementary value to the core offering. In doing so, each project may extend a customer's utility of using the platform's core offering.

This value creation is exemplified by a co-innovation project with Virtual Power Systems (VPS) focused on optimizing the use of energy in a data center. At the time of the project, SAP was running dozens of its own data centers around the globe.[25] A successful project outcome for VPS included SAP adopting the technology in its own datacenters and VPS capturing value from the technology adoption. Additionally, SAP could approach other partners and customers that were running data centers and encourage them to adopt the technology to lower their costs. By doing so, the partners and customers would either capture more value themselves (holding price constant) or distribute the additional benefits to their customers. The example illustrates the platform's ability to create and absorb an innovation and reflect it back out to the ecosystem.

Conclusion

Successful co-innovation platforms require a coherent strategy and an organizing logic that enables the platform to achieve its strategic objectives. Organizing to ensure productive collaboration can be challenging, especially when the relevant actors—the key sources of innovation—reside outside of the platform organization's boundaries. Lacking formal authority over these organizations, governance practices that establish incentives for participation, unbundle the complexity of co-innovation work, and provide equitable value distribution are essential to mobilizing and sustaining a productive microeconomy of innovators. Our observations and analysis of co-innovation projects reveals that a co-innovation platform's "hands-on" approach is a distinctive engine for innovation that fuels ecosystem growth. Will surprises arise? Yes. A robust governance system will help you navigate challenges and capitalize on new opportunities. But wait, there is more to the story. The value created and captured is not only about project outcomes. The "more" includes building co-innovation capabilities throughout the ecosystem and leveraging the platform's project portfolio to provide a broad narrative for the parent organization about how co-innovation can accelerate innovation, spawn new opportunities, and extend the organization's reach.

Key Takeaways

1. Transaction platforms, innovation platforms, and co-innovation platforms have distinct strategic objectives, involve different resources and capabilities, and vary in how value is created and distributed.
2. A co-innovation platform's primary strategic objective is facilitating innovation via collaborative arrangements among external actors as well as with the platform. A distinctive characteristic of the co-innovation platform model is curated access coupled with a high degree of resource openness—referred to as the hands-on approach: the platform provides external actors access to supply-side services to support the formation and execution of co-innovation projects *and* demand-side services to demo and showcase project results.
3. When considering developing a co-innovation platform, the questions that need to be asked are: (1) What innovation topics/areas play a strategic role in the parent organization's future?; (2) Are there opportunities to collaborate with external organizations to accelerate innovation?; and (3)

Can greater economies of innovation and complementarity be achieved through co-innovation with external organizations than by going it alone?.
4. A co-innovation platform's role is not as matchmaker, facilitating a transaction between co-innovators and customers. Instead, the focal task of the platform is to enable and support the development of co-innovation projects with and among diverse actors.
5. Identifying a platform's appropriate level of resource openness is driven by the platform's strategic agenda and invokes tradeoffs between enabling adoption and thwarting the ability of rivals to appropriate the value created by the platform.
6. The value created in co-innovation platforms relies on collaboration with, and among, firms external to the platform and that the platform owner does not control. Given the limited formal authority over these actors, a platform owner governs the platform-based ecosystem by playing the role of orchestrator rather than director. Successful ecosystem orchestration requires that a platform owner recognize its role is to shape, enable, and influence distributed innovation and to integrate complementary innovations into the ecosystem.
7. An effective co-innovation platform governance system specifies how the platform will design and manage four key areas: (1) Degree of Openness—Access and Resources; (2) Incentives: Mobilizing and Sustaining Participation; (3) Harnessing Complexity; and (4) Value Distribution.
8. Creating an environment where both the co-innovation project participants and the platform owner create and capture more value by working together, as compared to what the participants would achieve independent of the platform is vital to maintaining quality participation.

Questions, quibbles, comments? Please share your thoughts and ideas. We would value hearing your co-innovation story. You can reach us at: coinnovationstrategy@gmail.com.

Notes

1. Cusumano, M.A., Gawer, A., and Yoffie, D. B. 2019. *The Business of Platforms: Strategy in the Age of Digital Competition, Innovation and Power.* HarperCollins Publishers.
2. Rochet, J.C. and Tirole, J. 2006. Two-sided markets: A progress report. *The RAND journal of economics,* 37(3): 645–667. Shapiro, C.,

Carl, S., and Varian, H.R. 1998. *Information Rules: A Strategic Guide to the Network Economy*. Harvard Business Press.
3. Value distribution differs among platforms facilitating resource sharing. For instance, Uber and Airbnb both create significant economic value by providing non-price benefits and improving resource utilization. However, Uber's value creation involves both capital (automobiles) and labor (drivers) whereas Airbnb's value arises primarily from the sharing of capital (real estate). These differences have implications for the potential value that a platform can create. Markman et al. (2021) expand on the heterogeneity in value creation by considering differences in characteristics, such as asset utilization and asset value, across sharing economy platforms. See Markman, G.D., Lieberman, M., Leiblein, M., Wei, L., and Wang, Y. 2021. The Distinctive Domain of the Sharing Economy: Definitions, Value Creation, and the Implications for Research. *Journal of Management Studies*, online version-early access. https://doi-org.libproxy.scu.edu/10.1111/joms.12707.
4. Rohr, J. 2019. Keeping Highways Safe with RFID and Blockchain. SAP News Center, page 1–7; quoted text: page 3. https://news.sap.com/2019/10/sap-gs1-blockchain-rfid-safe-highways/, accessed May 10, 2021.
5. Cusumano, M.A., Gawer, A., and Yoffie, D.B. 2019. *The Business of Platforms: Strategy in the Age of Digital Competition, Innovation and Power*. HarperCollins Publishers.
6. Gawer, A., Cusumano, M.A. 2008. How Companies Become Platform Leaders. *MIT Sloan Management Review*, 49(2): 27–35; Eisenmann, T.R. 2007. Managing Networked Businesses: Course Overview note for educators. Harvard Business School Publishing, #807–104.
7. Williamson, P.J., and De Meyer, A. 2012. Ecosystem advantage: How to successfully harness the power of partners. *California Management Review*, 55: 24–46.
8. Teece, D.J. 2007. Explicating dynamic capabilities: The nature and microfoundations of (sustainable) enterprise performance. *Strategic Management Journal*, 28(13): 1319–1350; Tiwana, A. 2013. *Platform Ecosystems: Aligning Architecture, Governance, and Strategy*. Newness; Helfat, C.E., Raubitschek, R.S. 2018. Dynamic and integrative capabilities for profiting from innovation in digital platform-based ecosystems. *Research Policy*, 47: 1391–1399; Rietveld, J., Seamans, R., Meggiorin, K. 2021. Market Orchestrators: The Effects of Certification on Platforms and Their Complements. Forthcoming, *Strategy Science*; Rietveld, J., Schilling, M.A., and Bellavitis, C. 2019. Platform strategy: Managing

ecosystem value through selective promotion of complements. *Organization Science, 30*(6): 1232–1251.
9. Rohr, J. 2019. SAP Cloud Platform Helps Gerolsteiner Run Sustainability. SAP News Center. https://news.sap.com/2019/10/gerolsteiner-run-sustainably-sap-cloud-platform/, accessed June 24, 2021.
10. For a video summarizing the project, go to https://youtu.be/facfQ8eIOb0, accessed May 15, 2021.
11. Coalition for App Developers, https://appfairness.org/our-vision/, accessed March 25, 2021.
12. West, J. 2003. How open is open enough? Melding proprietary and open source platform strategies. *Research Policy, 32*: 1259–1285. Also see: Gawer, A., and Cusumano, M.A. 2002. *Platform Leadership: How Intel, Microsoft, and Cisco Drive Industry Innovation* (Vol. 5, pp. 29–30). Boston, MA: Harvard Business School Press; Boudreau, K. 2010. Open platform strategies and innovation: Granting access vs. devolving control. *Management Science, 56*: 1849–1872.
13. Boudreau, K. 2010. Open platform strategies and innovation: Granting access vs. devolving control. *Management Science, 56*: 1849–1872.
14. These activities are essential to effective ecosystem orchestration (Teece, 2007). Teece, D.J. 2007. Explicating dynamic capabilities: The nature and microfoundations of (sustainable) enterprise performance. *Strategic Management Journal, 28*(13): 1319–1350. See also: Helfat, C.E., and Raubitschek, R.S. 2018. Dynamic and integrative capabilities for profiting from innovation in digital platform-based ecosystems. *Research Policy, 47*: 1391–1399; Rietveld, J., Seamans, R., and Meggiorin, K. 2021. Market orchestrators: The effects of certification on platforms and their complements. Forthcoming, *Strategy Science*.
15. Parker, G.G., and Van Alstyne, M. 2017. Innovation, openness and platform control. *Management Science, 64*: 3015–3032.
16. See Ceccagnoli, M., Forman, C., Huang, P., and Wu, D.J. 2012. Cocreation of value in a platform ecosystem! The case of enterprise software. *MIS Quarterly*: 263–290.
17. For more on Apple's App Developer program, go to: developer.apple.com/support/ and developer.apple.com/programs/whats-included/, accessed March 16, 2021.
18. Boudreau, K. 2010. Open platform strategies and innovation: Granting access vs. devolving control. *Management Science, 56*: 1849–1872.
19. https://reg.sapevents.sap.com/flow/sap/sapphirenow2021/portal/page/home, accessed June 1, 2021.

20. Garud, R., Tuertscher, P., and Van de Ven, A. 2013. Perspectives on the innovation process. *Academy of Management Annals, 7*: 775–819.
21. For additional details on the Value minus Cost framework, see: Hoopes, D., Madsen, T.L., and Walker, G. 2003. Why is there a resource based view? Toward a theory of competitive heterogeneity. *Strategic Management Journal, 24*(10): 889–902; Peteraf, M.A., and Barney, J.B. 2003. Unraveling the resource-based tangle. *Managerial and Decision Economics, 24*(4): 309–323; Walker, G., and Madsen, T.L. 2016. *Modern Competitive Strategy*. NY: McGrawHill Education.
22. See Adner, R. 2013.*The Wide Lens: What Successful Innovators See That Others Miss*. Penguin.
23. In SAP's co-innovation platform, partners typically pay a nominal fee to access the platform; in some instances, resources might substitute for the fee. Partners capture the value created by their co-innovation projects minus the fee or expense of the partner's resource contribution.
24. Although Kore gained exposure to SAP customers, SAP eventually elected to pursue the bot market directly.
25. SAP has shifted to a new approach, SAP 4 + 1 strategy, involving 4 hyperscalers plus its private hybrid cloud or what SAP refers to as the converged cloud, the + 1.

3

Building a Co-Innovation Platform

> We live in an era of digital transformation where companies have to offer innovative solutions to reach the highest customer success. Integration of products and technologies on different levels from different vendors is critical for building these solutions, especially in the world of cloud and mobile technology. No single vendor can do this alone. Building strategic alliances and partnerships is essential for developing solutions and bringing them to market successfully. Companies need to work and innovate together on such solutions in a place like the SAP Co-Innovation Lab.
> —Roland Wartenberg, Sr. Director Strategic Alliances, NetApp

If you want to build a co-innovation platform, where do you start? A first step involves identifying the problem or opportunity the platform will address for your organization. Next, what does your organization want to achieve with the platform? Once the objectives and scope are established, attention shifts to building a platform activity system that supports the objectives: What resources and capabilities are needed? How will they fit together to enable and shape co-innovation? How will the platform be managed?

In this chapter, we discuss the core services, processes, and activities of a co-innovation platform. The platform's supply-side and demand-side services, and their associated resources and capabilities, allow co-innovation project teams to focus their energy on developing co-innovated solutions rather than on searching and acquiring the resources and capabilities needed to pursue projects and showcase results. Since innovation is a resource intensive process, providing innovators access to these services will accelerate the innovation process and yield performance benefits.

Setting the Stage: Why a Co-Innovation Platform?

Creating an environment to support productive collaboration begins with the mission and objectives of the platform. The objectives set the stage for how co-innovation work will get done and signal the platform's degree of commitment to enabling productive collaboration. For example, the mission and objectives guiding SAP's co-innovation platforms (see Table 3.1)[1] revolve around providing co-innovation-as-a-service by provisioning all required services to support collaborative innovation, connecting firms with complementary capabilities, and supporting marketing or demand-side initiatives. Over time, the objectives have become embedded in the firm's approach to innovation and growth. Rudi Held, Global Head of SAP's Co-Innovation platforms, framed it this way: "Co-innovation is part of our DNA here at SAP. It's been one of the foundations of SAP's success." Objectives, of course, may vary in scope. Some organizations may choose to adopt all aspects of the integrated model whereas others may seek a scaled-down approach. Both paths can advance co-innovation but of course, each choice involves different

Table 3.1 SAP Co-innovation platform: mission and objectives

Mission	Objectives
"SAP Co-Innovation Lab offers co-innovation-as-a-service across the globe with clear focus on appropriately securing the intellectual property for the collaborating parties. It provides all required services in an integrated project approach to accelerate the solution development".	• "Help turn your solution vision into a reality • Bring together the best minds in the relevant fields • Align stakeholders • Provisioning all required services for the solution build • Provide close interaction between solution build and go-to-market activities"

resource commitments. Not every objective requires a platform play. Clarifying what your organization wants to achieve in the short and long run is a crucial starting point. A second important activity is the "how" or a robust organizing logic to address the strategic initiatives.

The Core Services

Plenty of Silicon Valley urban lore describes one-of-a-kind ideas being scratched on the back of a napkin by two people sitting in a café that then changed the world. Yet, in the day-to-day pursuit of ongoing innovation, much is accomplished through project-based work. Project work requires resources and capabilities to turn an idea into productive, and revenue-producing, swipes and mouse clicks. The platform's core services include supply-side services to support the formation and execution of co-innovation projects and demand-side services to demo and showcase project results. Figure 3.1 shows the core service categories.

As the system's orchestrator, the operations management team (ops team hereafter) is listed at the top of the figure. The team manages and provisions all of the core services and provides support with innovation processes and

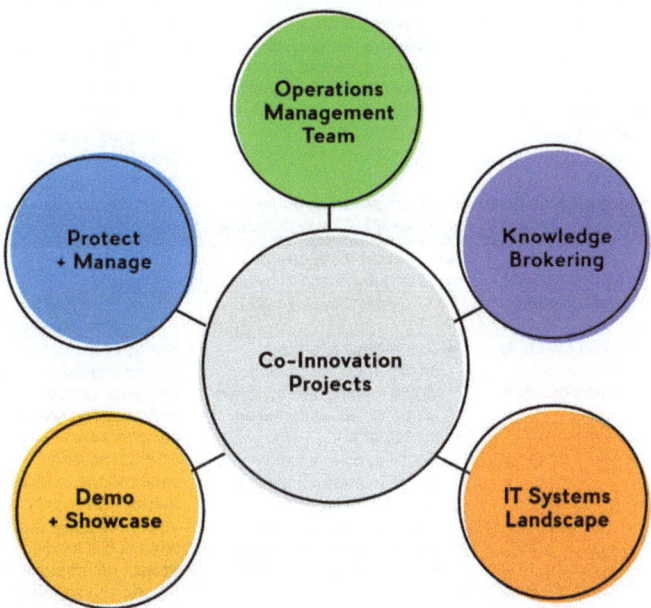

Fig. 3.1 Co-Innovation platform: core services

project management. Supply-side services specific to enabling co-innovation involve contract formation and management (referenced as "Protect and Manage"), information technology (IT) system landscape provisioning and management, and knowledge brokering. Demand-side services, "Demo and Showcase," focus attention on showcasing project results and advancing visibility through events, demos, and publications. In combination, the bundled services streamline the co-innovation process for a project. Table 3.2 summarizes the activities related to each core service; the term "actors" encompasses a variety of participants operating in different industries, sectors or institutions such as customers, competitors, complementors, entrepreneurs, and suppliers as well as public and non-profit organizations.

Table 3.2 Co-Innovation platform: core services

Supply-Side Services: Resources and Capabilities		
Operations Management Team • Delivers the supply-side services needed by each project, such as building out a suitable IT environment to meet a project's compute, storage and network requirements. • Responsible for managing and advancing the platform's project portfolio, supporting and overseeing project work, and providing assistance with changes to project scope.		
Protect & Manage	**Information Technology (IT) Systems Landscape**	**Knowledge Broker**
• Supports project contract formation using a simple, flexible contract approach (primary elements: frame agreements and statements of work). • Provides legal processes, clauses and negotiation options in support of contract formation.	• Provides all physical hardware and software for network and compute storage. • Provides access to software licenses and tooling in support of co-innovation project goals.	Services include: • Connecting existing solutions and problems with external sources of knowledge. • Facilitating connections among actors to fill a project's knowledge or resource gaps. • Enabling intersections among previously unconnected actors.
Demand-Side Services: Resources and Capabilities		
Operations Management Team • Provisioning demand-side services to publish and showcase project results.		
Showcase: Events	**Demo Development**	**Storytelling: Publications**
• Platform-hosted events to showcase co-innovation project work and problem solving. • Ecosystem events to showcase select projects.	• Capabilities to support electro-mechanical and virtual model making, demo scripting, and automation management. • Enabling co-innovation teams to build completely new architectures or integrate and test new features without seeming demo services from others.	• Narrative and storytelling of project activities and results: reference architectures, white papers, solution briefs, performance characterizations, certifications, podcasts, videos, live events, webcasts, blogs and other social media. • Project report publishing; reports shared internally and/or externally to enhance project visibility.

Before describing each core service, we provide a high-level overview of how the process works from project origination to showcasing results. The remaining parts of the chapter expand on the platform's supply-side services. Chapter 4, *Co-Innovation Storytelling,* discusses the demand-side services.

Co-Innovation Projects: From Origination to Demo & Showcase

Project Origination

Where do the project ideas originate? As Fig. 3.2 illustrates, projects typically emerge from four different sources or combinations: (1) Customer & Complementors: two or more firms or co-innovators propose a project with a joint customer; (2) Complementors & Ops Team: the operations management team brings together two or more firms to propose a project[2]; (3) Complementor & Complementor: two or more firms propose a project; (4) Platform & Complementor: the platform's organization, or the business unit where the platform resides within its parent organization, collaborates with one or more firms to propose a project.[3] Typically, projects emerge with an idea in place. Innovation activities thus tend to focus on experimentation, prototyping, and testing rather than early-stage brainstorming. However, additional services, such as design thinking workshops, assist project teams with skill building around the innovation process itself.

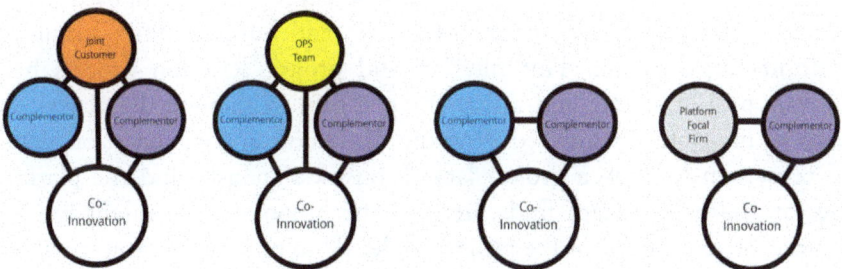

Fig. 3.2 Co-Innovation projects: origins

Project Phases

How do the services work together to support value creation and distribution? A co-innovation project involves four phases: Formation, Enablement, Project Work, and Demo & Showcase.

Regardless of a project's origin, the process kicks off when a project proposal is presented to the platform's operations team. A simple project proposal document: 1) identifies the project team (lead and key project members) and executive sponsors for the project; 2) briefly summarizes the project's objectives and alignment with the platform organization's objectives; 3) provides influence revenue projections for the partners and for the platform's organization; 4) details how the team plans to work together and includes a high level project plan; and 5) lists the resources committed by each partner and the services needed from the platform to support the project. The proposal includes all of the elements to write a project's formal statement of work (SOW).

As discussed in Chapter 2, *Platforms: Types, Governance, & Value Distribution,* proposed projects should align with the platform's objectives as well as the platform organization's strategic objectives. Alignment may be facilitated in different ways. When the platform is part of a large, multi-business organization, the platform or its parent organization might require that complementary innovators (project proposers) gain executive or senior-level sponsorship of a proposed project. This step ensures that co-innovation projects complement the platform organization's overall strategic direction and in turn, extend the possible uses, and use value, of the organization's core products and services. More broadly, it assures that a proposed project idea is of interest to a variety of executives and business units within the platform's organization. This filtering and project selection process helps cultivate project variety and assists the platform in shaping the ecosystem's scope of innovation while reducing the likelihood of fragmentation within the ecosystem.[4] When a project lacks a business sponsor and the platform director and/or ops team finds merit in the proposal, they might work to gain executive support for the project or decide to pursue the project without sponsorship. When a co-innovation platform is a standalone organization, a similar sponsorship requirement may be employed but the decision rests with the platform's director or leadership team. In both instances, publishing the organization's and platform's objectives as well as the organization's roadmap is critical to stimulating project proposals from complementary innovators.

Once sponsorship is settled, the ops team works with all parties to develop a contract. During the contract formation process, the ops team helps clarify

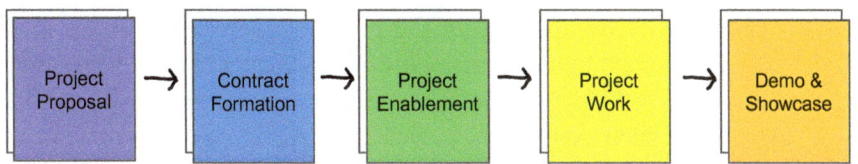

Fig. 3.3 Co-Innovation project process

the supply-side and demand-side services needed for the project and the project's partners become more familiar with the platform's services.

As Fig. 3.3 illustrates, the process kicks off with a project proposal; once approved, a contract is developed. Next, the project's enablement phase begins and primarily involves the operations management team provisioning the necessary services to support the subsequent project work phase. Depending on the type of project, the ops team might provide design thinking guidance to assist project teams with their innovation processes. Additionally, the ops team also is tasked with monitoring each project's progress and providing additional resource support when needed. For instance, as a project evolves, a project's partners may find that they lack the expertise needed to solve a particular problem. In this case, the operations management team will seek the relevant subject matter experts within, and/or external to, the platform organization to assist in problem solving. At completion, the partners have the opportunity to showcase and market the project results using the platform's various demand-side services.

Supply-Side Services

A distinctive feature of a co-innovation platform is its resource-open and hands-on approach to innovation. By providing heterogeneous complementary organizations access to supply-side services that enable co-innovation work, the platform is able to shape the ecosystem's innovation trajectory from the ground up. Additionally, the platform's activities contribute to mobilizing different types of actors, enabling value-creating interactions among varied complementary actors, and facilitating joint learning. As mentioned in Chapter 1, in combination, the activities strengthen the platform's generativity[5]—its capacity to produce new output from a wide range of different actors—a feature critical to maintaining ecosystem innovation and growth. Most studies of innovation-focused platforms devote less attention to how generativity occurs, especially when a platform filters complementor participation. A key feature of the co-innovation platform model is its ability to promote generativity by opening up the platform's services to complementors. Since the ops team manages the platform's services and orchestrates value creation, capture, and distribution in the ecosystem, we first highlight their key activities. We then describe how each supply-side service contributes to co-innovation.

The Operations Management Team (Ops Team)

The ops team is the heart of the platform and is actively engaged in all aspects of the platform. In this role, the team wears multiple hats such as consultant, coach, guide, enabler, manager, and knowledge broker to manage and advance the platform and its project portfolio. The ops team's primary activities and services are listed below. Through these various activities, the ops team orchestrates the system by coordinating and influencing the behaviors of complementors. The subsequent sections discussion each supply-side service and Chapter 4, *Co-Innovation Storytelling*, expands on the demand-side services.

- Enabling project formation and contract development
- Provisioning IT system landscape services
- Providing knowledge broker services
    - Purposively managing knowledge and resource flows by facilitating connections
    - Conducting supplemental research and analysis to support project work
    - Continuous knowledge building
- Managing and advancing the project portfolio
    - Supporting and overseeing project work
    - Change management
- Storytelling and showcasing project work and results (demand-side)

Protect and Manage

Platforms focused on enabling and accelerating co-innovation benefit from employing a simple and flexible contract approach. Typically, proactive management is needed to align the platform's simple contracts approach with its parent organization's established legal practices. In many cases, the established practices tend to add layers of contractual detail and complexity. Such practices can be a bit like Russian nesting dolls: the organization and its legal team start with a general agreement then add a service agreement, a partner agreement, a subscription agreement, addendums, and so on. As a result, established practices often constrain rather than enable rapid co-innovation. And when intellectual property is involved, as is often the case in co-innovation projects, we agree with the advice of Henry Chesbrough, the creator of the open innovation concept: "It's too important to leave it to the lawyers."[6,7]

Overcoming the various organizational challenges typically requires top-down support in addition to proactive management by the platform. When the platform employs less-balanced contractual terms, it sends the message that the complementors or co-innovation partners are working *for* the platform rather than *with* the platform. The '*for the platform*' mindset conflicts with the platform's objectives for productive multilateral collaboration and may raise a complementor's concerns about being exploited by the platform. Platform builders can mitigate these problems by working closely with their organization's executive leadership to ensure that the organization's legal staff supports contractual arrangements that align with the platform's objectives. When the platform is provided some degree of flexibility, fewer frictions and time delays occur in completing contracts for co-innovation projects. Navigating this process can be challenging and is easier when the organization commits legal staff to support the platform's operations. The platform-specific legal capabilities also can be used to guide project partners as they navigate the contract process.

Contracts. In the platform we studied, the contract formation process included simple templates for project proposals, statements of work (SOWs), and frame agreements. Each project begins with a proposal that: (1) identifies the project team (lead and key project members) and the project's executive sponsors; (2) briefly summarizes the project's objectives and their alignment with the platform organization's objectives[8]; (3) provides influence revenue projections for the partners and for the platform's organization[9]; (4) details how the team plans to work together and includes a high level project plan; and (5) lists the resources committed by each partner and the platform services needed to support the project.

Upon project approval, the ops team, as coach, works with each project team to formalize a project's statement of work (SOW) and frame agreement. The SOW builds on the project's proposal. Ensuring simplicity and flexibility is key: the standard template for the frame agreement and SOW should be designed to accommodate rapid project formation, learning, iterative development, and in turn, potential adjustments to project work. The frame agreement identifies the parties agreeing to collaborate; specifies the vision for the project; introduces definitions, contract terms (including limited liability clauses) and taxes; and addresses a variety of other areas of interest, such as brand use. The agreement also may contain specific clauses relevant to the use of intellectual property (IP) owned by the firm providing the platform as well as the background IP owned by co-innovation project partners. Similarly, the agreements specify how IP created during a project is owned and shared. The SOW, appended to the frame agreement, defines a project's scope, activities, deliverables, and timeline, as well as who is responsible for different aspects of the project and the actions to be taken when commitments are not upheld. IP clauses in the frame agreement specify how IP generated from the project is managed beyond details described in the project's SOW. Other appended documents list the platform's "house rules," including terms such as agreements not to share platform or project resources with unauthorized participants and not to reverse-engineer existing products or services. The simple and flexible features of the contract approach enable partners to move rapidly from project idea to project formation and execution. For example, in the platform we studied, the frame agreement used a template-based approach with standard language and terms, enabling participating partners to sign "as is," and avoiding contract redlining or negotiation.

A crucial part of the contract formation phase involves the platform's operations management team working with project partners to clarify project expectations. An operations manager from SAP's co-innovation platform noted that partners often come to the platform mesmerized by its rich resource base and success stories and, as a result, assume that it is impossible to fail. In some cases, the partners are so driven that they tend to gravitate to anything that might bring them closer to achieving their project goals. This behavior can lead partners to constantly seek more services, expanding a project's scope beyond the initial contract.

Two activities can help manage these conditions. First, during the contract formation process, the platform's ops team should be very transparent and explicit regarding how the platform can contribute to the project. Second, during the project work phase, the ops team should communicate frequently with project partners regarding a project's status, milestone achievements (or lack thereof), timeline, and any changes in scope. When a project evolves beyond its original scope, the operations management team typically works with the project's partners to revisit the frame agreement and/or SOW. In some cases, scope changes warrant gaining additional stakeholder buyin. In general, the ops team plays a critical role in shepherding and nurturing co-innovation projects.

Information Technology (IT) System Landscape

More and more, customers seek platform services that provide seamless integration, robust security, and high degrees of system resiliency. Software meant to codify business processes and support productive, secure transactions and workflows increasingly is needed to perform at scale in an always-on environment. As a result, the capabilities of a platform's IT system landscape are vital to the platform's success. The landscape includes a set of software, hardware, and facility elements configured to support the platform's operations. This core service provides participants access to physical hardware and software for network and compute storage as well as access to software licenses and tooling to support project goals. Tapping into the platform's IT services means that a project team does not have to scramble around trying to insource or outsource the necessary IT resources and capabilities, find additional budget resources, or manage a purchase request to get the necessary software and hardware.

As a co-innovation platform builder, you will set the course for the services the platform can provision reliably to project teams depending on what you choose to build and how. For example, you might opt to run physical hardware in the platform environment rather than build out a set of IT landscapes using a public or private cloud infrastructure. Regardless of the approach, the platform should be designed to operate as a multi-tenant model.[10] The platform's ops team also must ensure that the project portfolio does not over-extend the system's capabilities. Establishing service level objectives and key performance indicators for the IT system assists the ops team in balancing resource needs across the project portfolio. In general, one project should not be able to draw down resources so readily from the system that it compromises other projects.

Who Gets What? Provisioning and Needs Assessment. During SOW development, the platform's ops team works with each co-innovation project team to identify a project's IT requirements. For instance, a typical project requires replicating scale-up or scale-out architectures and workloads. When interacting with the ops team, the co-innovation team also learns about the platform's compute capabilities, storage network features, and systems technologies. This process also might reveal IT resource needs that exceed the platform's capabilities. Under these conditions, the ops team, wearing its knowledge broker hat, seeks support and resources from ecosystem participants, often bringing in an additional partner with the relevant complementary resources (see the Monsta case below).

Familiarity with the system's capabilities enables project partners to take immediate advantage of the platform's IT services. Co-innovation partners however, may lack expertise with the IT system's capabilities or lack an understanding of how the platform's system may be leveraged. The ops team is pivotal in helping teams understand their needs and the options available to meet those needs. The ability to hit the ground running with the platform's IT landscape resources accelerates project completion and often, provides partners additional time to explore a project stretch goal. For example, Bluecoat Systems, a WAN acceleration solution provider, pursued a co-innovation project aimed at improving connectivity performance for its customers and optimizing its network for SAP business analytics workloads. Understanding the characteristics and functionality of the platform's IT system landscape helped Bluecoat rapidly configure its system to work with the platform's software applications and in turn, demo its project results ahead of schedule. The demo was shown frequently and stimulated additional project work as well as customer exposure for Bluecoat.

Knowledge Broker Services

The ops team provides the platform's knowledge broker services. A rich knowledge brokering system allows the platform to tap subject matter and domain experts from its ecosystem to support novel co-innovation that engages actors from different industries and/or technology domains. An alternative is to staff the platform with the relevant experts but doing so may require significant resources and even then, not allow the platform to achieve its objectives. If the focus is on innovating around established products, local knowledge may be sufficient. But, if the vision is more expansive such as to advance the ecosystem by mobilizing many different types of economic actors to create and recombine ideas, and to enable the development of those ideas, a firm cannot go it alone.[11]

The services include capabilities to expose co-innovation participants to different actors, knowledge, resource pools, and patterns of innovation activity. Since knowledge sharing is imperfect, the ops team serves as a mechanism for connecting existing solutions and problems with external sources of knowledge, facilitating connections among actors to fill a project's knowledge or resource gaps, and fostering value creating intersections among previously unconnected actors. For instance, solutions or ideas associated with an existing or past project might solve a problem identified in a project running concurrently or a future project but only if a connection is made. These kinds of unique combinations tend to generate novel outcomes.[12] As a result, the ops team plays a vital role in shaping and promoting co-innovation opportunities by actively managing and blending knowledge flows internal and external to the platform. Developing knowledge broker capabilities is a first step.

Building Knowledge Broker Capabilities. In this outside-in form of open innovation, the ops team needs to develop an ability to recognize and assimilate external sources of knowledge and innovation—referred to as absorptive capacity.[13] This requires a commitment to continuously build deep intelligence on technologies, industries, and arenas by exploring local and distant knowledge domains; developing breadth in knowledge supports identifying novel connections. A variety of exploration-oriented activities help the team build its knowledge broker capabilities and promote inbound innovation. These activities include participating in industry and technology association events (tradeshows, symposia); hosting brown bag lunch-and-learn events; attending quarterly business reviews; meeting with innovation practitioners; formal technology upskilling and training; and engaging in research on technology trends and innovation activities related to the ecosystem. As the team members learn and engage with other actors, they develop formal and informal ties throughout the ecosystem and adjacent arenas. Connections with this community of innovation-minded professionals serves several purposes.

Filling Knowledge Gaps. Over time, through learning from others as well as learning by doing, the ops team accrues expertise that equips it to provide supplemental research and analysis to assist a project's development. At SAP's co-innovation platform in the Silicon Valley, project teams frequently sought information on topics such as IoT, big data, and artificial intelligence (AI). In response, the ops team invested time in researching sensor technologies including optimal ways to capture and route sensor data as well as other technologies such as augmented reality, virtual reality, and mixed reality. As another example, a co-innovation team pursuing a project focused on the large scale-out of an IT system began with a host of questions related to how load generation for testing could be conducted given the scale. Did they need to use a specific tool? Would an enterprise-based tool work in the cloud? Could the same requirement be met or delivered as a service from a third party? These types of questions as well as the need to investigate the capabilities of particular tools or technologies are common. In this case, the ops team researched the questions and assisted the team in project execution.

Bridging Resource Gaps. When a co-innovation project team lacks critical subject matter expertise or talent, the ops team will tap their networks for the relevant resources. A robust example stems from the Monsta BOE 4.x Project which began with two partners, RedHat and SAP (see Appendix). The project was formed to examine concurrent use levels, upwards of ten thousand users, of an SAP product (SAP Business Intelligence (BI) 4.0™). The ops team recognized that the project would stress the platform's IT system capabilities. As a result, they searched for a partner that could fulfill the project's technology needs and identified Supermicro, a tertiary server provider. At the time, Supermicro was contemplating joining the co-innovation platform as a step to building a stronger relationship with SAP. Supermicro was willing to support the Monsta project but to do so they needed access to semiconductor microprocessors with the appropriate capacity for their servers. To address this need, the ops team brokered an agreement between Supermicro and Intel and Intel provided the necessary components. The connection enabled Supermicro to engage in the Monsta project. Once the first stage of the project was completed, the ops team demonstrated the project outcomes to Intel. The project's success reinforced the value of Intel's collaboration with Supermicro as well as the platform's value to Intel. Searching, identifying and onboarding a new partner also saved the project team and the ops team from having to draw system time from other co-innovation projects to support the Monsta project's activities. The next phase of the project required additional technical equipment and the ops team brokered a connection with another firm, F5. The project, leveraging the load balancing capabilities of F5's technology, demonstrated the ability to achieve ten thousand concurrent users on the SAP BI 4.0 platform. The performance exceeded previous testing and validation results and helped the Monsta team establish a new threshold for concurrent user query performance. Riding the waves of their collaborative success, Supermicro and Intel subsequently pursued a second project with the platform.

The Monsta saga illustrates how bridging resource gaps and brokering relationships among unconnected actors creates value for project participants while also advancing the system's generativity. Brokering connections among unconnected actors however, requires skills in influence and persuasion. While Intel was willing to support the project, external actors may not always be willing to engage as partners or subject matter experts. As an example, a four-star general approached the co-innovation platform located in Silicon Valley and was interested in pursuing a project related to disaster management in Haiti. At the time, one of SAP's employees was a subject matter expert in the Creole language and was frequently contacted when there was a disaster in Haiti. The general sought the employee's expertise to support the creation of a technology that would provide soldiers with instant language translation when they were going door-to-door in a war zone. The platform's director spent many hours trying to convince the SAP subject matter expert to participate but he was reluctant and ultimately, did not support the project. In platform-based ecosystems, a critical challenge is managing influence over actors that are outside of the platform's hierarchical control.

Generativity via New Combinations. The notion of generating something novel by combining distant or diverse content (knowledge or subject matter) or by combining existing content with a new idea has a long history in the study of innovation.[14] A variety of studies demonstrate how the "carrying out of new combinations" yields breakthrough innovations.[15] For instance, Sarah Kaplan and Keyvan Vakili's study of recombination in breakthrough innovation shows that recombining diverse and distant knowledge advances economic value.[16] In a study of how science affects technological advance, Lee Fleming and Olav Sorenson find that breakthrough innovations tend to arise when inventors engage with, and synthesize, a broad range of knowledge elements.[17] Rebecca Henderson and Kim Clark's classic study of innovation in the photolithographic alignment equipment industry shows that invention arises by reconfiguring existing combinations of components.[18]

Over time, as knowledge brokers accrue an understanding of various domains and expand their networks, they learn how to identify and connect ideas, knowledge and/or technologies emerging from different sources. For instance, a result or idea from a past or existing project may be reused in a new project; alternatively, results or ideas may be combined with knowledge emerging from concurrent projects or organizations external to the platform. In some cases, new connections and projects propagate relatively quickly; in other cases, outcomes trigger new ideas downstream. Whether described as synthesis, integration, symbiosis, or recombination, the underlying idea is similar: creating something new by intersecting and blending existing and/or new knowledge, subject matter and/or ideas. By identifying unique intersections among a diverse set of actors and domains, the ops team uncovers non-obvious, value creation opportunities for established as well as new complementors. Doing so enhances the value the platform creates for project partners while also contributing innovation that extends the use value of the platform's core offering.

Building Organizational Memory. Related to the above, the ops team and platform benefit by building an organizational memory. The latter is achieved by retaining knowledge from interactions with different actors as well as knowledge about past projects, typically using digital resources (blogs, papers, images, videos, website summarizing projects), physical demo examples, and artifacts. Keeping demos "alive" in the platform's physical and digital space is a way to build awareness and stimulate interest in the platform's innovation activities and often, triggers the repurposing project results.[19] For instance, one of the projects we studied resulted in a demo for a mining business unit. Three years after the original project was completed, an executive learned about the project's results and contacted the platform director to ask if the project's demo remained available. The executive was interested in tapping the prior project's results to support a new project.

In summary, since a co-innovation platform's projects stem from a diverse set of actors and industries, its pool of knowledge and ideas exceeds that held by any one firm or actor. By fostering relationships with and among complementary actors spanning a wide range of industries, the knowledge broker capabilities extend the platform's scope of innovation activity. Over time, the platform organically, and fairly rapidly, becomes a point of intersection for subject matter or domain experts. In combination, the platform's knowledge broker system and its demand-side services, focused on project storytelling, stimulate the interest of new project seekers as well as repeat collaborators (see Chapter 4). In this way, the platform's knowledge broker system promotes the system's generativity by advancing complementary innovation among different, autonomous actors. Table 3.3[20] summarizes the key activi-

Table 3.3 Co-Innovation platform: knowledge broker activities

Category	Activities	Examples
Explore and Expose	• Build intelligence on different technologies, industries and arenas. • Expose actors to a wide range of industries and knowledge domains.	• An ops team member reads an article on an emerging technology and follows up with the author to learn more.
Learn	• Learn about different domains as well as the state of the art surrounding projects. • Learn by doing and learn from others. • Build and retain knowledge and ideas (the platform's organizational memory).	• An ops team member learns about sensor technology from a subject matter expert and shares the knowledge with partners in a co-innovation project. • The ops team creates and curates a digital repository of project reports, videos, etc.
Identify, Combine & Connect	Form new projects by capitalizing on unique intersections: • Identify non-obvious connections among co-innovation projects (past and present), existing partners and/or new partners. • Indirect Influence: Encourage and persuade actors to participate, engage, share and support projects. • Combine and repurpose ideas, results and knowledge from projects and different domains.	• The ops team co-opts a complementor (example: Monsta project, Supermicro and Intel). • An ops team member works with a project team to combine results from a past project and the team's technology.
Support project work	• Provide connections to fill capability or resource gaps. • Learn by doing.	• An ops team member cold calls a subject matter expert to fill a resource gap.

ties of the platform's knowledge broker system in supporting and advancing co-innovation.

Operations Management Team: Additional Activities

Managing and Advancing the Project Portfolio. As the glue that connects all aspects of the platform and keeps it running, the ops team understands the state and needs of the platform's project portfolio and core services at any given point in time. Overseeing the portfolio in support of the platform's objectives involves at least three activities: managing scope, managing scale, and managing relationships among projects. In terms of scope, the central question is how diverse should the portfolio be? Diversity is critical to maintaining a generative ecosystem.

To advance diversity, the platform should organize the portfolio using a mix of dimensions such as technology trends (IoT, cloud, analytics, big data, AI, etc.), industry verticals, *and* business functions or activities (marketing, manufacturing, supply chain, finance, IT, sourcing, commerce, etc.). Using multiple dimensions to inform the portfolio's project diversity assures that the platform's participants are exposed to a variety of experience and knowledge domains and supports the platform's capacity to produce new output from a wide range of different actors. A project roadmap or aggregate project planning tool also can be used to guide strategic thinking about the portfolio. The tool is guided by a series of questions: What types and mix of projects are needed to achieve the platform's objectives? Which projects have priority? What gaps exist in the portfolio relative to the platform's objectives? Is the scope too narrow or too broad? Do any projects not align with the objectives? The portfolio's projects are vehicles for executing the platform's objectives.

Some projects might be more derivative, such as an innovation improving the performance of an existing application, whereas others may involve exploring how an emerging technology might be used to inform a business. For example, a multi-phase co-innovation project with OSIsoft and SAP began as somewhat incremental and expanded (see Appendix for the case brief). The purpose of the project was to create an SAP HANA IoT connector that enables enterprise customers to gain insights from business assets, physical assets, and operational data. The jointly developed solution used open database connectivity (ODBC) architecture to provide fast performance and the simplest, most direct connection to SAP HANA. The partners collaborated to enable access to operational data with advanced analytics and visualization capabilities. Early phases of the project explored feasibility and the team worked to enable integration of the OSIsoft PI data with SAP's

IoT platform. In subsequent phases, OSIsoft extended its PI infrastructure to allow streaming sensor events captured by PI managed sensors to flow into SAP HANA. Next, the iteration of the adapter was built to capture, store, and analyze the sensor events into SAP Sybase ESP. Subsequent phases explored expanded functionality, new use cases and data visualization.

In general, you want a diverse mix of projects with some covering cutting edge topics. This approach also reinforces the role of strategy in defining the portfolio and resource allocation rather than resource allocation dictating strategic direction. As such, the platform's objectives and roadmap guide resource allocation priorities. At SAP, regional influences also informed the project portfolios at each platform location—both the Palo Alto, California (USA), and Berlin (Germany) locations pursued more IoT and AI/ML projects; the Moscow (Russia) location engaged in more ERP and analytics projects surrounding oil and gas; and the Zurich (Switzerland) location had many projects in retail. Additionally, an engineering team in Waldorf, Germany, provided back office support for co-innovation activities, such as provisioning the capabilities of five data centers across fifteen platforms, and participated in a lot of manufacturing-based projects.

Regarding scale, how large should the portfolio be? How many projects can the platform manage? The portfolio size will depend on your platform's objectives as well as the amount of resources and services you dedicate to concurrent project support. In SAP's co-innovation platforms, spanning fourteen years of activity, the size of project portfolios ranged from 13 to 20 projects per platform annually. Each platform location set goals for the number of projects per month, quarter or year. While some platforms eventually grew to 18 to 20 projects per year (~4–5 per quarter), growth was influenced by each the platform's capacity, including computing and infrastructure capacity. For instance, at SAP, co-innovation platforms' ops teams were tasked with managing the consumption of virtual SAP HANA instances; project proposals needing SAP HANA resources required an additional layer of approval to address consumption and schedule needs. The ops team actively monitors project requirements to verify that all projects receive sufficient support and to avoid bottlenecks in service provisioning. For example, you may have eight concurrent projects all needing more capacity than you can reliably provide. Additionally, when a project is in a hot topic area, finding subject matter experts to support the project also can be challenging. And if any projects hiccup in some way, the ops team may need to rebalance its service allocation plan. A platform's project roadmap along with project status updates provide the ops team a vehicle for communicating the platform's progress and pipeline to its parent organization as well as to the ecosystem community. In combination, scope and scale inform the project selection process. Not every project gets a green light. The ops team is tasked with directing a finite set of resources to the most relevant projects, ensuring the success of each co-innovation project, and extending the use value of the platform organization's core products and services.

A related activity is about managing the portfolio's scope, including relationships among projects, partners, and initiatives within the platform's parent organization. What synergies exist among current and past projects? Are there potential synergies with other activities within the parent organization? What opportunities exist for joint learning and capability building? This activity assists the ops team in uncovering new project opportunities and novel intersections among unconnected partners. For instance, the team might observe intersections between an IoT project, a blockchain project, and a sustainability project and bring the various partners together to discuss a potential project. A customer might approach the platform with an idea and the ops team might bring together partners with different knowledge and expertise to explore the idea; initial discussions may reveal potential or not. While this integration activity falls within the ops team's role, synergies among projects also might be identified from a variety of sources such as project teams working concurrently, audiences at showcase events, customers and partners reviewing the platform's publications, and managers from the platform's parent organization. The ops team can use simple tools to foster and track potential connections to initiatives within the parent organization. For instance, when IoT projects were a priority for SAP's co-innovation platform in Palo Alto, the ops team identified other SAP (non-platform) partnerships, initiatives, and points of contact to support the IoT agenda. This information was used to market and showcase IoT focused co-innovation projects to other parts of the organization with the intent to generate influence revenue. Overall, the ops team's integration skills play a crucial role in shaping the future agenda and ensuring the combined value created by the platform and its community of co-innovation partners is greater than the sum of its parts.

Given the portfolio management approach, the platform's success is not dependent on the success of a single project but stems from its portfolio of projects, allowing the platform to diversify risk. For instance, as a thought exercise, assume co-innovation projects, on average, have a 60% likelihood of failure; under these conditions, the likelihood of the platform failing when 8 projects are in the portfolio is (0.6^8) or less than 2%. As the number of projects in the portfolio increases, the estimates of worse case and best case performance become less meaningful and the expected value becomes increasingly important. Of course, given the diversity of projects, project failure or success rates will vary. Additionally, the platform's focus on co-innovation helps it manage risk associated with solving an industry-wide problem. For example, the mining industry aspires to become a zero-harm industry. The platform is not interested "going it alone" and assuming all of the risk associated with solving the mining industry's challenges. Instead, the platform shares risk in two ways. First, by bringing together organizations to co-develop the relevant solutions. Second, by connecting organizations with the relevant actors (subject matter experts, customers, etc.) to support and enhance solution development. In this way, the platform advances the development of co-innovation capabilities while also helping its customers tackle thorny, complex problems.

Key performance indicators (KPIs) are informed by what the platform and its parent organization seek to achieve. General metrics, assessed at different intervals, include items such as the number of projects by technology category/year, number of days partners are engaged in co-innovation projects/quarter, number of events showcasing projects/quarter, number of follow-on projects/year, partner survey responses, number of visitors to the platform/quarter or year, number of publications/quarter, project contributions—direct and influence revenue/year, and annual budget. For instance, SAP's co-innovation platforms had a common KPI of pursuing at least one big data project, IoT project, and/or HANA project per quarter. A similar metric existed for events—each platform was required to hold at least one half day or full day event per quarter that attracted an audience of 50 attendees or more. A full "co-innovation day" showcased partners and their projects. A typical event might begin with a keynote discussing a topic of interest—such as IoT, AI/ML, big data, virtualization, cloud computing, digital retail, sustainability, etc. Project partners are provided the opportunity to present their work to an audience of ecosystem partners, other project teams, field personnel, and usually, customers. Platforms sponsors also might co-host an event, symposium or week of activities on a focal topic such as virtualization or cloud computing. Shifting to outcomes, since many co-innovation projects are in an early stage of development, hard revenue targets might constrain achieving the platform's co-innovation objectives. As a result, demonstrating influence revenue requires the platform's director or ops team collaborate with other parts of the organization to support adoption of project outcomes—typically, solutions that extend the platform's parent organization's core offerings. For instance, at SAP, the ops team would demonstrate a project's proof of concept (POC) to a field team within the parent organization and in turn, track whether and when a solution extension was booked with the field team's customer.

How much does it cost to build a co-innovation platform? It depends on what you want to achieve with the platform: How can a co-innovation platform help your organization? Do you want to understand how a range of emerging technologies might extend your solutions and affect your customers' industries? Or are you seeking a more focused approach—staying informed about two to three cutting-edge topics or technology areas? Alternatively, is your strategy more about developing new solutions for established markets? While we have described a fully enabled co-innovation platform, your strategic objectives will influence how you implement the platform and the budget to do so. The platform benefits from all service categories but each category may be tailored to fit your agenda. At a minimum, consider the amount of diversity needed in the portfolio; the number of partners and co-innovation projects needed quarterly to support your goals; the number of projects you can service concurrently; and whether you will use a sponsorship approach to jumpstart the platform and help address its resource needs. Of course, the platform also incurs baseline administrative and operating expenses associated with activities such as cloud services, operations management, space equipment and maintenance, event support, publishing reports, demo development, and so on. Other organizations have imitated the platform in different forms. A large multinational launched a co-innovation network and replicated parts of the co-innovation platform's design. More recently and on a smaller scale, Sam Lakkundi, Vice President, Innovation and Head of BMC Innovation Labs, BMC Software, indicates that he has replicated parts of the model to spur co-innovation at BMC; Sam was the SVP and CIO of Kore.ai when he engaged in co-innovation projects at SAP's co-innovation platform in Palo Alto, California.

Project Management and Change. The ops team's easiest job is helping co-innovation teams with project management when needed. As discussed in the contract formation section, each project's SOW defines a project's scope, activities, deliverables, and timeline, as well as who is responsible for different aspects of the project. Most project participants have experience in working in project teams and rarely need assistance in executing the SOW. As a result, the ops team takes more of a back seat role, periodically checking on each project's status, needs, and milestone progress. The ops team, however, tends to play a more active role in helping manage changes to project scope.

The discovery-based stage of many projects means that change is inevitable. Iterative development facilitates learning that often warrants adjustments in project scope and needs. In some instances, experimentation results in a team redefining the focal problem to be solved; in other cases, a team learns they need a particular type of software, tool or technology to move a project forward. The co-innovation platform is designed to support the co-evolution of knowledge in co-innovation projects. Building sufficient time in project schedules for co-innovation teams to engage in creative friction, absorb knowledge, and think through ideas is essential. This process is not an open door to persistent change but more of a tolerance for failure and less of a tolerance for incompetence. In other words, changes to a project's statement of work are feasible and often necessary but should not be a daily occurrence. Various steps can help the ops team manage project changes. At the SOW stage, project partners are encouraged to develop a project schedule that allows sufficient time for experimentation. The ops team also benefits from adopting a simple process for assisting teams in adjusting scope and adapting project development. Of course, a large number of change requests occurring concurrently across projects can quickly overwhelm the ops team. Monitoring each project's journey helps the ops team anticipate shifts in resource needs and informs adjustments to the allocation of services across the project portfolio.

Where Do We Collaborate?

Numerous books and academic articles identify the ideal organizational conditions to amplify and incent innovative thinking. It is widely accepted that collaboration for innovation benefits immensely when individuals have opportunities to interact and exchange knowledge face-to-face or in-person. The colocation of individuals also tends to increase adhoc or unplanned face-to-face communication, enabling socialization and knowledge recombination. Establishing innovation spaces where teams can collaborate also promotes knowledge generativity.[21] And as Henry Chesbrough's work on open innovation advocates, proximity is critical given the platform's outside-in approach to co-innovation where collaborators from different organizations are sharing knowledge.[22]

To capitalize on these opportunities, the physical space for co-innovation work needs to be designed to promote formal and informal interactions among partners participating in different projects. This is not about creating a glass walled room and assuming everyone who enters immediately is creative or an innovator. Instead, it is about establishing an environment where teams can engage in project work, exchange knowledge about their projects, and share insights on innovation processes and emerging technologies. Specific ideas such as creating a common gathering space, whether it be a communal table or enticing coffee/snack area, can spark informal conversations. These conditions increase the likelihood that individuals will interact and develop social relationships.[23] For concurrent project work in a large open space, rolling chairs and desks that rotate facilitate interactions among project teams whereas moveable whiteboards or walls allow the space to be reconfigured to multiple private spaces quickly. Also important is providing workspace where projects, such as a building a physical demo for testing, can remain in place while in development. The platform's showcasing activities benefit when the space easily can be reconfigured to host events and demonstrations. Of course, ensuring the availability of basic infrastructure resources such as sufficient WiFi, power, and collaboration tools also matters.[24] Christine Puccio, Vice President, Global Cloud Alliances & GTM Programs, F5 Networks, commented on the platform's interactive space: "A great place to try things out. More companies need to do this. There is not a place for us to go and tinker; not a place to go where the whole focus is to think out of the box." Additionally, establishing a set of house rules that guide how the space may be used by co-innovation teams helps promote a productive innovation environment. Lastly, virtual access to many of the platform's services is feasible but should be considered a complement rather than a substitute for the activities that occur in the physical space. Although firms have adapted to virtual work due to the covid-19 pandemic, we have missed the opportunity for the unplanned and planned face-to-face or in person interactions that are vital to productive co-innovation.

With multiple and diverse project workstreams running concurrently, the platform's physical space is a buzz of activity. The co-innovation teams we spoke with valued the platform's physical space for several reasons: opportunities for spontaneous interactions with other project teams, potential for learning and knowledge spillovers, access to collaboration tools, and the general functionality of the work space. Kathy Barboza, Head of Google Cloud Sales, Net App, reflected on her experiences at SAP's co-innovation lab in Palo Alto: "You had the tools to collaborate, meeting space, areas for everyone to come in to collaborate; not just a stuffy conference room, but an environment for people to think outside of the box, to promote creative thinking." She viewed the platform as "Ahead of its time in collaboration tools for companies to come together." Kathy was the Director of Software Alliances at Intel when she participated in multiple co-innovation projects at SAP's co-innovation platform in Palo Alto, California.

Spillovers from these interactions foment new co-innovation projects with the platform as well as new business relationships among firms, internal and external to the platform. Even in small samples, strong generativity is evident. For instance, considering a random sample of fifteen co-innovation projects, eight firms pursued two or more additional co-innovation projects with the platform and four of these firms worked with different partners or sets of partners to support nineteen additional co-innovation projects. For example, Intel pursued its first project with SAP's co-innovation platform in 2009 and participated in twelve more co-innovation projects between 2010 to 2014.[25] An Alliance Manager at Intel commented on a project that occurred in 2014: "This project outcome is the result of companies working cooperatively in a true co-innovation style that was built on the backbone of the COIL [co-innovaton platform] at SAP. I can't wait to see what we do next."

Among the fifteen projects, nine firms indicated that connections they made through the platform contributed to new partner relationships outside of the platform environment. An Alliance Manager at Citrix reflected on the opportunity to build additional partnerships with the platform and beyond: "COIL offers us the unique combination of collaboration with SAP and other partners, working with them on customer-driven solutions, projects and proof-of-concepts and hence extending and creating new partnerships beyond an already existing ecosystem." Between 2009 and 2013, Citrix had participated in five co-innovation projects with the platform. A Principal Enterprise Architect at Red Hat stated: "Working with SAP COIL enables Red Hat to participate in world leading innovative projects, in collaboration with not only SAP but also other partners." As another example, a project involving collaboration with SAP NS2 (SAP's U.S. proxy entity), spawned multiple projects internal and external to the platform. NS2's CTO explained: "Our work in COIL started in 2013 based on collaboration with SAP NS2 focused on building an engineered solution on SAP HANA that specifically leverages the HANA Spatial engine. This work has led to additional projects within COIL to leverage more SAP HANA spatial capability, SAP Mobile, and SAP BI; all aimed at accelerating adoption of the emerging spatial technologies across the SAP stack within the SAP customer base. It further resulted in expanded relationships with other key SAP Partners and SIs. Without the collaborative work in SAP COIL, this extension and creation of new partnerships as well as marketplace adoption of these technologies would have taken much longer." Reinforcing these effects, another executive noted, "The COIL has provided more than sustained infrastructure. The COIL has opened doors that helped [my firm] build enduring relationships internal to SAP and with external SAP partners."

The Zoo Effect

In our interviews, project partners also identified the visibility of the platform's office location as a benefit. In SAP's Silicon Valley location, the co-innovation platform was located off the main lobby entrance to SAP's building 1 in Palo Alto, California. As Image 3.1 shows, glass walls provide transparency into the space, digital content is displayed on monitors behind the glass and the rails for the lobby staircase are captured in the lower right corner of the image. At any point in time, the ops team might be running a demo and showcasing real-time data from a project. As a result, any visitor to building 1 is exposed to the platform's daily hub of activity, is likely to glimpse a project or two, and has a clear view of a wide array of infrastructure technology. Kathy Barboza referred to it as the "zoo effect": "as you walked up the stairs, you could see all the servers and everyone could see this is where hardware and software comes together. Every time I brought an executive and we passed the stairs with the glass, I would point out Intel's technology in the COIL space. In those moments, there was a bit of puffing out the chest." A second layer of visibility occurs within the platform space itself where co-innovation teams are exposed to other projects showcased in digital displays, prototypes, or demos. Artifacts such as interactive displays

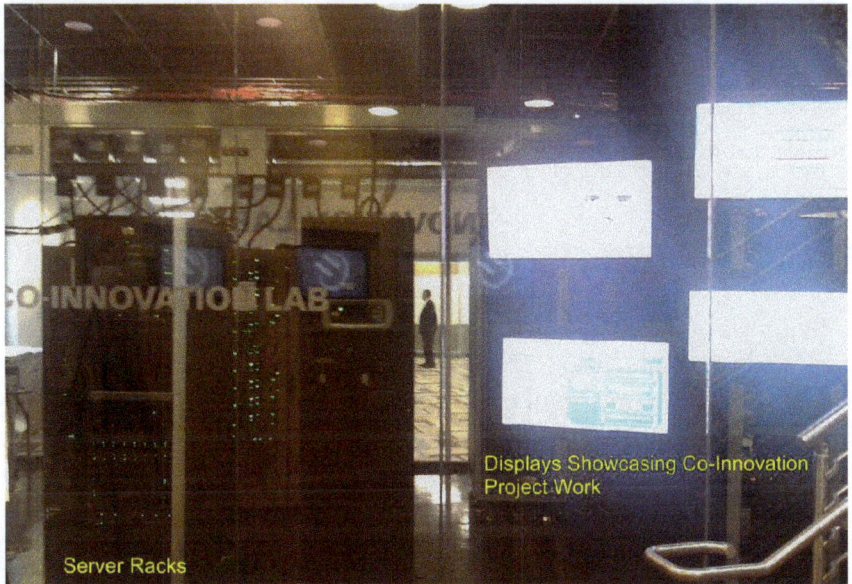

Image 3.1 The zoo effect: a view from the lobby

and always-on automated demos make the space sticky and a frequent visitor attraction.

The Value of a Co-Innovation Platform

Firms are continuously seeking ways to innovate. We could say that doing so today is more important than it was in the past but this mantra rings true for every generation of managers and firms. What is distinctive today? The ability to collaborate for innovation or to develop a co-innovation capability. Successful navigation of volatile, complex, uncertain, and/or ambiguous environments is difficult to do alone, especially in the face of rapid technological change and digital transformation. By adopting an outside-in approach to innovation, a co-innovation platform purposively manages inflows and outflows of knowledge to shape its ecosystem's innovation trajectory. The chapter lays out how the platform's core supply-side services enable co-innovation. In our view, simply provisioning digital marketing resources to complementors is not going to make co-innovation happen or cultivate meaningful variety in an ecosystem. But, equipping your organization with all the service elements also is not enough. The platform's innovative capacity stems from the integration of services, resources, and capabilities—the key is how the services work in combination to facilitate, enable, and showcase co-innovation. The ops team, as the system architects of the platform, is the engine underlying this integration. In the next chapter, we describe and illustrate how the platform's demand-side services contribute to showcasing co-innovation project results.

Key Takeaways

1. By provisioning supply-side and demand-side services to complementors to enable co-innovation projects, the platform's hands-on approach to innovation is distinct from other innovation platform models that employ a hands-off approach with limited resources. The integrated system of services inspires actors to join and makes it easy for them to create and capture value from their co-innovation work.
2. The orchestrating concept pops up frequently in the context of platforms and ecosystems yet, studies are less precise about how to make it happen. The co-innovation platform model solves this problem by detailing how

the ops team, through an integrated set of services and activities, coordinates and influences the innovation activity of a variety of ecosystem actors.
3. The co-innovation platform model promotes generativity in platform-based ecosystems by connecting two or more firms and equipping them with the supply-side services, resources and capabilities, from contract formation to launch, to enable successful co-innovation.
4. Encouraging co-innovation projects from different origins assures that the platform is continuously engaging diverse actors and in turn, expanding the ecosystem's scope of knowledge and resources for creating new combinations.
5. Engaging in co-innovation with the platform is an experience not an event. The platform provides an environment where formal and informal interactions facilitate knowledge sharing and problem solving among diverse actors to support joint knowledge creation and capability building.
6. The co-innovation platform's knowledge broker services are vital to shaping and advancing co-innovation in a platform-based ecosystem. Using indirect influence to fill knowledge and resource gaps, the platform's knowledge brokers cultivate variety by uncovering novel project opportunities, fostering connections among unconnected actors, identifying non-obvious project intersections, building relationships within and beyond the ecosystem, and managing the platform's organizational memory.
7. Value created by co-innovated solutions extends the use value of the platform's core offering while creating new sources of value capture for co-innovation partners. In combination, co-innovation platforms and co-innovation project teams generate more value than the participating actors could create individually.

Questions, quibbles, comments? Please share your thoughts and ideas. We would value hearing your co-innovation story. You can reach us at: coinnovationstrategy@gmail.com.

Notes

1. Turning Vision into Value with Co-Innovation, SAP Co-Innovation Lab, https://www.sap.com/documents/2020/07/84d1846f-a67d-0010-87a3-c30de2ffd8ff.html#page=7. Accessed May 1, 2021.

2. For example, the ops team might identify an opportunity and engage with a startup to develop the idea. Alternatively, based on its experience and oversight of the platform's projects, the ops team might identify a unique opportunity that could be addressed by combining the complementary resources of previously unconnected partners.
3. As an example, the ops team could propose a project to a product manager or business unit manager. When a proposal was of interest, a manager would evaluate the resources he could commit to the project; lacking resources, interested parties often agreed to serve as stakeholders.
4. Studies of platform-based ecosystems are relatively silent on how this process is managed. We offer one approach.
5. Per Chapter 1, for a detailed discussion of ecosystem generativity, see Cennamo, C. and Santalo, J. 2019. Generativity Tension and Value Creation in Platform Ecosystems. Organization Science, 30 (3): 617–641; Wareham, J., Fox, P.B., and Giner, J. 2014. Technology ecosystem governance. *Organization Science, 25*: 1195–1215.
6. Page 42, Chesbrough, H. 2020. *Open Innovation Results: Going Beyond the Hype and Getting Down to Business*. UK: Oxford University Press.
7. Of course, the conditions have changed given the widespread proliferation of application program interfaces (API) in the cloud era. This is the cornerstone of the digitization occurring today.
8. Objectives should be proximate—identifying a target that the team expects to achieve. Robust proximate objectives provide clarity and help focus a team's energy.
9. Influence revenue is revenue generated when a co-innovation project outcome assists a sales or presales manager, field representative, and/or business development manager close business with a customer. For example, a project outcome might be offered as additional functionality to address a customer need. The platform is not a sales unit; instead, it enables project teams to develop outcomes that might generate direct revenue for the participating partners.
10. The type of technology and equipment needed to support a co-innovation platform is a function of the platform's objectives. The platform we studied began by leveraging the hardware of technology partners such as Intel, Cisco, Fujitsu, NetApp, HP, IBM, Lenovo, Hitachi Data Systems (HDS), PureStorage, and others, to build large-scale architectures and a multi-tenant private cloud. The IT landscapes deployed to project teams typically involved different-sized virtual machines (ranging from two to four CPUs) with NSF-based, SAN storage options to

support deployments of the platform organization's business suite software. Co-innovation project teams access the landscape, deployed as a virtual lan (VLAN), via a VPN gateway. Other connectivity options, such as encrypted LAN-to-LAN, often are used to securely access partner resources during a project or demo.

11. At SAP, each platform location had a staff of about 3–5 people; each location leveraged experts across SAP and the broad ecosystem (spanning multiple industries) to enable co-innovation projects.
12. See Hargadon, A., and Sutton, R.I. 1997. Technology brokering and innovation in a product development firm. *Administrative Science Quarterly*: 716–749; Fleming, L., and Sorenson, O. 2004. Science as a Map in Technological Search. *Strategic Management Journal, 25*: 909–928; and Kaplan, S., and Vakili, K. 2015. The double-edged sword of recombination in breakthrough innovation. *Strategic Management Journal, 36*: 1435–1457.
13. Cohen and Levinthal (1990: 128) define absorptive capacity as a firm's ability "to recognize the value of new, external information, assimilate it, and apply it to commercial ends" and view it as critical to a firm's innovation capabilities. In the original discussion, the emphasis was on the importance of using internal research to capitalize on external knowledge and technology. Cohen, W.M., and Levinthal, D.A. 1990. Absorptive capacity: A new perspective on learning and innovation. *Administrative Science Quarterly*: 128–152.
14. For instance, the German edition of Schumpeter's The Theory of Economic Development (1911) refers to entrepreneurs as identifying new combinations whereas Schumpeter's subsequent version (1934) emphasized that innovation arises from the "carrying out of new combinations" (Schumpeter, J.A. 1911. *Theorie der wirtschaftlichen Entwicklung* (1st edn). Duncker & Humblot: Leipzig; Schumpeter, J.A. 1934. *The Theory of Economic Development. An Inquiry into Profits, Capital, Credit, Interest, and the Business Cycle*. Harvard University Press: Cambridge, MA). See also: Nelson, R., and Winter, S. 1982. *An Evolutionary Theory of Economic Change*. Cambridge, MA: Belknap Press; and Becker, M., Knudsen, T., and March, J.G. 2006. Schumpeter, Winter and the sources of novelty. *Industrial and Corporate Change, 115*(2): 353–371.
15. The phrase is attributed to a translation of Schumpeter, J.A. 1911. *Theorie der wirtschaftlichen Entwicklung* (1st edn). Duncker & Humblot: Leipzig.

16. Kaplan, S., and Vakili, K. 2015. The Double-Edged Sword of Recombination in Breakthrough Innovation. *Strategic Management Journal, 36*: 1435–1457.
17. Fleming, L., and Sorenson, O. 2004. Science as a Map in Technological Search. *Strategic Management Journal, 25*: 909–928.
18. Henderson, R.M., and Clark, K.B. 1990. Architectural innovation: The reconfiguration of existing product technologies and the failure of established firms. *Administrative Science Quarterly, 35*: 9–30.
19. See Hargadon, A., and Sutton, R.I. 2000. Building an innovation factory. *Harvard Business Review*, 156–166, #6102: page 156.
20. Adapted from Hargadon (1998). Refer to Hargadon and Sutton (1997) for a more thorough treatment of promoting innovation through knowledge brokers. Hargadon, A. 1998. Firms as Knowledge Brokers: Lessons in Pursuing Continous Innovation. *California Management Review, 40*(3). Hargadon, A., and Sutton, R.I. 1997. Technology Brokering and Innovation in a Product Development Firm. *Administrative Science Quaterly*: 716–749.
21. For example: Caccamo, M. 2020. Leveraging innovation spaces to foster collaborative innovation. *Creativity and Innovation Management, 29*(1): 178–191.
22. See Chesbrough, H. 2020. *Open Innovation Results: Going Beyond the Hype and Getting Down to Business.* UK: Oxford University Press.
23. A variety of studies reinforce the role of geographic proximity in the formation of social relationships. In a classic study, Zipf (1949) suggests the "principle of least effort" where the lowest cost interactions are among co-located actors. A recent study by Kleinbaum, Stuart and Tushman (2013) shows that individuals with similar characteristics tend to form stronger social relationships when employed and co-located in the same office as compared to individuals employed and located in different offices. Kleinbaum, A.M., Stuart, T.E., Tushman, M.L. 2013. Discretion Within Constraint: Homophily and Structure in a Formal Organization. *Organization Science, 24*(5): 1316–1336.
24. As an example, SAP's co-innovation platform in Palo Alto houses a computing and network data center featuring two rows of 42U-sized racks (approximately 19 racks in total) with twenty tons of cooling capacity from its heating, ventilation, and air conditioning (HVAC) system and runs inside of a glass room adjacent to other co-innovation collaboration and event space. The platform's IT system landscape is surrounded by four collaboration rooms as well as a multi-purpose space

that could be configured for 50-plus-person events, multiple breakout team work spaces, and live demos.
25. Independent of the co-innovation platform, SAP and Intel had previously collaborated to build functionality for SAP's HANA system (an in memory, column-oriented, relational database management system). This effort and the SAP HANA technology fueled a variety of related, co-innovation projects that added additional value to the platform. SAP HANA converges platform, database, data processing capabilities, spatial and textual data analysis and provides libraries for predictive planning and business analytics all in a single platform with a built in application and web server. It blends together innovations in hardware architectures, columnar and row databases, text analytics and parallel processing, in a real-time data processing platform.

4

Co-Innovation Storytelling

I still remember when we worked on several projects in Mining, Construction, and Oil & Gas, involving a number of partners, designing and architecting the complete demos from scratch. Spending time in such an environment, for the design thinking sessions and exploring ideas was priceless, but after the demo was built, I was really impressed by the approach the platform team took to show the result with the physical assets and the software solution, through storytelling. This innovative storytelling approach was very powerful as it puts the listening audience in the context of the industry and the personas, and clearly helps to understand the value of the solution and how the ecosystem working together is essential for a successful co-innovation. I can't express how memorable and powerful this experience has been in my innovation mindset.
—Merlin Yamssi, Lead Solutions Consultant, Google

The co-innovation platform's demand-side services, referenced as Demo and Showcase, are designed to generate awareness and demand through various methods of storytelling.

The platform and participating actors benefit when the platform's operations management team (ops team) and a project's partners can tell a story about a project's journey with the platform. Storytelling is used not only to capture the attention of stakeholders but also to give project partners the opportunity to learn from current and past projects. Compelling co-innovation stories or narratives knit together material artifacts, actors' behaviors, and context to convey information and experiences. Building and retaining narratives about co-innovation experiences enables knowledge to accrue in a way that stimulates thinking about new ideas and options. As individuals learn a project's story, they draw inferences and lessons that inspire action. Additionally, stories about multiple co-innovation projects expose individuals to different activities and ideas and facilitate the building of connections among different knowledge domains.[1] As a result, they enhance the co-innovation experience and project work while also stimulating new project development.

Co-innovation project stories stem from different sources, leverage different methods or materials, and inform the platform's memory of co-innovation experiences. Stories can arise from any stage of a project's evolution, such as proposal development, project enablement, project work, or demo and showcase. For instance, narratives about a co-innovation project's journey provide a translation of the collaborative process that occurs in project work,[2] making the unobservable more tangible. Stories that are retold and demos that are reshared contribute to new opportunities as individuals connect the past with a new idea. As a result, compelling innovation storytelling is sticky and generative and provides a tool to help sustain innovation.

This chapter describes the platform's storytelling activities. We begin with the operations management team's (ops team) role in storytelling. Next, we expand on the different sources of, and methods for, project narratives over the course of a project's lifecycle. The subsequent sections use case examples to illustrate the platform's various methods of storytelling with a focus on live events and demos.

Storytelling and the Ops Team

Developing a process for generating stories or narratives about co-innovation projects and the platform plays an important role in supporting the platform's goals of advancing ecosystem generativity. The platform's ops team, in collaboration with project teams, has four overarching tasks when it comes to the storytelling aspect of demand-side services:

- Outcome Story Development: Developing narratives about the value created by a project outcome.
- Process Story Development: Developing narratives about the collaborative process throughout a project's lifecycle (including activities such as contract formation, collaborative problem solving, co-innovation project workstreams, etc.).

- Platform Memory Management: Retaining, curating, and sharing narratives about projects.
- Showcasing the Platform: Broadcasting the platform's activities and success stories.

First, the ops team helps project teams develop narratives about the value derived from a project outcome. Assistance includes how to craft stories in a way that will resonate with a broad audience. On the process side, the ops team also tells the story of how things were discovered, learned, tried, tested or proven. This content is born from an array of team activities over the course of a project. As such, the ops team has the advantage of being able to tell a more complete story about how a combination of technologies, processes, context and people solved a problem. Third, the narratives about outcomes and process are retained, contributing to the platform's organizational memory and informing future projects and their development. Lastly, the ops team also devotes time and energy showcasing the platform's activities and building the platform's reputation for co-innovation throughout the ecosystem.

Storytelling Sources and Opportunities

Figure 4.1 identifies some of the types of stories that can be told during a project's lifecycle. Storytelling spans all stages of a co-innovation project

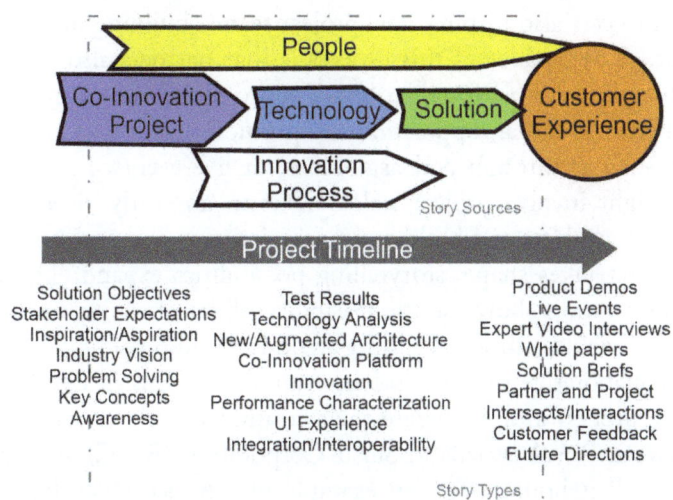

Fig. 4.1 Storytelling: sources and opportunities

beginning with project formation. It's somewhat akin to when a new film is introduced to the market. Before the film is distributed, producers share things such as who is signed to a film, unique behind the scenes stories such as how special effects were created, movie images (posters or digital) or sneak peaks, and actor interviews on talk shows and social media. The combination of artifacts (posters, images), actors and context, generate awareness, provoke interest, and stimulate demand. In our experience, project participants valued learning from stories and viewed the opportunity to tell stories about a project at any stage of a project as complementary to other marketing activities.

Beginning with the contract formation process, opportunities exist to explore, examine, and share the story of the co-innovators themselves and what they seek to achieve. Although the contract formation process (proposal, SOW, frame agreement) is designed to be simple and flexible, potential partners often seek information about how the process unfolds. As detailed in Chapter 5, *Enabling Co-Innovation as Behavior*, this stage of the process is critical to building relational attachments among project participants. As participants share their backgrounds and motivations for a project, they begin to build a mutual understanding and trust. Serving as a coach, the ops team facilitates these conversations. Having worked with multiple project teams, the ops team is well versed in the contract formation process and in a position to share "best practices" that have emerged from past projects to support the process. Sharing stories about activities such as how successful teams overcame differences, developed a work plan, or decided how to manage potential project changes, enables partners to gain an understanding of how other projects built a foundation for effective collaboration. Learning about successful projects also inspires new project teams, building momentum and excitement. A byproduct of this process is that partners also become more comfortable with the platform's contract approach. Once a contract is finalized, the platform has an opportunity to promote the project externally and internally, such as through podcasts, blogs, or live events. For example, the platform might involve project stakeholders in an "early view podcast" to showcase new projects and build awareness, interest, and enthusiasm.

As a project takes shape, storytelling possibilities expand. The details of a project's evolution showcase the feasibility of transforming an idea into a commercially viable solution. Gaining an understanding of how another team managed collaborative problem-solving can assist teams in developing their co-working process and accelerate their co-innovation activities. A collaboration between Royal Swaziland Sugar Corporation (RSSC) and established SAP partner Britehouse offers an example of a project's development. The project focused on solving a problem encountered in sugarcane harvesting and transport. RSSC's sugar mills run 24/7 requiring a continuous supply of cane; halting and restarting a production line is costly. Cane also must be burnt in the field before it is transported to a mill for processing and longer transport times compromise the sugarcane's sucrose content. The entire process must be efficient and continuous. The team began by identifying the project requirements. SAP and Britehouse also spent time with RSSC discussing how their joint knowhow could help RSSC streamline its operations; they also participated in a design thinking workshop. To provide proof of concept and value for RSSC, Britehouse recognized that they needed a system landscape for application development and reached out to SAP's co-innovation platform. The platform's team provided the environment for solution configuration and testing. The solution involved placing a geotag vehicle management device on each of RSSC's harvesting vehicles. Britehouse software engineers provided the interface software to capture data from the geotag or IoT devices. The solution provided RSSC the ability to monitor the status of harvesting vehicles (harvesting, down, in repair, etc.) in real time using a dashboard. RSSC's vehicle management realized improved efficiency as well as transparency. These types of stories show new project teams how successful outcomes are achieved.

The storytelling opportunity continues with a project's final stage. At this point in a project's lifecycle, project partners and their organizations' marketing teams take the lead in developing marketing content and marketing activities to showcase project results and their implications. Storytelling allows marketing teams to develop a deeper connection with their audience. Support also may be provided by the ops team and other product or partner teams within the platform's parent organization. As the various case examples illustrate, projects vary in scope and objectives and in turn, the timing of when they contribute to go-to-market goals. For example, some projects serve as a validation step for a technology's capability (Monsta) or a larger initiative (such as highway safety—see the tire retread example below), another set of projects yield solutions that are immediately implemented by a customer (Britehouse, RSSC, and sugar cane), other projects contribute to revenue associated with a downstream activity (Bluecoat, Monsta), and others support a more traditional go-to-market trajectory (such as a complementary service offering). As a result, project teams are exposed to a wide variety of project narratives, expanding their understanding of what is possible with the platform.

For example, recall the Monsta project shared in Chapter 3, *Building a Co-Innovation Platform*. The project's objective was to establish customer confidence in large scale business intelligence deployments using off-the-shelf commodity hardware and software. The project's targeted benchmark of serving ten thousand users concurrently was viewed as a business intelligence platform differentiator that would provide guidance for engineering and field representatives. The project achieved its objectives, demonstrating that business intelligence platforms for visualization, data reporting, and analytics could sustain up to ten thousand concurrent users with an architecture based on commodity hardware. At the time, a load of ten thousand concurrent users had never been tried before in any known internal or external testing (for additional details, see the Monsta case in the Appendix). Exceeding the established threshold with commodity components was a significant achievement. The result allowed field representatives to share this outcome with customers, many who were seeking the new high performance capability.

In Chapter 2, *Platforms: Types, Governance and Value Distribution*, we shared the truck tire retread case integrating blockchain and RFID technology to digitize truck tire retread activities. One project objective was to provide more accurate information for repair and warranty; another was to enhance highway safety by avoiding truck accidents due to tire problems. The project generated a tire lifecycle management prototype—tires are equipped with an RFID device that identifies the tire while a blockchain records tire mileage and maintenance. A tire repair organization can scan the RFID tag and capture a tire's maintenance and usage history, including information about retreads. GS1, the project partner and a non-profit global standards setting organization, showcased the result at various industry and supply chain events and attracted the attention of managers in different industries including automotive, rail, transport, and logistics. The project allowed GS1 to gain a stronger understanding of how new technologies could be used and the role they could play in solving problems for a variety of industries worldwide.

Demand-Side Services

Storytelling about co-innovation projects relies on a variety of demand-side services, referred to as Demo and Showcase. Table 4.1 lists each service, provides examples of content or materials associated with each service, and identifies the responsible actors (typically, the ops team and a project's partners). The content is published and distributed via digital channels, events, and traditional marketing channels. The services focus on building demand by capturing the attention of customers as well as other ecosystem participants. The subsequent sections offer examples of practices associated with each service.

Table 4.1 Demand-side services supporting project storytelling

Services	Description	Participating Actors
Demo Development	Design, build, run, & manage demos with project teams.	Platform ops team & Project partners; subject matter experts may be solicited.
Document Development	Develop solution briefs, blogs, white papers, technical reviews, press releases, case briefs &/ or use case summaries.	Platform ops team & Project partners; additional support may stem the organizations' marketing teams.
Podcasts and Video Content Creation	Create multiple short segment feature stories for public consumption.	Platform ops team & Project partners.
Event Hosting & Participation	Host or sponsor live events such as panel discussions, symposia, keynote events, & demo expos. Create and support exhibits at industry conferences or company-sponsored conferences/events.	Platform: Director & Ops Team Project: Partners, partner organization's marketing & communications representatives. Platform Organization: Executive briefing teams, Public Relations representatives.
Marketing Content Creation	Project specific examples: sales decks complemented by project documents (white papers, solution briefs, etc.). Multi-project examples: hosting events to showcase projects to customers and other partners.	Project partners & their organizations' marketing teams. Additional support may stem from the platform's ops teams and various groups within the platform's organization (product teams, partner groups, marketing teams, centers, etc.).

Demos: Build, Run and Host

Demo development involves the design, build, and management of a physical object that exhibits the functionality of a project's solution in real time. The demos are used to develop, test, and showcase a project and results are shared in the platform environment, at platform events, and via digital channels. Demos bring a project to life. By making results more tangible, demos foster a deeper connection with audiences. They also showcase the platform's unique capabilities.

In our observations, SAP's co-innovation platforms leveraged the ops teams' skills and prior experience to support demo development. For example, some members of the ops team at the co-innovation platform in Palo Alto, California, had experience in manufacturing whereas others had craftsman skills related to electro-mechanical devices. Complementary skills in theatrical settings, prop design, lighting, sound, model building, and carpentry also added value. The ops team often took some leaps of faith in its ability to convert prior experiences and latent skills into sophisticated demo design and development. In other words, you might be able to accomplish more than you think with existing staff.

A mining demo serves as a prime example. Firms in the mining industry want to develop a zero-harm work environment. To support this goal, Vandrico Solutions Inc., an industrial IoT and wearables software startup, collaborated with Illumiti, an SAP systems integration and management consulting company, to develop a MineSafe Smartwatch (for additional case details see Chapter 5, *Enabling Co-Innovation as Behavior* and the Appendix). The project used an IoT communications system and wifi to interact with mine-specific IoT data stemming from wearable devices and sensors placed throughout a mine. The solution provided an ability to help miners identify and respond to emerging safety issues in advance of a catastrophe. The fully functioning demo, displayed in Images 4.1a & b, showcased the project's solution. The demo was designed to support multiple industry use cases and to expand in features as solutions evolved.

How was the demo created? The ops team used stacked styrofoam to build the foundation for the mine environment and a hot knife and sculpting tools to excavate shafts. As Images 4.1a & b show, sensors, lighting, and a working

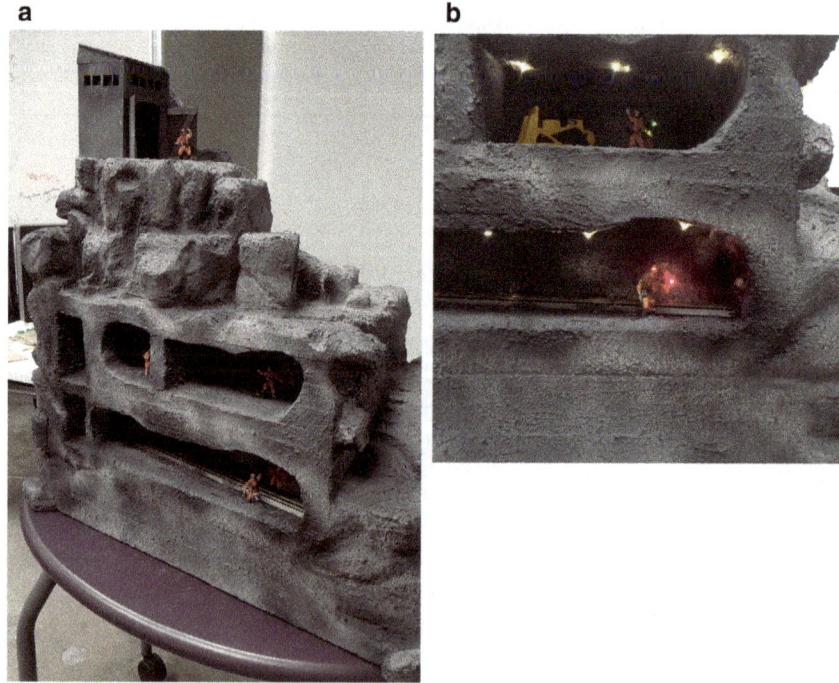

Image 4.1 IoT and the mining industry: **a.** Co-Innovation project demo. **b.** Zoom in of co-innovation project demo

elevator were added for testing purposes. A Raspberry Pi with a breadboard and wiring harness was hidden in the rear of the demo and supported all sensor and two-way communication needs. The base of the mine sat on a hidden springboard that simulated seismic events. Design to deployment took about six to eight weeks and the demo was active and on display for months. The demo captured the attention of multiple project teams, project sponsors, and visitors and it made a sticky imprint—three to four years after the project was completed, potential partners voiced interest in testing other mining scenarios. While the demo was housed in the platform's space, videos were created to share its performance with various audiences. Image 4.2 illustrates the setup; the image in the background of the photo is a mine shaft. Recordings provided a low cost way of sharing the demo and project and were popular with project teams and other ecosystem actors.

Image 4.2 Co-Innovation project demo recording IoT and the mining industry

A second demo example stems from an oil and gas industry project (see Image 4.3) involving multiple partners: Dell EMC, Pixel Velocity, Mtell, SAP Industry Business Unit (IBU), SAP Asset Management, and SAP Partner Management. The demo system replicated common problems experienced in an offshore rig and showcased how the integration of IoT, edge computing, and machine learning could be used to solve or anticipate problems. The system provided real-time situation awareness and had the capability to act on patterns and anti-patterns of data. Results contributed to improved operational integrity of rig assets and the safety and security of rig workers. By offloading the design, build, and test of a complex demo, the project team was able to devote more attention to refining its understanding of edge computing

Image 4.3 Co-Innovation project demo: simulator for IoT application in oil and gas industry

requirements for remote, asset intensive, and high-risk operating environments. In sum, the action filled demo enthralled audiences and attracted ongoing interest in the co-innovation project. Refer to the Appendix, Case: Edge Computing and IIoT, for additional details.

As the demo images and stories illustrate, development is more about creativity and bricolage—creating something with available skills, tools, and equipment versus acquiring expensive resources and capabilities. A lack of resources often leads to creative solutions that become part of the storytelling process.

In conclusion, project demos provide a unique experience that far exceeds the storytelling that can be accomplished with a power point deck, solution brief or white paper. Demos captivate target audiences and are highly valued by project partners and their marketing teams. The capability to build, run, and host demos also is a differentiating service feature that generates demand for the platform and makes the storytelling more salient.

Documenting Project Activities and Results

Project stories also are documented using a variety of media including solution briefs, blogs, white papers, technical reviews, case briefs or use case summaries, press releases, podcasts, and video.[3] The materials are co-developed by the ops team and project partners. This content is shared in multiple channels such as social media, company websites (including those operated by the platform, the platform's parent organization, and each project partners' organization), and showcase events as well as traditional marketing channels. Some activities, such as live events, benefit from sharing a combination of materials such as physical demos accompanied by a project case and solution brief.

Events

Stories also can be communicated through a variety of events. The showcase aspect of demand-side services includes live events, such as panel discussions or symposia, keynote events, and demo expositions, to showcase co-innovation projects and/or to explore a topic. Industry conferences or industry events sponsored by the platform or its parent organization also provide an opportunity for sharing co-innovation projects and building the platform's reputation. To make this service category more salient, we begin with a story.

An SAP subsidiary, National Security Service (NS2), pursued projects at SAP's Palo Alto co-innovation platform for nearly ten years despite that its offices were in Virginia and its primary customers were located within the Washington D.C. beltway. The team's mission was to provide a reality based pathway for its customers to begin consuming more off the shelf software and hardware to implement and manage government business. SAP NS2's customers are avid consumers of high performance computing and sophisticated analytics however, their effective use of these tools is often complicated by factors such as geographic location. When the NS2 project team built its SAP HANA Data Fusion solution, it did so with consideration for one customer's necessity to operate the solution anywhere on earth. As a result, it teamed with Hitachi Data Systems (HDS) to build a 6U sized ruggedized container to house all of the compute, storage, and network capability (e.g., satellite) needed by an analyst in the field—where an analyst would need to power up and operate shortly after dropping by parachute in a remote locale. The co-innovation platform team, as part of its yearly exhibit at SAP's SAPPHIRE NOW, demonstrated one of these ruggedized containers on the show floor. The co-innovation platform's exhibit at SAPPHIRE NOW typically showcased about a dozen co-innovation projects and solutions. However, the ruggedized solution was an amazing magnet, attracting an incredible amount of attention on the show floor. As a result, it increased visibility for all of the other projects that were being showcased concurrently. The demo also captured the attention of other SAP hardware partners and triggered interest in how to build it. Some engineers took time carefully examining the unit—taking pictures and measuring its dimensions. The example underscores how a combination of artifacts and context make for a compelling innovation narrative that inspires curiosity and action.

Platform as Stage. When the co-innovation platform has sufficient physical space for meetings or events or access to meeting space, it can serve as a physical and virtual stage for showcasing co-innovation work. Under these conditions, the ops team can host a variety of events targeting technology and innovation topics relevant to partners and actors in the ecosystem. Examples include events such as partner days, technology focused sessions or symposia, and workshops for topics of interest such as emerging technologies. Live events can be streamed to accommodate remote viewership and recorded for distribution. Walk-up and hosted demo stations also can be easily deployed to any multi-purpose areas within the space, providing additional exposure during live events. Live demos almost always attract attention and questions from platform participants as well as any visitors to the platform's organization (recall the Zoo effect mentioned in Chapter 3). Lastly, when the space can accommodate a variety of demo displays as well as working teams, the ops team can offer tours to special guests and customers. This allows the stories to be communicated to multiple parties who otherwise might not be involved.

As an example of the importance of physical space to storytelling, SAP's co-innovation platform located in Palo Alto, California encompassed approximately three thousand square feet of floor space with a layout featuring a glass wall-enclosed data center; five collaboration rooms to accommodate project team meetings or event breakout sessions; a free form demo area to stage and showcase a variety of demos; and a large multi-purpose space that could host events with up to sixty participants and be configured to support interactive design thinking workshops or to produce content for demos or other marketing content. Image 4.4 shows the platform's multi-purpose space configured for a panel discussion with synchronous virtual participation.

Image 4.4 Co-Innovation platform space: panel discussion setup with virtual participation

Marketing Content

This service category includes activities to support individual projects and showcase multiple projects to customers. First, project teams collaborate with their organizations' marketing groups to share stories through direct marketing. Depending on the project, these marketing activities also may be supported by the platform's ops teams and various groups within the platform's parent organization (such as product teams, project sponsors, partner groups, marketing teams, centers, etc.). The platform's ops team continuously collects data on project activities and tracks outcomes and the content is valued by project teams and their marketing groups. Project-specific marketing content includes materials such as slide decks complemented by other materials listed in Table 4.1 (demos; documents such as solution briefs and white papers; podcasts and videos; etc.). Additionally, multi-project marketing involves activities such as customer events hosted by the platform that showcase a variety of projects using demos, videos, slidedecks and other materials.

Everyone enjoys a good story. In combination, the platform's demand-side services, its parent organization, and each project partner's marketing engine create and consume stories and output from co-innovation projects to promote awareness and demand. Collectively, the platform's demand-side services create memorable experiences for project participants and their customers.

Storytelling About the Platform

Although the demand-side services supporting project storytelling contribute to the platform's reputation and that of its parent organization, a parallel story is told about the platform itself. Documents (blogs, white papers), demos, multi-media content, and traditional marketing materials are used to share stories about the platform's activities and achievements. For instance, a blog posted on the parent organization's website might share stories about the variety of technologies and solutions emerging from co-innovation projects.[4] Project case studies and interviews with project partners illustrate the platform's ability to accelerate solution development. As such, the materials provide proof points to senior managers, customers, and other ecosystem actors that co-innovation makes a difference. In sum, storytelling at the project level and the platform level contributes to the platform's reputation, and that of its parent organization, for advancing ecosystem growth via co-innovation.

Key Takeaways

1. A co-innovation platform's demand-side services, referenced as Demo and Showcase, are designed to generate awareness and demand of co-innovation project activities and outcomes through various methods of storytelling.
2. Demo and showcase services supporting co-innovation projects include demo development, document development (solution briefs, blogs, white papers, technical reviews, press releases, case briefs, and/or use case summaries), podcasts and video creation, event hosting and participation, and traditional market content creation.
3. Co-innovation project storytelling spans all stages of a co-innovation project's lifecycle.
4. Compelling co-innovation stories knit together material artifacts, actors' behaviors, and context to convey information and experiences. Building, sharing, and retaining stories about co-innovation experiences enables knowledge to accrue in a way that stimulates thinking about new ideas and options and, in turn, inspires action.
5. The platform's ops team, in collaboration with project teams, has four tasks to support storytelling: outcome story development, process story development, platform memory management, and showcasing the platform.
6. Compelling co-innovation stories are sticky and generative and provide a tool to help sustain co-innovation and promote ecosystem growth.

Questions, quibbles, comments? Please share your thoughts and ideas. We would value hearing your co-innovation story. You can reach us at: coinnovationstrategy@gmail.com.

Notes

1. See page 115 of Bartel, C.A. and Garud, R. 2009. The role of narratives in sustaining organizational innovation. *Organization Science*, *20*(1): 107–117. For additional insights, see: Barry D., Elmes, M. 1997. Strategy

retold: Toward a narrative view of strategic discourse. *Academy of Management Review*, 22(2): 429–452; Garud, R., Dunbar, R.L.M., and Bartel, C.A. 2010. Dealing with unusual experiences: A narrative perspective on organizational learning. *Organization Science, 22*(3): 587–601; Lampel, J. 2001. Show and tell: Product demonstrations and path creation of technological change, in Garud, R., Karnøe, P., eds. *Path Dependence and Creation* (Lawrence Erlbaum Associates, Mahwah, NJ), 303–328.

2. Brown, J.S., and Duguid, P. 1991. Organizational learning and communities-of-practice: Toward a unified view of working, learning, and innovation. *Organization Science, 20*(1): 40–57.

3. For example, SAP's news website includes a case brief and video about the mineral water project with Gerolsteiner Brunnen GmbH & Co.: https://news.sap.com/2019/10/gerolsteiner-run-sustainably-sap-cloud-platform/.

4. For a website example, the link that follows includes a blog and video about the platform's activities: https://news.sap.com/2020/11/spotlight-sap-co-innovation-lab/.

5

Enabling Co-Innovation as Behavior

> Working with our partners and customers we want to find the best way to enhance the way they work and come up with agile solutions. To connect with them on an emotional, technical, and practical level.[1]
> —Vidya Gugnani, Program Director, SAP COIL Dubai

What do a dairy cooperative, a wildlife conservation nonprofit, and mining company have in common? Each has created and captured value from pursuing projects with a co-innovation platform. The leaders of these organizations recognized that given the rapid pace of innovation, they no longer can think of their capabilities in isolation. Each organization sought practices and partners with complementary capabilities to help them seize opportunities, accelerate the innovation process, and solve novel, tough to tackle business problems. But shifting from managing a "winner take all" culture within a hierarchy to one of co-creating knowledge with external partners is not easy to do. And the high failure rate of partnerships reinforces the challenge. Blending distinct cultures, objectives, and ways of working is complicated especially when collaborations span industries and managers have different assumptions about priorities, opportunities, critical growth drivers, and how other industries work. As discussed in Chapter 2, the uncertainty inherent in innovation projects adds another layer of complexity. This chapter shifts attention to the project level and highlights some of the processes and practices that enable successful co-innovation work. We begin with the contract formation process and then shift attention to practices that foster the desired behaviors for effective co-innovation work and dampen co-innovation project risk.

Simplify Contract Formation

Contracts and relational governance are viewed as the primary tools to manage interorganizational collaboration.[2] A distinctive and complicating aspect of co-innovation platforms is that external actors or third parties contract with each other and perhaps with the platform organization as well, depending on a project's needs. Co-innovation projects typically begin with an established idea, shared outcome objective and partners seeking resources to accelerate development. These collaborative arrangements are not about the platform gaining control over third parties participating in co-innovation projects. Instead, the focus is on ensuring agreement over how value is created and distributed. The complementarity of co-innovation partners aligns with this approach. Despite best intentions, however, exchange hazards[3] can arise in collaborative arrangements, especially those involving co-specialization or the co-mingling of partners' resources and capabilities. For instance, when complementary innovators are from different organizations and not under the hierarchical control of the platform, the separation of ownership and control gives rise to information asymmetries between the platform owner and partners and among partners. Information asymmetry is when one party holds knowledge or information that others lack and the knowledge is used for private gain. These conditions can lead to opportunistic behavior, where one partner attempts to exploit the other who has made co-specialized investments in a co-innovation project. Uncertainty and ambiguity magnify these conditions. If the threat of opportunistic behavior is high, firms respond to these potential exchange hazards by developing complex contracts.[4]

Platform services are designed to help mitigate exchange hazards. As a starting point, the platform provides simple templates for project proposals, statements of work (SOWs), and frame agreements, coaching from the platform's operations management (ops) team, and access to legal consultation, to make the contract development process easy and transparent. As discussed in Chapters 2 and 3, each project begins with a proposal that: (1) identifies the project team (lead and key project members) and executive sponsors for the project; (2) briefly summarizes the project's objectives and its alignment with the platform organization's objectives[5]; (3) provides influence revenue projections for the partners and for the platform's organization[6]; (4) details how the team plans to work together and includes a high level project plan; and (5) lists the resources committed by each partner and the services needed from the platform to support the project.

When a proposal is approved, the ops team, as coach, works with each project team to formalize the project's statement of work (SOW) and frame agreement. The SOW and the frame agreement are intended to foster stable partnerships where, by leveraging the platform, two or more parties create and capture more value by working together than then could achieve when working with other parties or going it alone. This process involves conversations with a project's team and helps to surface differences in expectations and understanding among the partners and the platform owner. The frame agreement identifies the parties agreeing to collaborate; specifies the vision for the project; introduces definitions, contract terms (including limited liability clauses), and taxes; and addresses a variety of other areas of interests, such as brand use. The frame agreement may also contain specific clauses relevant to the use of intellectual property (IP) owned by the firm providing the platform as well as the background IP owned by co-innovation project partners. Similarly, the frame agreement specifies ownership of IP created during a project. The SOW, appended to the frame agreement, defines a project's scope and work plan—including resource needs, how work will get done, who is responsible for specific activities, how IP will be used, deliverables, and a timeline. For example, legal sensitivity may surface when a project requires partners to integrate their software. When this occurs, the partners can rely on their co-developed SOW that describes the process for revealing items such as exposing proprietary source code or unpublished APIs and in turn, how the content will be used. During project work, the ops team steps in to help project participants understand and apply contract terms as questions arise. The SOW also describes the actions to be taken when commitments are not upheld.

While simple templates cannot themselves solve potential exchange problems, the repeated interactions that occur among partners and the platform's ops team in developing these documents set the stage for how partners will behave as they co-innovate. What types of behaviors can ensure productive collaboration? First, avoid abstract discussions throughout the contract formation process; instead, specify mutual obligations, coordination and communication processes, and terms for managing iterative development. The intent is to ensure that partners have agreed upon a shared vision, are motivated to support the project, and will fulfill their project commitments. Second, develop a mutual understanding of the similarities and differences among partners. Acknowledging differences at project initiation provides collaborators with an opportunity to discuss how their differences can be a source of advantage rather than a constraint. Complementarity is not sufficient to ensure success, partners also must be compatible and committed to the relationship.[7]

Repeated interactions among partners and the platform's ops team to develop the proposal, SOW and frame agreement, contribute to relational attachment among actors. By using an open dialogue with the ops team to discuss partner motivations and commitments, each partner begins to build confidence that the other party, and the platform, will fulfill its promises and not exploit vulnerabilities. When teams are aligned on a project's objectives or goals, they also tend to engage in more effective coordination.[8] Developing a mutual understanding of each partner's capabilities and what they want to accomplish can be a challenge. Pascal Hagedorn, co-innovation architect at SAP's Zurich Co-innovation lab explained: "Expectations, technologies, and requirements change in every project. But if it's done right, customers receive what was promised by the partner – plus the integrated and extended added value of their SAP installations."[9] Overtime, these social processes promote agreed upon norms of engagement and in turn, the enforcement of expectations, promises, and obligations. This trust-building contributes to relational governance which helps lower the costs of monitoring, enforcement, and adaptation in contractual arrangements.[10] One co-innovation project partner, Tom Turchioe, SAP CoE Spatial Expert (and co-innovation project partner while serving as CTO, Critigen) confirmed the importance of this process, "[It is] entirely possible that you step out of the co-innovation platform and nothing sees the light of day, but the value that companies gain is an increased level of trust. That cannot be accomplished in any other environment." When relational governance is associated with interdependencies among partners, it facilitates interorganizational coordination across the life of a project. Under these conditions and given the experimental nature of projects, partners typically are willing to use simple contracts to achieve their shared objectives. By promoting a streamlined contract process and relational governance, the platform's services also make the platform sticky to participants, promoting repeated engagement.

Promote Productive and Generative Co-Innovation

Although contracts play a pivotal role in co-innovation project formation, a more important aspect of the process is each partner's willingness to adopt an open innovation mindset and to work collaboratively to solve a problem. As a result, the platform's services assist with the project formation process, helping project partners build mutual understanding, common norms of behavior, and trust. Managers typically are trained with a winner-take-all view, where appropriating value from a firm's resources and capabilities requires protecting those factors from customers, suppliers, competitors, or emerging organizations. Our analysis of a variety of co-innovation projects finds that partners with a willingness "to access, harness and absorb flows of knowledge" and resources from external sources as well as a willingness to share knowledge and resources with other parties have a higher likelihood of achieving a co-innovation project's goals.[11] This is a simple statement but not always easy to put into action, especially when leaders view innovation as a way to distinguish themselves from competitors.

What practices lend to fostering an open and collaborative mindset focusing on "what can we do together"? Establishing expected norms of behavior that support trust-building and joint problem-solving such as a willingness to share, acting with honesty, fairness and integrity, and engaging in reciprocity is critical. To ensure all project participants are on the same page regarding expected behaviors, the norms should be shared with potential partners prior to the co-development of the SOW and frame agreement. In the platform context, such norms might be part of a platform's house rules and set expectations for how partners will behave as they co-work. Since co-innovation projects involve uncertainty and a need for flexibility, the norms serve as a foundation for deterring opportunistic behavior.

Co-Develop a Shared Vision & Capitalize on Different Motivations

As a first step, it is important for the ops team to engage a co-innovation project's participants in co-shaping the project's vision. This process involves clarifying why each party values the project to ensure a shared understanding of the importance of the project or what is at stake. Partners each bring different resources and capabilities to a co-innovation project and may vary in their motivations. Understanding and aligning motivations is complicated by the fact that the firms are not under hierarchical control. To understand how this unfolds, we studied a wide variety of co-innovation projects, such as projects using blockchain and RFID to keep highways safe, combining software and systems to improve energy and carbon management in manufacturing facilities, creating edge computing solutions for the Oil and Gas industry, and integrating IoT and AI to support "lights out" manufacturing. Our analysis revealed that the majority of partners were motivated by the need to gain access to non-generic complementary resources and capabilities—factors that a partner lacked or that it could not develop or acquire in time to act on an opportunity. Other partners were motivated by the opportunity to develop a relationship with the platform's parent organization. Collaborating organizations may begin with different motivations yet, developing a mutual understanding of the job to be done is vital to a project's success.

Building a Castle in the Air? An example of a co-innovation project with a clear shared vision involves a collaboration between a dairy cooperative, Schwarzwaldmilch, supporting milk dairies located in the Black Forest region of Germany and a digital consultancy, sine qua non (see Table 5.1). Schwarzwaldmilch wanted to improve the customer experience by providing more transparency of a product's production. However, Schwarzwaldmilch lacked expertise in how to leverage new digital technologies. SAP learned of the challenge and introduced Schwarzwaldmilch to sine qua non, a digital consultancy. Sine qua non was motivated by the opportunity to apply their smart digital technology in a new context. For them, demonstrating success in the milk industry served as a stepping stone to attracting a broader

Table 5.1 Co-Innovation projects: examples of shared vision and a co-innovated solution

Co-Innovation Project	Problem to be solved	Shared Vision	Co-Innovation Solution
Dairy Cooperative Using Smart Packaging Partners: • Dairy Cooperative Schwarzwaldmilch • sine qua non	Food Transparency: Consumers want to know where the products they buy come from.	Tell milk's journey from cow to store to provide transparency to the consumer: Who provided the milk? When did the milk leave the farm? How did the milk get to the store? When were the containers or cartons filled?	Smart packaging using digital twin technology. Milk cartons are assigned a digital ID (and include a QR code) and a digital copy is created for every milk carton. The digital twins capture data from automated milking machines, milk tankers, manufacturing equipment and distribution. Data associated with every stage in the food production process is captured on a cloud platform. By scanning a carton's QR code, consumers can find out which farm provided the milk, when the milk was collected from the farm, how big that farm is, how many animals the farm has, and when the milk carton was filled and sent to a store. For sine qua non, the project demonstrated that their digital technology could provide transparency in the supply chain for different consumer goods. As a result, the project helped them expand their network of clients and develop a digital transparency platform.

client base while also providing them additional experience with the technology. Different motivations and specializations yet, both organizations saw opportunities to create and capture value through collaboration.

The platform ops team worked with Schwarzwaldmilch and sine qua non to establish the co-innovation project's goals. The firms quickly converged on the project's vision: to provide more transparency to customers by telling milk's journey from source to store shelf. The project resulted in the adoption of smart packaging using digital twin technology[12] where each milk carton or bottle is assigned a digital ID (and a QR code) and a digital copy is created. The digital twins are used to capture data about the milk's journey from automated milking machines to delivery. Once the carton is on the store shelf, consumers can use the carton's QR code to learn information such as which farm provided the milk, when the carton was filled and when it was sent to the store.

A sine qua non manager stated that the co-innovation platform "…supported us and gave us access to infrastructure free of charge for an extended period of time so that we could build the product. Schwarzwaldmilch was our first customer, it would have been extremely costly for us to set up the infrastructure ourselves." Andreas Schneider, Managing Director, Schwarzwaldmilch, stressed that participating with the platform provided organizational value above and beyond the project itself: "SAP helped train the team in design thinking – focusing the effort on what is value add for the customer. We learned what data is needed and that 80% of the data was not worth sharing. This was our first digital solution and initially, there were some cold feet but ultimately it was successful and provided high visibility; we gained consumer feedback, media coverage, and innovation audience interest."

Although the project began prior to the start of the 2020 pandemic, the effectiveness of the solution gained attraction as scandals in the meat processing industry in Germany during the pandemic spurred demand for more transparency in the food industry. A sine qua non manager expressed it this way: "COVID-19 and the resulting difficulties in transnational supply chains as well as scandals in the meat processing industry have confirmed to us that we weren't building a castle in the air; we have a solution that can address relevant problems and challenges in the food industry." For Schwarzwaldmilch, the success of their first digital solution was a conversation starter in the cooperative and motivated them to apply the digital twin technology to oatmilk produced in the Black Forest region. Experience with one digital technology inspired them to explore others. At the time of our interview, Andreas stated that they are now "planning to apply augmented reality elements in mobile applications, allowing customers to gain an experience effect." In sum, both firms captured explicit and tacit value form the co-innovation project.

The Dairy Cooperative—Smart Packaging case makes co-innovation sound easy. Of course, not all partners might find common ground. What other actions can the platform take to strengthen the collaborative process?

Foster a Climate that Promotes Knowledge Sharing

Creating a platform environment where actors feel safe volunteering unique ideas, making mistakes, and openly disagreeing without negative repercussions is crucial to any collaborative arrangement but especially so when projects involve uncertainty. Individuals often hesitate to reveal their lack of understanding or ignorance in the face of experts from a different domain or industry. Individuals also may invoke stereotypes about technologies, other industries or domains and in turn, advance the cultural divide between organizations, making open dialogue difficult. Additionally, the performance of engineers or technical staff often is based on what they create, patent, or publish so foundationally, they may be less motivated to share knowledge or information. To reduce these behaviors and promote an open mindset among project partners, the platform should:

- Emphasize the experimental nature of projects.
- Frame partners' differences as complementary advantages.
- Facilitate ongoing interactions among partners and encourage face-to-face collaboration.
- Reiterate the platform's policy of equitable value distribution among project participants.
- Reinforce the platform's focus on working "with" external actors vs. actors working "for" the platform.

The ops team engages in a variety of activities to encourage and facilitate knowledge sharing among partners. By facilitating face-to-face and virtual interactions among partners throughout the course of a project, the ops team reinforces the social bonds, norms of interaction, and trust developed during contract formation. These attributes and the ongoing project dialogue help to break down communication barriers among partners and in turn, improve conditions for knowledge exchange and co-innovation. The platform's physical space supports these activities (see Chapter 3).[13] Second, recall that the ops team also provides the platform's knowledge broker services. In this role, the ops team supports knowledge integration by working with teams to identify ways they can connect ideas and resources. In addition to the activities discussed above, the platform's staff needs to model the expected behaviors by being inquisitive, exhibiting a willingness to share, and acknowledging the uncertain nature of co-innovation projects. In combination, these practices promote an environment where individuals feel safe sharing knowledge, resources, and capabilities.[14]

What type of sharing occurs in co-innovation projects? Projects vary in the scope of resources and capabilities shared among teams. Some projects involve multiple complementary resources contributed by all parties whereas others are somewhat narrow in scope, with each partner contributing a specific capability or resource. We illustrate the variety with a few case examples.

Returning to the mineral water sustainability case discussed in Chapter 2, INTENSE AG partnered with mineral water company, Gerolsteiner Brunnen GmbH & Co. The partners shared software development methods on SAP's cloud platform (SAP HANA). SAP's co-innovation platform team provided subject matter expertise including architecture consulting and development support, such as recommendations for managing queries using the in-memory database of SAP HANA. INTENSE AG also contributed software talent to write the solution code. Matthias Orth, INTENSE AG, noted that the SAP HANA development support was not generic but tailored to the team's needs: "Instead of trawling through SAP documentation, we received guided tours from the experts."[15]

Another project with Elephants, Rhinos & People (ERP), a wildlife preservation non-profit organization, sought help from SAP to protect and monitor endangered wildlife and deter poaching. The platform provided access to software and subject matter experts; ERP and the experts collaborated in the platform's environment to design a mobile app that leveraged various technologies including drones, cameras, AI algorithms, and SAP software capabilities. Digital images from drones and GPS data from animal collars are processed by AI algorithms to assess a threat in real time. When a positive threat is identified, the location data is shared with a drone and ERP's team. The drone flies to the location and users access real-time data for situation assessment. The solution is referenced as the ERP Airforce. ERP reports that poaching has decreased to zero in areas where ERP Air Force has an active drone presence.[16]

Encourage Iterative Learning

One of the strongest benefits to collaborative innovation is the learning that occurs from non-linear and iterative interactions. It is important for the platform to emphasize that projects involve experimentation and in turn, flexibility and agility is needed to adapt a project's direction as learning occurs. However, rapid experimentation and iterative development—testing, gaining insights, and refining—are less conducive to a traditional lock-step project management approach. Enabling agility requires establishing mechanisms for capturing and facilitating iterative development, including feedback processes. Additionally, in any co-innovation project, changes may be warranted. For instance, changes in scope suggest the original planning was insufficient whereas other changes might be unforeseeable, such as learning that yields new requirements or a new vision. By a project's proposal stage, most teams have identified the "right" problem to solve and have a preference for accelerating development. As such projects tend to be focused and short in duration (some as fast as 90 days, others ranging from 6 to 12 months). In our study of 225 co-innovation projects, learning often motivated additional experimentation and/or triggered an idea for a new project; in some cases, learning warranted adaptation to a project's shared vision or objectives.

A mining project provides a robust example of iterative development that stimulated adaptations in the project's scope (without a change in the project's shared vision). Firms in the mining industry aspire to develop a zero-harm work environment. To help tackle this challenge, Vandrico Solutions Inc., an industrial IoT and wearables software startup, collaborated with Illumiti, an SAP systems integration and management consulting company, to develop a MineSafe Smartwatch.[17] The project used Vandrico's Canary Platform, an IoT communications system designed for enterprise security and scale. The Canary Platform communicates mine-specific IoT information via wifi using data from wearable devices and sensors placed throughout a mine. By enabling real-time communications between the watches and a mine's central control system, the MineSafe Smartwatch helps miners identify and respond to emerging safety issues. When a concern arises, the system can locate miners and transmit alerts and solutions where needed. Vandrico's CEO, Gonzalo Tudela, explained: "Mine workers can use a one-touch distress call feature to send an urgent notice to the surface. The surface system is designed to send immediate alerts to key personnel and emergency responders based on the type of incident being reported – which can enhance response time and reduce risk to other workers."

In the beginning, the watch design allowed the team to show proof of concept for the real-time situation awareness function. However, the team wondered whether a watch was the optimal wearable format for the setting. In consultation with industrial customers, the team learned that miners often operate in Tundra-like conditions, requiring them to wear several layers of clothing as well as thick gloves. Accessing a watch under this gear may not always be convenient. Additionally, when a miner is around heavy equipment with names like "cutter," she needs to be mindful about the gear she wears, a misstep or entanglement could be deadly. A cutter looks like a giant drum with sharp teeth located all over it.[18] Given the feedback from customers, one project scope iteration involved exploring other types of wearable technology such as helmets and vests. This exploration confirmed that the watch was the most appropriate device for the setting. The project's initial phase generated a physical demo designed to model the use of wearables in an industry setting; the demo had the ability to sense and receive data related to employee safety and when coupled with machine learning, could process edge data in real time to predict risk and reduce harm.

As the project progressed, other questions arose that prompted an additional phase of experimentation and testing. For instance, what type of sensor data was optimal for predicting and analyzing operational risk? To address this question, the team simulated data collection from seismic sensors as well as fire/smoke/gas detection sensors. As a result of this inquiry, a second project phase was planned to examine sensor data from machines and tools in operation. The team thought that expanding the type of sensor data collected would allow a company to categorize levels of risk throughout a mine. For example, two junior miners might be operating heavy equipment in a shaft where a ripper[19] or cutter had not received regular maintenance. Cutters are notorious for scattering shrapnel when their teeth break loose. The team wondered whether the MineSafe system could be used to assign risk scores for a situation using a combination of data—such as maintenance records and worker experience level. In sum, the iterative nature of the project advanced learning, helped the team refine its original design, and stimulated new project ideas.

Is It All Good?

Throughout the co-innovation process, there are possibilities for partners to be at odds. We highlight three potential areas of friction that can complicate a project's development and execution.

Fostering Buy-In

Friction between the platform and a project's partners may arise when the partners do not buy-in to the platform's approach to contract formation. The platform faces the task of convincing project partners to use the platform's simple, flexible, and standard SOW and frame agreement approach. As noted, most partners join the platform to accelerate development of an idea or a go-to-market initiative. As a result, project teams want the contract formation phase to move smoothly and quickly. However, pushback may arise for various reasons. Although the majority of partners readily agree to use the platform's standard contract templates (SOW and Frame Agreement), some question whether a project would be better off with a specialized, built from the ground up, agreement. Large, established organizations with partnership experience may favor a customized contract that aligns with their own contracting practices. Alternatively, since a co-innovation project's success depends on gaining commitment from one or more other project participants, some partners are skeptical of using a standardized approach.

While the contract templates are designed to be signed as is, partners are required to have their organizations' legal teams review contracts. Each partner's legal team tends to be more experienced with contracts aimed at protecting the partner's resources as opposed to sharing them. On occasion, these reviews generate extensive conversations among partners, extending the contract formation process. When the process is prolonged by persistent iteration, it is critical that the platform's ops team and/or director remind the partners why they are pursuing a project with the platform. Under these conditions, reorienting the participants to the project's objectives and expected outcomes is vital to moving the project forward. This type of prompt reminds the partners that as they spend time debating a statement or clause, they may miss a window of opportunity for creating and capturing value—the main reason they are working with the platform in the first place. Our analysis of a wide variety of co-innovation projects shows that project outcomes were not compromised when partners agreed to adopt the platform's standard, simple contract templates.

Co-Innovation Project Risk

Despite the benefits, co-innovation also is associated with risk. In some projects, the probability of achieving the outcome is unknown; in other cases, the likelihoods of outcomes may be known to the decision maker. The co-innovation platform model is designed to support projects that are narrow in scope, short in duration and focused on activities such as validating concepts, integration requirements, and/or technical feasibility. These types of projects are less encumbered by potential go-to-market requirements.[20] Given the project characteristics, project outcomes are used in different ways; examples include: an outcome might inform another project at a partner's organization, stimulate additional project work in a focal area, trigger thinking about new strategic directions, and/or contribute to downstream go-to-market goals. As a result, the project characteristics limit the amount of risk associated with each project. We are not suggesting that project-specific risk does not exist but rather pointing out that the platform's objectives, and specifically, the type and scope of co-innovation projects that the platform will pursue, informs how much risk the platform, and co-innovation partners, are willing to take on.

An additional layer of risk is associated with the partnering process and partner behavior. Each partner assumes that their collaborators will participate in good faith and in line with resource commitments, project work, and schedule. Even with these good intentions, a variety of exchange hazards may arise in the gray area of contracts. As the contract formation section discussed, a partner could misrepresent their skills, shirk responsibilities, and/or act opportunistically attempt to appropriate more value from a co-innovation project. As discussed in Chapter 2, the resulting relational complexity is mitigated by the platform's structures, processes, and services. For instance, the repeated interactions and ops team coaching during proposal development and contract formation facilitates establishing norms of interaction, social-bonding, and trust-building among collaborators and in turn, enhances relational performance.

Intellectual Property: Who Gets What?

The platform's open innovation approach also raises questions about rights around intellectual property (IP). Frictions arise when parties feel they have been treated unfairly. When building a co-innovation platform, it is essential that the platform team coordinate with its parent organization's legal team for endorsement of the platform's simple contract approach (including templates). Inevitably, the conversation with legal turns to protecting background IP owned by the platform's parent organization and concerns around managing IP developed in co-innovation projects (foreground IP). At the project level, the contract elements (SOW and Frame Agreement) describe the multi-lateral ways ideas, knowledge, resources, and IP will be used to support a project. Contracts require terms that address both background and foreground IP. During contract development, partners typically are in agreement as to the ownership of any background IP contributed to a project. As a result, more time is spent considering ownership and licensing agreements surrounding foreground IP. It is important to note that while the platform might benefit from a co-innovated solution that adds value to its core offerings, project partners decide how IP created in a project will be assigned among participating organizations. In other words, who owns "what" once the project is completed. How this comes together will vary across organizations and industries. In the era of cloud and API-based integration where IP often is consumed through subscribed metered services, a co-innovation project contract may not need to address ownership or licensing where an activity, such as integration, will be completed by accessing published APIs. In the cases we observed, rarely did concerns arise over "who owns" versus "who licenses" a piece of foreground IP originating in a project. Project teams deemed long-term ownership as less important than right of use and how successfully the solution will fulfill downstream customer requirements. We offer the following guidance to inform your thinking around IP management:

1. As you develop and implement a co-innovation platform:

    - Gain buy-in from your parent organization's legal staff regarding the platform's contract and IP management approach. The platform does not require its own legal staff but benefits when the parent organization provides a lawyer to assist the platform when needed. The lawyer tapped for this role should be familiar with the platform's co-innovation strategy and objectives and in turn, understand the rationale for simple, flexible contracts.
    - Develop the platform's ops team's expertise regarding IP management practices and ensure the team is familiar with how different firms view and manage foreground IP. The team's expertise informs the platforms supply-side services.

2. When coaching project teams:

    - Keep the project participants focused on the project's objectives—reminding partners of their original motivations for pursuing co-innovation with the platform.
    - In contract discussions with project partners, discuss how IP will be used to achieve a project's objectives and avoid introducing commercial terms associated with go-to-market goals. Co-innovation project results frequently are inputs to a future go-to-market initiative.

Conclusion

Co-innovation is not achieved by a process, contract, or agreement. Collaboration for innovation requires careful consideration of the resources, practices, and environment that promote and enable the desired behaviors. It is not always easy; everyone likely has a story to tell about a difficult partnership or a collaboration that failed. Although contracts matter, the partners' behaviors can make or break a project. A productive co-innovation platform's contract formation services, including coaching, help project teams bond, develop a common ground, capitalize on differences, problem solve, and build trust. Contracts reinforce collective responsibility as well as partner accountability. The practices and guidance discussed in this chapter work in combination with the co-innovation platform's equitable value distribution—reinforcing the mindset that partners are working "with the platform" vs. "for the platform."

Key Takeaways

1. A distinctive aspect of successful co-innovation platforms is that actors external to the platform contract with each other and may contract with the platform as well, depending on a project's objectives.
2. The co-innovation platform model is designed to enable projects that are short in duration, narrow in scope, and focused on exploring an early stage idea.
3. Co-innovation is a behavior. Creating a platform environment where project partners feel safe volunteering unique ideas, making mistakes, and openly disagreeing without negative repercussions is vital to successful co-innovation.
4. The co-innovation platform's contract approach includes a project proposal, statement of work, and a frame agreement; coaching by the platform's ops team as well as legal support ease the contract development process easy. The platform's services are designed to enable relational governance and mitigate exchange hazards that may arise in co-innovation partnerships.
5. The use of simple, flexible contracts aligns with the non-linear and iterative nature of collaborative innovation and supports the platform's objective to accelerate innovation to advance ecosystem growth.

6. A co-innovation platform's objectives, and specifically, the type and scope of co-innovation projects that the platform will pursue, inform how much risk the platform is willing to assume.
7. While a co-innovation platform might benefit from a co-innovated solution that adds value the platform organization's core offerings, project partners decide how IP created in project will be assigned among the partner organizations. Collaborative arrangements in co-innovation platforms are not about gaining platform control over external actors (complementors, customers, suppliers); instead, they focus on ensuring multilateral agreement over how value is created and distributed.

Questions, quibbles, comments? Please share your thoughts and ideas. We would value hearing your co-innovation story. You can reach us at: coinnovationstrategy@gmail.com.

Notes

1. Rohr, J. 2020. Roll Up Your Sleeves: Spotlight on SAP Co-Innovation Lab. SAP News Center, accessed June 18, 2021. https://news.sap.com/2020/11/spotlight-sap-co-innovation-lab/.
2. Contracts are used to organize two or more firms into a binding agreement and are designed to safeguard a party from a counterpart's opportunistic behavior as well as risks and future contingencies. A wealth of articles and books discuss the contract provisions, governance mechanisms and practices that enable productive partnerships and alliances. For example, see: Dyer, J., Singh, H., and Hesterly, W.S. 2018. Relational view revisited: A dynamic perspective on value creation and value capture. *Strategic Management Journal, 39*: 3140–3162; Kale, P., and Singh, H. 2009. Managing strategic alliances: what do we know now, and where do we go from here? *Academy of Management Perspectives, 23*(3): 45–62; Oxley, J.E. 1997. Appropriability hazards and governance in strategic alliances: A transaction cost approach. *The Journal of Law, Economics, and Organization, 13*(2): 387–409; Reuer, J.J., and Ariño, A. 2007. Strategic alliance contracts: Dimensions and determinants of contractual complexity. *Strategic Management Journal, 28*(3): 313–330; Reuer, J.J., and Ariño, A. 2002. Contractual renegotiations in strategic alliances. *Journal of Management, 28*(1): 47–68; Inkpen, A.C., and Tsang, E.W.K. 2007. Learning and strategic alliances. *Academy of Management Annals, 1*: 479–511.

3. Exchange hazards are influenced by the degree of asset specificity, appropriability, or observability of outcomes characterizing a transaction among two or more parties. For a review, see Shelanski H. A., and Klein P.G., 1995. Empirical research in transaction cost economics: A review and assessment. *Journal of Law, Economics and Organization, 11*: 335–361.
4. These conditions increase transaction costs or the costs of conducting an exchange. Oliver Williamson is recognized as developing transaction cost theory; his seminal works include Williamson, O.E. 1975. *Markets and Hierarchies*. NY: Free Press; Williamson, Oliver E. 1985. *The Economic Institutions of Capitalism: Firms, Markets, Relational Contracting*. London: Free Press; Williamson, O.E., 1981. The economics of organization: The transaction cost approach. *American Journal of Sociology, 87*(3): 548–577. For classic empirical studies see: Walker, G. and Weber, D. 1984. The transaction cost approach to vertical integration. *Administrative Science Quarterly, 29*: 373–391; Masten, S. 1984. The organization of production evidence from the aerospace industry. *Journal of Law and Economics, 27*: 403–417.
5. Objectives should be proximate—identifying a target that the team expects to achieve. Robust proximate objectives provide clarity and help focus a team's energy.
6. Influence revenue is revenue generated when a co-innovation project outcome assists a sales or presales manager, field representative, and/or business development manager close business with a customer. For example, a project outcome might be offered as additional functionality to address a customer need. The platform is not a sales unit; instead, it enables project teams to develop outcomes that might generate direct revenue for the participating partners.
7. Three attributes are critical to the success of a partnership or alliance: complementarity, compatibility, and commitment (Kale and Singh, 2009). Kale, P., and Singh, H. 2009. Managing strategic alliances: what do we know now, and where do we go from here? *Academy of Management Perspectives, 23*(3): 45–62.
8. For example see: Levesque, Laurie L., Jeanne M. Wilson, and Douglas R. Wholey. 2001. Cognitive divergence and shared mental models in software development project teams. *Journal of Organizational Behavior: The International Journal of Industrial, Occupational and Organizational Psychology and Behavior, 22*(2): 135–144; Mathieu, J.E., Heffner, T.S., Goodwin, G.F., Salas, E., and Cannon-Bowers, J.A. 2000. The influence

of shared mental models on team process and performance. *Journal of Applied Psychology, 85*(2): 273.
9. Rohr, J. 2020. Roll Up Your Sleeves: Spotlight on SAP Co-Innovation Lab. SAP News Center – Ecosystem. https://news.sap.com/2020/11/spotlight-sap-co-innovation-lab/, accessed May 10, 2021.
10. When firms trust their partners will behave fairly, the need for monitoring and enforcement declines; costs of adjusting a project's scope also are lower since partners are willing to be flexible in response to unexpected insights or events that emerge as a co-innovation project evolves. See Kale, P., and Singh, H. 2009. Managing strategic alliances: What do we know now, and where do we go from here? *Academy of Management Perspectives*: 45–61.
11. See page 30 of Chesbrough, H. 2020. *Open Innovation Results: Going Beyond the Hype and Getting Down to Business.* UK: Oxford University Press.
12. Sine qua non's refers to their smart digital technology as YoY. Rohr J. 2020. German Dairy Cooperative Uses Smart Packaging to Tell Milk's Story. SAP article, accessed July 12, 2020. https://news.sap.com/2020/09/schwarzwaldmilch-german-dairy-cooperative-smart-packaging/.
13. The 2020 Covid-19 pandemic and resulting work-from home (WFM) policies limited face-to-face collaboration and in turn, forced partners to collaborate virtually. Although the pandemic environment motivated co-innovation among distant actors in areas such as PPE distribution or vaccine development, an empirical question remains regarding whether the forced virtual work practices helped or hindered collaboration for innovation. For instance, distractions of a work-from-home environment may compromise listening and attention or focus. In contrast, studies conducted prior to the pandemic suggest that, under certain conditions, remote work can strengthen creativity and ideation within teams (for instance, see Thompson, L. 2013. *Creative Conspiracy: The New Rules of Breakthrough Collaboration.* Boston: Harvard Business Review Press. As we completed this book, many firms were in the process of developing hybrid work models that combine face-to-face office work with remote work.
14. It is widely recognized that enabling psychologically safe environments is foundational to facilitating innovation, creativity, and risk taking. For readings on the topic see: Edmondson, A. 1999. Psychological safety and learning behavior in work teams. *Administrative Science Quarterly, 44*(2): 350–383; Edmondson, A.C. 2018. *The Fearless Organization: Creating*

Psychological Safety in the Workplace for Learning, Innovation, and Growth. Wiley.
15. Rohr, J. 2019. SAP Cloud Platform Helps Gerolsteiner Run Sustainability. SAP News Center. https://news.sap.com/2019/10/gerolsteiner-run-sustainably-sap-cloud-platform/, accessed June 24, 2021.
16. Campbell, S., and Tully, A. 2019. Improving People's Lives: Saving Elephants and Rhinos. SAP New Center. https://news.sap.com/2019/03/erp-air-force-saving-elephants-and-rhinos/, accessed June 24, 2021.
17. Illumiti press release, November 5, 2015, Illumiti and Vandrico Launch MinSafe Smartwatch Running on the SAP HANA Platform; accessed June 14, 2021. https://www.prnewswire.com/news-releases/illumiti-and-vandrico-launch-minesafe-smartwatch-running-on-the-sap-hana-platform-300172952.html.
18. As background, a cutter or cutting machine, usually used in coal mining, cuts a 10 cm to 15 cm slot in a mine; the slot allows room for expansion of broken coal. Workers who operate these machines also may be referred to as cutters. For additional details, see: http://www.coaleducation.org/glossary.htm and https://www.freepatentsonline.com/5013093.html, accessed June 18, 2021.
19. A ripper is a coal extraction machine that works by tearing coal from the exposed area of a coal bed—where coal is being extracted. A universal ripper includes a cutter head. http://www.coaleducation.org/glossary.htm, accessed, June 18, 2021.
20. When a project seeks to include go-to-market requirements, the contract formation process lengthens, consuming time, and attention that could be allocated to co-innovation work.

6

Bringing It All Together

What have we said so far? Table 6.1 provides a snapshot of the book's key tenets. The core contribution is the introduction of the co-innovation platform—a platform that enables hands-on co-innovation with external actors using curated access and an open resource approach. As we pointed out, thinking strategically about developing a co-innovation platform begins with diagnosing the problem an organization is trying to solve. This diagnosis informs three strategic questions relevant to a co-innovation platform: (1) What innovation topics/areas play a strategic role in the parent organization's future?; (2) Are there opportunities to collaborate with external organizations to accelerate innovation?; and (3) Can greater economies of innovation and complementarity be achieved through co-innovation with external organizations than by going it alone? The answers to the above questions lead to strategic choices regarding the relevant actors and platform governance.

As we shared in Chapter 1, hype around the ecosystem concept abounds, yet managers often struggle in understanding the actions relevant to promoting and sustaining ecosystem growth. A co-innovation platform addresses this problem. The platform's integrated system of services are explicitly designed to support three activities necessary for ecosystem generativity: *mobilizing many different types of economic actors, enabling interactions among diverse, loosely connected actors,* and *facilitating joint learning*. A set of governance mechanisms that establish incentives for participation, unbundle the complexity of co-innovation work, and provide equitable value distribution underlie these activities (Chapter 2). In the co-innovation environment,

Table 6.1 Co-Innovation platforms: core tenets

Chapter 1 Introduction: Co-Innovation Platforms	Chapter 2 Platforms: Types, Governance, and Value Distribution	Chapter 3 Building a Co-Innovation Platform	Chapter 4 Co-Innovation Storytelling	Chapter 5 Enabling Co-Innovation as Behavior
Strategic Ecosystem Activities: Mobilizing a diversity of actors; Enabling Interactions; and Facilitating Joint Learning	Transaction, Innovation, & Co-innovation Platforms: Core differences	Co-Innovation Platform: Objectives	Core Services — Demand-side: Demo & Showcase	How do we collaborate?
Platform-based Ecosystems: Strategy, Tactics & Questions	Co-Innovation Platform: Network Relationships	Core Services — Supply-side: Protect & Manage, Operations Management; Knowledge Brokering; IT Systems Landscape	Storytelling sources and opportunities; modes of storytelling	Simplify project and contract formation; Engage in services and activities to promote relational governance
Hands-on approach to co-innovation via provisioning supply-side & demand-side services	Co-Innovation Platform Strategy: What, Who, & How?	Project origins, phases, and process	Platform as Stage: Showcasing & Events	Co develop a shared vision & capitalize on different motivations
Strategic and organizational benefits for co-innovation project partners and the platform	Governing the Platform: Curated Access & Resource Open Approach; Incentives; Mobilizing & Sustaining Participation; Harnessing Complexity; Equitable Value Distribution	Operations management team as coach & orchestrator	Guidelines for demo development	Create an environment that embraces knowledge sharing, experimentation and iterative learning
	Fostering a Mindset: Working 'with the platform' vs. 'for the platform'	Where do we collaborate? Platform Environment & the Zoo Effect	Building project awareness throughout the ecosystem	Potential Frictions? Risk; Buyin; & IP Management

a productive governance system embodies and promotes a mindset where complementors are "*working with*" *the platform* as opposed to "*working for*" *the platform*. In combination, the platform's services and governance mechanisms support effective orchestration of the platform-based ecosystem and contribute to a self-reinforcing, positive feedback loop within the platform's growing network of relationships.

What types of services matter? As compared to hybrid platforms or innovation platforms, a unique feature of a co-innovation platform is that it provisions supply-side services—including physical resources and capabilities—to external actors to enable productive co-innovation. The value creation is not simply about the individual actors but their complementary interactions. The *supply-side services*, as detailed in Chapter 3, include *Protect & Manage* (associated with partnership formation and contract development), *Operations Management Team, Knowledge Brokering*, and *IT System Landscape*. The hands-on approach assists actors in forming co-innovation partnerships and provides them with resources and capabilities to enable and support project work. The approach differs from traditional innovation platforms that provide complementors access to some digital services but not resources and capabilities to assist with project formation, project execution, and productive collaboration. Additionally, the platform's curated access plays a strategic role by guiding project selection and in turn, shaping the ecosystem's innovation trajectory. Lastly, co-innovation project outcomes are less useful if they are kept a secret. The platform's *demand side services, Demo and Showcase*, facilitate different forms of storytelling to generate awareness and demand (Chapter 4). Effective story telling is sticky; compelling narratives inspire action by conveying information and experiences, connecting ideas and activities, and providing insight into the co-innovation process. As such, the platform's demand side services are generative—stimulating new ideas and project options.

Chapter 5 shared two platform activities critical to enabling co-innovation projects: coaching partners through a simple contract formation approach and taking actions to promote the desired behaviors for productive collaboration. Even though contracts are important, partner's behaviors can make or break a project. As a result, engaging in activities to promote mutual understanding and build trust among partners begins with the proposal development process and persists throughout contract formation and project execution. For example, through repeated interactions among partners and the ops team during proposal and contract development, partners learn about each other's motivations and capabilities, form norms of interaction, and build relational attachments. These activities support trust-building and in turn, relational governance—which facilitates interorganizational coordination and mitigates exchange hazards. Equally important is establishing an environment where partners feel safe volunteering ideas, making mistakes, and openly questioning ideas without repercussions. Reinforcing the experimental nature of projects, encouraging iterative learning, and reminding project teams of the platform's equitable value distribution approach sets the stage for successful co-innovation. Nonetheless, frictions may arise among partners. Chapter 5 concludes with some guidance regarding co-innovation risk and IP management.

Value Creation and Value Capture

Throughout the book, we have shared the nontraditional ways a co-innovation platform creates value for co-innovation project partners as well as for the platform and its ecosystem. In this section, we elaborate on some of the less obvious and/or intangible benefits, beginning with the platform.

The chapter recap underscores the platform's impact and highlights the strategic benefits gained by operating a co-innovation platform (see column 1, Table 6.2 [previewed in Table 1.2 from Chapter 1]). Building experience with

Table 6.2 Strategic and organizational benefits for the platform owner

Strategic Benefits for Co-Innovation Platforms	Organizational Benefits for Co-Innovation Platforms
Ecosystem Growth – Beyond tradition • Extending the network of ecosystem participants • Expanding strategic scope via co-innovation projects spanning different technologies, industries, and sectors • Seeding new growth paths • Identifying and capitalizing on unique intersections • Advancing the platform's reputation • Promoting ongoing value creation, capture and distribution	**Learning from Co-Innovation Enablement** • Partner identification and selection • Multi-lateral contract formation • Partnership governance and execution • Building organizational memory
Shaping and Accelerating Innovation • Enabling co-innovation • Developing and managing a co-innovation project portfolio • Extending the use value of the platform's technological system • Showcasing co-innovation outcomes & the platform's portfolio	**Capability Development** • Orchestration • Fostering generativity • Platform governance and management • Relational governance • Knowledge brokering • Co-innovation

co-innovation enablement and ecosystem growth, also yields several organizational benefits for the platform and its parent organization (see column 2, Table 6.2). For instance, through repeated contract formation processes and partnership enablement, the platform team develops capabilities in building partnerships based on relational governance. Studies suggest that repeated experience with partnerships contributes to learning capabilities as well as capabilities in mitigating exchange hazards.[1] As a result, the platform's experience with, and templates for, multi-lateral contract formation can inform best practices and be shared with other parts of the platform's parent organization to expand co-innovation activities. Additionally, through repeated enablement, the platform develops capabilities for ecosystem orchestration and generativity. Orchestration requires a different way of thinking. In the role of orchestrator, the platform's ops team relies on a host of services to influence and incent a variety of loosely connected actors to participate in mutual value creation. Successful orchestration, in turn, promotes generativity. In sum, many large enterprises have developed innovation programs, such as labs, incubators, or accelerators, with a focus on startups. Few have established programs that enable different sized enterprises to collaborate on project topics that range from solution validation to the creation of services that realize immediate and tangible customer value.

Shifting attention to partners, as previewed in Chapter 1, co-innovation project partners gain much more from participating with the platform than the value they capture from a project outcome. The additional benefits, listed in rows two through seven in Table 6.3, often surprise partners. As the Table shows, each benefit is not limited to one case example but replicated across multiple cases. For instance, the collaboration between the dairy cooperative, Schwarzwaldmilch, and a digital consultancy, sine qua non, yielded additional opportunities for both firms. At Schwarzwaldmilch, the positive customer and media responses to using QR codes to tell a milk product's journey from farm to shelf sparked conversations about other technologies the cooperative might explore to enhance the customer experience, including augmented reality in mobile applications. For sine qua non, the project demonstrated that their digital twin technology could provide transparency in the supply chain for other consumer goods. As a result, the project helped them expand their network of clients and recast their offering as a digital transparency platform.[2] Given the co-innovation platform's collective benefits, many partners become serial co-innovators, engaging in multiple projects with the platform and in turn, advancing the ecosystem's scope and growth. Appendix provides additional case examples. In combination,

Table 6.3 Partner benefits and chapter examples

Benefits for Partners	Some Examples from Chapters
• Enabling the pursuit of projects that otherwise would not be feasible	Bluecoat Systems; Gerolsteiner Brunnen GmGH & INTENSE AG; Kore.ai; Monsta Project; Telit & Stellium; Schwarzwaldmilch & sine qua non; Britehouse and RSSC
• Exposure to project opportunities not on the roadmap	Telit & Stellium; Schwarzwaldmilch & sine qua non
• Developing novel intersections through connections with unfamiliar partners	Elephants, Rhinos & People; Gerolsteiner Brunnen GmGH & INTENSE AG; GS1 & Tire Retreads; Montsa Project; Schwarzwaldmilch & sine qua non; Telit & Stellium; Britehouse and RSSC
• Expanding the network of potential clients and partners	Bluecoat Systems; Kore.ai; sine qua non; Virtual Power Systems
• Learning & Knowledge Acquisition: Vicarious learning; Spillover exposure	Demos, Showcase Events, Platform Physical Space, Project Stories Oil & Gas; Mining; NS2
• Learning & Knowledge Acquisition: Recombinatory learning; Knowledge sharing, Experiential learning and Iterative development	Britehouse and RSSC; Elephants, Rhinos & People; GS1 & Tire Retreads; Monsta Project; OSIsoft; Oil and Gas; Schwarzwaldmilch & sine qua non; Telit & Stellium; Vandrico & Illumiti;
• Capability Development: Problem Solving; Co-Innovation; Project Management	Britehouse and RSSC; Elephants, Rhinos & People; Kore.ai; Monsta Project; Schwarzwaldmilch & sine qua non; Vandrico & Illumiti

the strategic and organizational benefits for partners and the platform reinforce a co-innovation platform's distinctiveness relative to other innovation platforms.

The Next Phase of Co-Innovation

Co-innovation is a constant. Executives view innovation and ecosystems as critical to future growth yet many lack the necessary capabilities to orchestrate an ecosystem—including how to engage in co-innovation with a diverse set of firms.[3] The book details how a co-innovation platform can help firms address this challenge. How can co-innovation itself advance value creation and growth? Where can it help solve complex problems confronting firms? We explore these questions in the context of digital and cloud-based business transformation. Next, we conclude the book with some final thoughts on co-innovation strategy.

Digital and Cloud-based Business Transformation

We see co-innovation as playing a dominant role in ongoing digital- and cloud-based business transformation. As digital transformation evolves from industry 4.0 to 5.0 and beyond, firms will continue to seek growth from solutions built on technologies, such as IoT and artificial intelligence (AI), that are increasingly becoming dependent on cloud services. IoT is not just about simple connectivity but enables decentralized intelligence. Business leaders view IoT, AI, and cloud infrastructure as the technologies that will have the largest impact on business in the near future.[4] The installed-base of active IoT connected devices is expected to reach 30.9 billion units by 2025, as compared to approximately 12 billion units in 2020.[5] To co-develop solutions and/or business models leveraging these technologies, firms will need partners with the relevant capabilities, as well as expertise in edge computing and machine learning. In this fast-paced context, cloud providers also see value in collaborating to support innovative solution development. When discussing SAP's future cloud strategy, Christian Klein, CEO, stated, "Instead of doing everything ourselves, *we are co-innovating.*"[6] Judson Althoff, Executive Vice President, Worldwide Commercial Business, Microsoft, explained: "…digital technology must be the servant of business outcomes, allowing organizations to realize efficiencies across their business, harness data to deliver differentiated customer experiences, make collaboration seamless wherever employees are located and thwart emerging security threats. This is the foundation of *co-innovation* with our customers…"[7] Meanwhile, Amazon AWS has established a Cloud Innovation Center (CIC) to help public sector organizations *co-innovate* to solve their critical challenges and explore new ideas.[8]

Many organizations are developing, or have developed, a multi-cloud strategy whereas others find themselves in a "multi-cloud by accident" scenario. In a multi-cloud environment, an organization may have different applications and workflows running on multiple public clouds such as Amazon AWS and Microsoft Azure, to support different activities or functions. The "multi-cloud by accident" scenario occurs in situations where cloud adoption was not guided by a coordinated strategy and instead, emerged through choices made in different parts of an organization at different points in time. For instance, departments within an organization may adopt different cloud providers to address unique or department-specific needs. As time accrues, a firm realizes that it is using multiple cloud providers without a cohesive or coordinated approach. The situation also might arise when a firm acquires a cloud provider or acquires other firms that are using different cloud providers relative to the acquirer. Hybrid cloud environments, where a company operates both a private cloud and a public cloud, also pose significant challenges.[9]

Although a well-crafted multi-cloud strategy may allow a firm to access the best-in-class service offerings for specific activities and avoid dependence on any single cloud provider, firms face a host of development and execution challenges. We begin by highlighting some of the problems firms and managers encounter as they navigate digital- and cloud-based business transformation and suggest ways that co-innovation can help.

A common obstacle with any organizational change initiative is overcoming the past. As firms try to accelerate moving to the cloud, they often begin with a "lift and shift" approach—replicating a technology stack [10] from their enterprise data center in a public cloud infrastructure instead of re-platforming to build an architecture designed to take full advantage of a public cloud environment. The implication is that firms often treat public cloud providers or hyperscalers as infrastructure-as-a-service providers rather than consuming cloud native services designed to make optimal use of cloud technology. Consider a basic case where lift and shift results in deploying a firm's software architecture into a public cloud but the firm only installs to a single availability zone (single country or region) offered by a cloud provider. A disruption to service in the single availability zone could have significant business impact. In contrast, designing a landscape from the start with the capability to manage failures more adeptly by employing multiple availability zones reduces dependency on any one zone and, in turn, lowers risk from a service outage or impairment.[11]

A second challenge stems from differences among cloud providers. Multi-cloud environments require more oversight due to heterogeneity among cloud providers. Cloud providers innovate and excel in different areas. As a result, managers must keep track of what their firm is trying to accomplish with each cloud provider while also maintaining awareness of the provider that offers the best-in-class services for specific applications. Complicating matters, cloud providers, such as Amazon AWS, release frequent updates. The sheer volume of updates can be overwhelming. For instance, as devOps engineers[12] chase the latest update, they may lose sight of a project's core requirements. Additionally, all public cloud providers offer a common set of infrastructure services but each tailors these services to their cloud. For instance, automation and scripting tools tend to be unique to a particular provider's cloud infrastructure. This problem might be solved by talent with deep expertise across multiple cloud environments but such talent is scarce. And while cloud services are by subscription, managers can choose from a menu of offerings—from top tier to basics—within a single service category. Expenses can creep up as managers across different parts of an organization opt for more advanced services; this situation suggests the need for more systematic management of a firm's multi-cloud approach. Lastly, ensuring data portability and interconnectivity also warrants consideration. Cloud to cloud connectively is feasible but typically, expensive. Some cloud providers charge for data delivered to another hyperscaler, increasing the costs of data transfer. In a multi-cloud environment, organizations may need to connect islands of resources. Innovation will be critical for future portability. In sum, multi-cloud environments involve managing significant heterogeneity and complexity and, in turn, require more oversight, talent, and support.

Organizations rarely start a digital transformation or multi-cloud journey with all the talent, time, and resources they need and desire. Even if a company wants to take on the above challenges alone, it may not be able to access the necessary talent to do so. In a 2020 survey of four hundred IT decision makers at mid to large size enterprises, 86% of respondents indicated a cloud talent shortage will delay projects.[13] Another 2020 survey of 1500 industry professionals (e.g., CTOs, CIOs, IT VPs, directors, executives, COO/LOIBs) from mid to large sized enterprises offered similar results: 56% of respondents indicated that identifying or building the necessary expertise to successfully manage data beyond enterprise data centers will be challenging or extremely challenging and another 30% viewed the activity as somewhat challenging.[14] A 2020 cloud computing study by IDG, surveying 551 IT decision makers, reported that 67% of respondents plan to add new roles, such as cloud architect and cloud systems administrators, to help manage their expanding cloud activities.[15] The cloud talent drought may get worse given accelerated cloud adoption. Complicating the situation is the persistent need for agility. Customers' expectations include continuous improvement in services, streamlined integration, and support. These expectations also hold true for internal stakeholders who rely on cloud services for their operations. When organizations need to execute faster than they have in the past to keep up and the necessary talent is scarce, increasing innovation budgets or investing in new technologies will not be enough.

How might co-innovation help firms cope with these challenges? First, in order to accelerate solution development, firms will need to be open to accessing the necessary complementary capabilities through co-innovation with a wide range of partners (platform providers, system integrators, technology companies, domain experts, etc.). Success will require developing capabilities in building and executing partnerships for rapid co-innovation. Another alternative is tapping into or developing a co-innovation platform with a focus on enabling projects oriented toward enhancing cloud operations. Second, motivated toward building operational excellence, a firm's devOps teams may find co-innovation with public cloud providers a fruitful method for enhancing scalability or facilitating re-platforming—moving from an on premise enterprise architecture to one designed for an always on environment to improve uptime and resiliency. An organization's cloud team also might consider collaborating with managed service providers (MSPs) to co-develop services and solutions. As part of these co-innovation activities, organizations may gain new insights regarding how different technologies artificial intelligence, machine learning, and automation can be deployed to enhance their operations. Third, the pain points discussed above may motivate organizations to co-innovate with complementors to develop overlay solutions aimed at coordinating across public clouds in a more agile, orchestrated way. Some cloud providers, such as Amazon, Microsoft, and SAP, already collaborate with a host of 3rd parties, such as managed service providers, co-location providers, independent software vendors, and hardware suppliers, to support customer needs. Imagine what co-innovation among these hyperscalers might generate for their customers, especially those operating in hybrid or multi-cloud environments. Lastly, some future ecosystem growth will be driven by increasing integration and consumption of platform APIs. Organizations will continue to seek deeper integration of applications and solutions supporting all aspects of their operations—both upstream and downstream. Coordinating and managing APIs might begin as a relatively straight forward process but requests for new APIs, or extensions to existing APIs, translates into more process and approval actions with the cloud provider. Each new API and extension require a cloud provider to provide robust API management and have structures in place to facilitate engagement, integration and innovation. Firms pursuing a multi-cloud strategy must understand how the process works across multiple providers and adapt. Given the talent drought and pressure to act quickly, co-innovation with complementors offers one route to developing and integrating API accessible microservices.

Co-innovation among a variety of stakeholders within the cloud ecosystem is certain to evolve as business strategies, models, technologies, and customer requirements change. Undoubtedly, there are many ways co-innovation can be applied to technology challenges up and down the technology stack. While we cannot predict all aspects of the future, multiple co-innovation opportunities are present today that can yield performance advantages in navigating digital- and cloud-based business transformation.

Final Thoughts

We conclude by revisiting the important role that diversity in actors, projects, technologies, and industries plays in ensuring co-innovation contributes to ecosystem expansion. We also offer some guidance regarding different forms of the co-innovation platform.

Is there a sweet spot to achieving ecosystem generativity? A co-innovation platform provides a way to generate new output by engaging a diversity of actors, projects, technologies, and industries. Value creation is not about the individual elements but their interactions. Our collection of case examples demonstrates that the co-innovation platform approach is not simply a matter of advancing one type of technology, firm, or industry. Instead, a co-innovation platform is designed to solve a wide array of problems or challenges across vastly different contexts using collaboration. Co-innovation projects are not limited to co-creation with customers—the most common starting point for firms beginning a digital-based business transformation journey. Instead, they span a diverse range of activities. As shared in our case examples, some projects focus on solving an industry wide challenge—such as seeking zero harm in the mining industry (Illumiti and Vandrico) whereas others address industry challenges that also benefit the public—such as developing a solution to keep highways safe (GS1 and tire retread). Other projects focus on firm-level objectives such as creating a novel solution and validating its capabilities (Monsta, Bluecoat), optimizing supply management (mineral water case), solving an operations/supply chain challenge (sugarcane transport), and using a new technology to create unique customer value (dairy cooperative and digital twin technology). See Appendix for additional co-innovation cases.

Enabling collaboration among firms from different knowledge domains provides them an opportunity to combine ideas and knowledge in new ways. This activity is vital to ecosystem growth but requires managers to think differently about the sources of innovation that will support their organizations' future. For instance, say your company produces snack foods and is seeking ways to enhance the customer experience. Would you know who to partner with to explore how unfamiliar technologies, such as digital twin technology or augmented reality, could be used to create value for the customer? And if you do, would a short term co-innovation project focused on rapid development and test of a solution be more advantageous than a traditional approach which requires you to search for a partner in a domain where you lack expertise? The unique value co-innovation platforms create is underscored by the case examples and this thought exercise.

How can these ideas be applied in small or medium sized enterprises? While the chapters demonstrate that all elements of a co-innovation platform play a prominent role in its success, we offer some guidance for developing one with a less resource intensive approach. Governance policies and mechanisms supporting curated access, resource-openness, incentives to mobilize participation, and equitable value distribution are essential. However, the scale and scope of supply-side and demand-side services may vary. For example, demand-side storytelling services might be streamlined by focusing on a subset of storytelling activities and using alternative methods to simplify activities, such as providing templates for press releases, solution briefs, and white papers rather than using an ops team to co-develop content. On the supply-side, priorities are simple contract formation, knowledge broker services, and IT system resources. Since co-innovation is the guiding focus, a hands-on approach to contract formation is vital to project success. Knowledge broker services are needed but the role could be assumed by the platform director, rather than an ops team. In our experience, teams significantly valued rapid access to IT system resources for project work but the amount of service and support provided for this category will be informed by your co-innovation objectives. Reducing the scale and scope of services comes with tradeoffs. Your choices will be informed by a clear understanding of the problem you are trying to solve and your answers to the three strategic questions relevant to a co-innovation platform (see paragraph one of this chapter).

Platforms and ecosystems will continue to increase in prominence across industries and sectors. Existing platform types will evolve and new variants may emerge, changing the way individuals interact, firms innovate and operate, and industry boundaries evolve. Complex business problems, the persistent drive for success, and the wickedly fast rate of technological change will continue to motivate firms to seek collaboration as a problem-solving tool. Co-innovation platforms offer a systematic approach to enabling collaborative innovation and orchestrating an ecosystem. Our goal in this book is to offer practical guidance on how to use, as well as develop, a co-innovation platform. We hope that this book inspires you to think about new ways co-innovation can be used to assist your organization's strategic directions and growth.

Questions, quibbles, comments? Please share your thoughts and ideas. We would value hearing your co-innovation story. You can reach us at: coinnovationstrategy@gmail.com.

Notes

1. Anand, B.N., Khanna, T. 2000. Do firms learn to create value? The case of alliances. *Strategic Management Journal,* March Special Issue 21: 295–315. Delios, A., Henisz, W.J. 2000. Japanese firms' investment strategies in emerging economies. *Academy of Management Journal, 43*: 305–323.
2. https://www.sine-qua-non.biz/index.php/de/component/k2/item/43-transparenzplattform-mondo-del-caffe-wird-teil-von-yoy, accessed June 21, 2021.
3. In a 2018 survey of business leaders, Accenture found that 76% of business leaders believe their business models will dramatically differ by 2023 and that ecosystems will be the force driving change and growth. However, only 40% of respondents indicated they had the capacity and experience to execute an ecosystem strategy. Lyman, M., Ref R., and Wright, O. 2018. Cornerstone of Future Growth: Ecosystems. Accenture Strategy, pages 1–14.
4. The Fourth Industrial Revolution: At the intersection of readiness and responsibility. 2020. Deloitte Insights: page 18. Source data: September, 2019 Deloitte survey of 2029 business leaders in technology. https://www2.deloitte.com/content/dam/Deloitte/de/Documents/human-capital/Deloitte_Review_26_Fourth_Industrial_Revolution.pdf, accessed June 21, 2021.; Mehta, D., Seen-Kalb, L. 2021. In-depth: Industry 4.0 2021, *Statista* (#did-66974-1), pages 1–110. https://www-statista-com.libproxy.scu.edu/study/66974/in-depth-industry-40/ accessed June 21, 2021. The results are referenced on page 17 of the report; the report refers to the survey source data as a September 2019 Deloitte survey of 2029 business leaders in technology.
5. Lueth, K. L. 2020. Stat of the IoT 2020: 12 Billing IOT connections, surpassing non-IoT for the first time. IoT Analytics (report publication date: November 19, 2020). https://iot-analytics.com/state-of-the-iot-2020-12-billion-iot-connections-surpassing-non-iot-for-the-first-time/,

accessed June 21, 2021. Also see, Vailshery, L. S. 2021. Internet of Things (IoT) – Statistics and facts. Statista (report publication date: May 11, 2021). https://www-statista-com.libproxy.scu.edu/topics/2637/internet-of-things/, accessed June 21, 2021; https://www-statista-com.libproxy.scu.edu/statistics/1101442/iot-number-of-connected-devices-worldwide/, accessed June 21, 2021.
6. Dignan, L. 2020. SAP Charts new course to accelerate cloud shift, co-innovation, one data model. ZDNet, October 26, 2020. https://www.zdnet.com/article/sap-charts-new-course-to-accelerate-cloud-shift-co-innovation-one-data-model/, accessed June 21, 2021.
7. Althoff, Judson. 2021. How Microsoft cloud technology and co-innovation approach are driving business value for customers across industry. Microsoft: Official MS Blog, April 26, 2021. https://blogs.microsoft.com/blog/2021/04/26/how-microsoft-cloud-technology-and-co-innovation-approach-are-driving-business-value-for-customers-across-industry/, accessed June 26, 2021.
8. https://aws.amazon.com/government-education/cloud-innovation-centers/, accessed June 26, 2021.
9. Cloud Computing, Statista Dossier. https://www-statista-com.libproxy.scu.edu/study/15293/cloud-computing-statista-dossier/, accessed June 21, 2021.
10. A technology stack is the set of technologies used to run an application or project and includes a variety of elements—programming languages, frameworks, database, front-end and back-end tools, servers, operating systems, and applications connected via APIs. https://www.sumologic.com/glossary/technology-stack/, accessed June 30, 2021.
11. A firm can organize use of its cloud provider's infrastructure, in part, based on the provider's regional footprint and the proximity of the provider's infrastructure resources to end customers. Cloud providers offer regional coverage spanning one or more countries and each region can include multiple availability zones. The zones contain physical data centers controlled by the cloud provider; cloud providers operate zones directly and/or by partnering with a local co-location provider or managed service provider (MSP). For example, a firm with customers spread across France, Switzerland, and Germany might organize its cloud infrastructure around the Europe, the Middle East and Africa (EMEA) region where the firm can select availability zones in the closest proximity to customers to minimize network latency arising from data traveling long distances.

12. A devOps engineer uses tools, processes, and methodologies to manage a variety of activities throughout the software development lifecycle. DevOps is the integration of tools, processes, and methodologies designed to strengthen an organization's capabilities in delivering services and applications and to do so at a faster pace than traditional software development processes.
13. Reported in "Challenges of Cloud Transformation", Logicworks Report; the survey was conducted by Wakefield research (see page 4 of the report). https://go.logicworks.com/2020-cloud-transformation-challenges, accessed June 30, 2021.
14. Cloud Computing, Statista Dossier. See pages 49 and 88. https://www-statista-com.libproxy.scu.edu/study/15293/cloud-computing-statista-dossier/, accessed June 21, 2021.
15. IDG Cloud Computing Survey, 2020. https://www.idg.com/tools-for-marketers/2020-cloud-computing-study/, accessed June 30, 2021.

Appendix: Co-Innovation Project Case Briefs

This appendix includes a variety of co-innovation project cases drawn from projects at SAP's co-innovation platform in Palo Alto, California. Each case provides a project overview, highlights project details and challenges, and concludes with project outcomes. As Table A.1 shows, the cases span different industries, involve the integration of different technologies, and vary in size from two partners to five partners. Several cases involve collaboration between a complementor and one or more units within SAP, such as an industry business unit, product unit, or business unit. The cases were developed from a variety of materials such as project proposals, project result documents (solution briefs, white papers, blogs, project reports, etc.), and interviews with project participants.

Table A.1 Co-Innovation project case briefs

#	Co-innovation Project Case	Partners	Context
1	Empathy for Shoppers Improves Enterprise Procurement	eBay, SAP Ariba	Enterprise Procurement: integrated corporate and personal buying experience Application: multi-industry
2	Monsta - Business Intelligence at Scale	RedHat, Supermicro, Intel, F5, SOASTA, SAP Business Intelligence Software Development	Performance characterization for business intelligence applications—demonstrating concurrent services for 10 K users with commodity h/w and s/w Application: Multiple industries
3	Wide-area network (WAN) Acceleration of SAP applications	Bluecoat Systems, SAP Business Analytics Group	WAN acceleration and enhancing the remote business analytics user experience Application: multi-industry
4	The Perfect Plant: Energy and Carbon Management	OSIsoft, SAP Solutions	Sustainability and operational efficiency in manufacturing Application: Manufacturing
5	IoT and Zero Harm for Mining	Vandrico Solutions, Inc., Illumiti, SAP Industry Experts	IoT, Edge computing and real-time situational awareness in the mining industry Application: Mining industry; asset intensive industries
6	IoT Enterprise Bots	Kore.ai, SAP Partner Management	Using bots to interact with IoT sensor data. Application: Multiple industries
7	Moonraker: Improving the Remote Compute Experience	Citrix, Nvidia, SAP 3D Visual Enterprise Product Team	3D Visual Animation applications Application: Manufacturing and asset intensive process industries
8	IoT and AI for Manufacturing	Telit, Stellium, SAP Analytics, SAP Data Warehouse Product Management	Integrating IoT, Artificial Intelligence, & Big Data. Application: Manufacturing and Asset intensive Industries
9	Expense Management Analytics Integration Project	Tangoe, SAP HANA Product Management	Using enhanced analytics, IIOT and online transaction processing (OLTP) capabilities to optimize IT assets and expenses. Application: Multiple industries

(continued)

Table A.1 (continued)

#	Co-innovation Project Case	Partners	Context
10	Edge computing and IIoT	Dell EMC, Pixel Velocity, MIntelligence (Mtell), SAP Industry Business Unit (IBU), SAP Asset Management, SAP Partner Management, SAP Data Science	Real-time situational awareness and edge computing solutions. Application: Oil and Gas industry
11	Accelerating Financial Analytics Performance	Vendavo, SAP HANA Product Management, SAP Partner Management	Optimizing pricing using artificial intelligence (AI), machine learning (ML) and columnar in-memory database technology. Application: Multiple industries
12	Unified Computing for Big Data Analytics	Cisco, Intel, SAP HANA Development	Integrating hardware and software to simplify architecture and improve big data analytics performance. Application: Multiple industries
13	Creating automated workflows to accelerate development of high-powered database applications	RedHat, SAP Sybase Product Development, SAP Partner Management; SAP ASE, IQ and SQL Anywhere product teams	Making it easier for RedHat's applications developers to access and use SAP enterprise database technologies. Application: Multiple industries
14	SAPNS2 HANA Intelligent Data Fusion	Axon AI, SAP National Security Service (NS2)	Real-time situational awareness and edge computing. Application: Government, public and private sector, and process industries
15	Software-defined data centers and managing hot, warm and cold data	Vmware, Hitachi Data Systems, SAP Product and Partner Management	Software defined networks & micro-segmentation; Virtual network design. Application: Multiple industries

Empathy For Shoppers Improves Enterprise Procurement, February 2015

Partners

eBay and SAP Ariba.

Co-innovation Project Overview

Sometimes, mundane or basic activities, such as employees ordering office supplies, are overlooked for innovation. Of course, even boring activities or processes can represent complexity. The advent of cloud, software-as-a-Service (SaaS) and IoT have motivated firms to embrace new ways of working that are not always provided by an IT department. At the time of the project, enterprise IT shops began to label such behaviors as shadow IT.

Given the proliferation of e-commerce solutions, it should come as no surprise that if Kenya in accounting wants a particular type of stapler or highlighter not found in the company's procurement catalog, and she has a pre-approved spend account, Kenya might decide that purchasing her item on eBay makes sense. But, what are the implications if hundreds or thousands of employees in a company use the same approach? Over time, the company's local IT report, which is informed by the formal procurement system, would provide an inaccurate view of the company's spending on particular supplies and resources. Not an ideal outcome. How can a company address this problem? Block all ecommerce web traffic on the network? Set policy prohibiting purchases from non-qualified vendors? Fortunately, a more productive approach is possible.

An SAP Ariba executive and one of his lead development managers approached the co-innovation platform team to discuss a potential project with an ecommerce development team from eBay. The problem resonated with SAP procurement staff. SAP recognized that it was not capturing a high-fidelity picture of its total procurement. Internal research and audits of expense reporting and end user survey work revealed that other frequent purchasing channels were being tapped. Already in partnership, SAP and eBay used a design thinking approach, facilitated by the platform, to identify how to provide access to eBay shopping via SAP's Supplier Relationship Management (SRM) application.

Project Detail

The solution needed eBay seller functionality to integrate seamlessly with the SAP procurement system. It also needed to preserve a user's shopping experience and the retailer's traditional shopping catalog architecture while including advanced features from the eBay marketplace such as additional shipping options, inventory checks, and rich content. The design thinking approach kept the focus on the user experience.

Some co-development work occurred prior to the co-innovation project proposal, streamlining contract formation process. The co-innovation team had a solid understanding of the platform services they needed to fulfill the project's objectives and benefitted from using the platform's supply-side and demand-side services. The project team relied on the ops management team to assist with project management and made repeated use of the platform's physical space. For instance, the platform's flexible meeting spaces allowed the project team to bring together a variety of teams for workshops and events. The platform's demo and showcase services were used to share the team's work and solution with partners and customers and supported all workshops or field facing events hosted by the project team.

Challenges

Legacy systems include the people responsible for making them run and work. Significant changes to mission and business critical systems are rarely quick. One initial rollout challenge was gaining buyin among operating managers of the existing procurement systems within SAP.

Outcome

The project demonstrated how adapting systems to capture users' procurement shopping behavior contributes to more efficient and accurate procurement reporting while also enhancing a user's interface experience. The ops team supported the launch of the new capability for SAP's procurement system. Blogs, podcasts, and demos at SAP SAPPHIRE NOW and other sponsored events showcased the project's results. The new capability was made available to SAP end customers and contributed to additional value capture for SAP and eBay.

Monsta: Business Intelligence at Scale October, 2012

Partners

RedHat, Supermicro, Intel, F5, SOASTA, SAP Business Intelligence Software Development.

Co-innovation Project Overview

The "Monsta" project was formed to conduct performance characterization for a business intelligence application—demonstrating concurrent service for ten thousand end users with a scale out architecture using commodity hardware and software. The collaboration also provided an opportunity to explore how various elements, such as operating system (OS) management and load balancing, informs the overall optimization of scale out architecture. Additional activities focused on providing reliable and cost effective load generation as well as testing for concurrent use.

The project name "Monsta" originated from an engineer with the SAP Business Objects software quality team. The inspiration was a monster truck image with the logos of all the partners who were taking part in the project. It eventually morphed into a drawing of a green "Monsta" to further accentuate the size and scope of the endeavor as well as to reflect some of challenges in managing a large co-innovation project team.

Regarding the partners: RedHat is an enterprise open source solutions provider; Supermicro provides server solutions; F5 offers a variety of application services (application delivery networking, network security, access and authorization, application availability and performance, multi-cloud management); Intel is a semiconductor company; SOASTA, is a subsidiary of Akamai Technologies and offers testing services for websites and website applications; SAP Business Intelligence Software provides a suite of services for data reporting, visualization, and sharing.

Project Details

The project's overall objective was to establish customer confidence in large-scale business intelligence deployments. As background, the SAP Business Objects Business Intelligence (BI) platform and database technologies were configured to run over a standard enterprise-ready open-source operating system from RedHat (RHEL 6), using enterprise data center–ready Intel Xeon processor-based hardware from Supermicro (TwinBlade and SuperServer) and an application delivery control system from F5.

The project scope included a variety of subgoals:

- Demonstrate scalability and performance of SAP Business Objects Business Intelligence (BI) platform, release 4.
- Improve customer satisfaction and implementation success with enhanced deployment guides and best practices documentation for large scale deployments.
- Provide in-depth training for services, support, and sales teams that are supporting and selling enterprise BI solutions.
- Provide tools to support an ecosystem of services and reseller partners.
- Validate and optimize Business Objects Enterprise architecture.
  - Provide guidance and documentation for engineering teams on enhancements to ease deployment and system administration.
  - Provide specific recommendations for improving platform architecture by leveraging underlying middleware and hardware.
- Accelerate revenue by supporting the SAP Business Object's business unit and its Open Platform initiative.
  - Demonstrate continued commitment to invest in BI for large enterprise customers.
  - Target offering to ninety-seven companies with 100K+ employees operating around the globe.

The targeted benchmark was viewed as a BI platform differentiator; it would provide future engineering projects with the level of concurrency and performance that might be attained with particular software architectures and server configurations.

Supermicro provided a 42U Rack featuring its TwinBlade architecture to create an eighty-core system. Each twin blade possessed four CPUs and forty-eight gigabytes of RAM. F5 provided the project landscape with its load balancing appliances offering tailored configurations for managing traffic flowing to and from the deployed Tomcat Servers responding to concurrent user queries. F5 also contributed its BIG-IP management software and backend support for landscape change management. The ops team installed and managed the SAP Business Objects Business Intelligence (BI) platform landscape and coordinated configuration and change management with Supermicro, RedHat, F5, and SOASTA.

RedHat initially configured its Rhel 6 release to accommodate testing by a sustainability team; the team wanted to measure data center energy management running SAP workloads. This sustainability dimension of the project was eventually declared out of scope due to subject matter expert resource constraints. As a result, RedHat shifted attention to another aspect of the project—building an optimal environment for running high concurrent software application consumption. This activity included configuring its Satellite software to illustrate effective management of Linux resources in the environment and to perform non-disruptive updates.

To achieve the projects goals, load testing needed to scale up to concurrent use volumes. SOASTA provided the project team with its high-volume testing solution that was cost-effective, available, and scalable. This contribution spawned a separate Intel-Supermicro co-innovation project with SOASTA examining load generation for large scale SAP Business Objects Enterprise (BOE) deployments.

Each of the Monsta project partners contributed fundamental elements to the project. The team had a mutual understanding of the use case context and the degree of scale out that was achievable using the available off the shelf resources.

Challenges

All five partner teams agreed to the project's mutual objectives. However, each partner also had its own specific project requirements and expectations. One challenge posed by the multi-party project was getting all partners on boarded to the project's system landscape and keeping everyone in sync with the project work.

Whether your project demands scale up or scale out hardware capability, securing the equipment needed to pursue a large project is rarely a small undertaking. The co-innovation platform contributed a mix of its own equipment along with equipment provided by Intel, Supermicro, and F5 to meet the project's compute, storage, and network capability needs.

The Monsta project team was fortunate that Intel was interested in the project and agreed to participate (the connection was made by the platform's knowledge broker). Intel provided Supermicro with the cores needed to support the project's compute and storage capacity requirements. The project outcomes validated Intel's participation in the project. Intel also generated a KPI to show how its contributions to the project enabled Supermicro to meet its revenue growth targets.

The team also encountered challenges in maintaining focus on delivering benchmark quality scale out test results. The platform's knowledge broker was actively engaged in acquiring technology needed for the project. This is not always easy; the project required an expensive test environment. Additionally, the scope increased with iterative learning as well as evolving expectations of different partners. The project also attracted a lot of attention within SAP. At one point, another internal stakeholder requested to participate. The stakeholder wanted to assess energy use of the system and to develop optimizations to reduce energy use by a large SAP Business Objects Business Intelligence (BI) platform 4.x deployment. The request was deferred given the complexity of the project but reinforced the project's value and the potential for broad application.

A final challenge was that the project lacked a committed developer resource. While there were two development teams principally responsible for the BOE 4.x product, both offered limited support. They claimed backlog challenges limited their ability to dedicate resources to the project.

Outcomes

The project met the objectives—demonstrating that the software could sustain up to ten thousand concurrent users. The team achieved an upper bound of around 11,800 users before instability ensued running queries. The theoretical number of max concurrent users was fifty-thousand. At the time of the project, a load of ten thousand concurrent users had never been tried before in any known internal or external testing. The only prior benchmark attempt was a scale up architecture featuring an IBM system running PowerPC; a whitepaper described this effort as a proof of concept (POC) sustaining up to eight thousand concurrent users. Exceeding the established threshold with commodity components was a significant achievement. The platform director was actively engaged with all the development teams as they engaged in iterative development and problem solving to clear roadblocks in the configuration—as a step to get to the next larger query load. The project work involved a lot of tacit knowledge exchange, iterative learning, and learning from failures.

After the environment had been tested and scaled up to ten thousand users, the project team noticed that resource consumption of the environment was relatively low:

- Tomcat: ~ 12% CPU on average
- Web Intelligence: ~ 25–30% CPU on average

- CMS: ~ 12% CPU on average

To raise the average resource consumption without impacting throughput and performance, the project team and ops team immediately began seeking ways to reduce hardware through consolidation of server tiers onto fewer hosts.

The project team was hopeful the work would continue and a "Son of Monsta" project was approved but ultimately, did not gain traction due to reorganizations a year later. The team felt it could reach upwards of fifteen to twenty thousand concurrent users through fine tuning as things were installed and configured, but there were indications that the software architecture needed changing in order to achieve these goals.

Project partners benefitted in other ways. Each partner gained lessons about effective project management and partner management. They also learned from each other and found value in the platform's knowledge broker capabilities. The platform gained experience with knowledge brokering as well as with managing a large, multi-partner, multi-objective project.

Glossary

CMS: Central Management System, Business intelligence sub-component admin tool and system repository.
PowerPC: IBM CPU.
TomCat: open source database.

Wide-Area Network (WAN) Acceleration of SAP Applications, January 2010

Partners

Bluecoat Systems, SAP Business Analytics Group.

Co-innovation Project

The purpose of this project was to demonstrate how WAN acceleration benefits the SAP business analytics user by providing an appliance-based WAN endpoint solution that improves performance and latency experienced by the user and requires little to zero disruption of existing network infrastructure routers and switches.

Project Overview

In 2010, network computing experienced increased demand from business analytics users for a better user experience as well as improved performance for situations where intensive analytics are performed and users are remote to their headquarters local area network (LAN). Bluecoat Systems, a WAN Acceleration solution provider, was introduced to SAP's co-innovation platform by the SAP PartnerEdge program. Bluecoat pursued a relationship with SAP to address the connectivity performance needs of Bluecoat customers who also are SAP customers. The project proposal focused on building an optimized business network configuration for SAP Business Analytics workloads. Customers in multiple industries were interested in the solution given their analytics workforces were broadly distributed rather than concentrated in one locale. For this project, Bluecoat provided two of its endpoint appliances (one for each end of the WAN link for instance, home office, satellite office). It later provided two more of its appliances to support the SAP demosat SAP SAPPHIRE NOW. Bluecoat partner managers collaborated with an SAP partner management team to certify its appliance-based product for operating within a standard SAP landscape. Certifications for physical hardware were regularly facilitated using co-innovation platform resources.

Project Details

Using connections provided by the platform, the Bluecoat project team worked with an SAP Business Objects subject matter expert to build a complete LAN-to-LAN and Client-to-LAN reference architecture featuring Bluecoat caching technology. The technology submitted transmit packets with updates to the cache. Standard SAP landscapes for Analytics applications are provided by the platform and the ops team provides a standard configuration for each landscape component. The default hardware allocation typically was a 2 CPU, 8 GB RAM MS Windows or Linux server unless the project team specified different requirements. The platform's ops team tapped several internal SAP channels to introduce various SAP analytics subject matter experts to the Bluecoat team. The Bluecoat team collaborated with the subject matter experts to optimize data flow caching over WANs between Bluecoat appliances.

Using a network measuring capability provided by the ops team and sponsored by Shunra Systems, the project team was able to replicate an array of circuit configurations (private leased lines) and could simulate transoceanic leased lines. Within the provisioned project landscape, the ops team and business objects experts built both server and client-side SAP environments. They also created load generation from various user driven business analytics work (database queries) to test latency, application responsiveness, hardware performance, and user experience. Additional testing explored concurrent use capacity and WAN security.

Challenges

The project found traction with SAP Business Analytics and with a number of product and field stakeholders. The project team faced two challenges: (1) how to sell direct to SAP analytics customers and (2) how to demonstrate that its WAN technology was not disruptive to applications and could quickly improve performance and the end-user experience. Nearly everyone with tradeshow experience is aware that wifi or general network performance can be either be "ok" or not. To showcase the solution's performance, the team ran the demo on a tradeshow exhibit floor. Individuals who explored the demo lauded its responsiveness, speed, and performance as compared to the responsiveness, speed and performance of other demos they had examined at the tradeshow.

Outcomes

The outcomes from extensive testing and documentation led to a whitepaper (produced by the platform) and a standing demo presented at platform events such as SAP Virtualization Week, SAP TechEd, and SAP SAPPHIRE NOW. The demo created by the project team and hosted by the platform stimulated the interest of an internal manager, a business objects expert, participating in a different co-innovation project related to analytics and SAP HANA. The manager was introduced to Bluecoat at a previous co-innovation event and wanted to leverage the project's demo to simulate the ability to accelerate priority network traffic to machines on a showroom floor. The request to expand the project's scope occurred before the team had achieved the project's primary goals. The manager collaborated with the Bluecoat team to create and run a show floor network architecture where all of the demos (about ten) exhibited on the show floor also were running reliably back at the platform location in Palo Alto, California. For Bluecoat, the add on project was advantageous; it was exhibited at the event and attracted customers from the SAP data analytics exhibit. Each demo station had SAP co-innovation platform and Bluecoat branding with information regarding how to learn more.

Unfortunately, due to some show floor wide network latency, there were moments when the only demos one could see operate in a booth on the show floor (not installed on a local demo machine) were Bluecoat's demos. The demos performed as expected with impressive screen refreshes and load times of some large data sets. The project demonstrated the value of the platforms Demo and Showcase services—specifically, the awareness building associated with the platform's events. On the supply-side, the project illustrated the benefits of the platform's knowledge broker services.

The whitepaper co-written by the project leads and the ops team provided a comprehensive proof of concept (POC) covering test results for LAN to LAN and Client to LAN scenarios using various SAP business warehouse user actions and processes. For Bluecoat, the project allowed it to win a multi-million-dollar deal with a large North American retailer. The retailer accepted the white paper as a POC, allowing Bluecoat to skip the retailer's default POC process and reducing the sales cycle by six months.

Glossary

Mpls: a telecommunications network that directs data using labels versus lengthy network addresses serving to speed up traffic flows.

The Perfect Plant: Energy and Carbon Management, December, 2010

Partners

OSIsoft and SAP Solutions.

Co-innovation Project Overview

The project was developed to illustrate how combining OSIsoft and SAP Solutions can enhance a firm's ability to measure and manage its carbon footprint.

Project Details

OSIsoft provides a data management platform for industrial operations. For this project, OSIsoft contributed integration capabilities and access to its OSIsoft PI System. SAP provided access to SAP software, Manufacturing Integration and Intelligence (MII), Business Objects Xcelcius, and SAP Carbon Impact. MII is an SAP application for synchronizing manufacturing operations with both back-office business processes and standardized data. It also includes analytics and workflow tools for identifying problems in the production process and managing its performance. Xcelsius was Business Objects Dash boarding (it's use concluded with the end of life of Adobe Flash and it was reformed using HTML 5 via SAP Lumira). Carbon Impact was a solution acquired by SAP in 2009 to aid in reducing CO_2 emissions.

The platform team provisioned several virtual machines in the landscape to host all of the different components and provided the systems interoperability needed by the nodes in the architecture. Leveraging these resources, the project team developed and deployed a platform to collect real-time energy consumption information gathered from the building where the co-innovation platform resides. The team analyzed the data, generated a set of reports, and presented a dashboard of the key results for decision-making. Additionally, the platform, through its services, provided a direct source for energy data via its Starline Bus energy management system.

The key components were integrated as a combined software solution, creating what the project team referred to as the "Perfect Plant." The team's first step was to collect plant floor data from different sources, such as solar installations on a plant's roof and data on power consumption. The platform ops team coordinated with facilities' leads to capture data from the solar panel system. The data was fed into OSIsoft's PI System infrastructure (simulated in the co-innovation platform's provided landscape). Next, the team injected this data into SAP HANA. Using the PI System software, a steady stream of data was continuously monitored and stored. Summary data was then distributed to SAP MII for time-of-day reporting and also to SAP Carbon Impact for carbon footprint reporting. The reporting gave SAP users the ability to view and correct energy consumption problems as they occur.

Challenges

The project's challenges were typical for complex co-innovation project work. First, finding the right subject matter experts to support the project needs took longer than anticipated. At the time of the project, sustainability was an emerging hot topic and it spawned many projects across multiple business units impacting the ability to find experts available to support the project. Subject matter experts were needed to help the partner software architects understand how to seamlessly integrate the software with various SAP software applications, such as MII and Carbon Impact, within the co-innovation platform's system landscape. The project team also faced challenges in determining how all of the various technical components would work together and in turn, yield a solution for collecting, analyzing, and presenting energy data. Another challenge was tied to organizational constraints, such as the availability of project team members to support parts of the project. As an example, individuals were needed to collaborate with local facilities leads to identify and capture data from various building elements like four-hundred solar panels on the building's roof or from the building's heating, venting and air conditioning electromechanical systems management.

Outcomes

Advancing Value Creation Through Co-Innovation and Capitalizing on Intersects: The project achieved go-to-market success. The team published a whitepaper describing the project and informing customers how the solution could be used to improve access to energy information and to gain a more robust view of asset performance.

Extending the network of Ecosystem Participants – Seeding ideas: The project work and supporting project landscape spawned an array of white papers, podcasts, demos, and live events across multiple industry solution spaces; practitioners continue to build on the team's co-innovation work.

Glossary

Adobe Flash: A multimedia software platform to produce animations for web applications, mobile devices, games and offered full streaming of audio and video.

HTML5: Hypertext markup language. A markup language used to create structure to present content on the World Wide Web.

PI: real-time data storage, normalization, analytics, and notification engine. As described in the use case, the platform was used for managing and delivering sensor-based data.

Starline Bus: Starline Bus refers specifically to the Starline Track Busway which is an electric power distribution system for a data center. It offers several possible configurations for outlets, drop cords, and circuit breakers, plus power metering.

IoT and Zero Harm for Mining, April 2015

Partners

Vandrico Solutions, Inc. (An industrial IoT and Wearables Software Startup), Illumiti (SAP Systems Integration and Management Consulting Company), SAP Industry Experts.

Co-innovation Project

Illumiti, an SAP partner and boutique SAP HANA Systems Integrator and reseller, proposed a project with start-up firm Vandrico, to bring an IoT solution to the mining industry and support the industry's goal of zero harm mining. The partners planned to integrate Vandrico's real-time situational awareness platform with SAP HANA to ingest and process continuous feeds of sensor data from a mine as well as from miners and assets underground. Using wi-fi-based two-way communication, data from smart sensor laden wearables would provide a mine's back or central office operators with a connection to, and the status of, all personnel underground. All sensor data would be correlated and analyzed to assess the degree of risk to employees or assets in real time.

Project Overview

The mining industry has a business goal of zero harm to its workforce and assets. To help tackle this challenge, Vandrico collaborated with Illumiti to develop a MineSafe Smartwatch. The project's digital solution used Vandrico's Canary Platform (built on SAP HANA), an IoT communications system designed for enterprise security and scale, as well as wireless mobile 2-way communications and in-memory database technology to perform real-time analytics to monitor and predict riskof harm. The Canary Platform communicates mine-specific IoT information via wi-fi using data from wearable devices and sensors placed throughout a mine. By enabling real-time communications between sensors, smartwatches, and a mine's central control system, the MineSafe Smartwatch helps miners identify and respond to emerging safety issues.

Every human and every asset in a mine originate data. As an example, sensors on a diesel engine driving a cutter[1] emit temperature, pressure, vibration, and rotation data whereas sensors embedded in tunnel infrastructure capture everything from the presence of noxious chemicals and heat to seismic energy. When a concern arises, the system could locate miners and transmit alerts and solutions where needed. Vandrico's CEO, Gonzalo Tudela, explained: "Mine workers can use a one-touch distress call feature to send an urgent notice to the surface. The surface system is designed to send immediate alerts to key personnel and emergency responders based on the type of incident being reported – which can enhance response time and reduce risk to other workers."[2]

All participants contributed complementaryresourcesand capabilities. Illumiti was adept at bringing interested customersto the project. As part of an IoT Kickstarter Program developed by the platform's ops team, the 90-day project work included multiple design thinking sessions with 3 large Canadian and U.S. Miningcompanies. SAP applied its rich design thinking competencies to work alongside of the systems integrator to identify and validate the voice of the customer in the solution design.

Lessons learned from the design thinking activities and customer interviews informed additional exploration. For example, although the MineSafe Smartwatch allowed the team to show proof of concept for the real-time situational awareness function, the team wondered whether a watch was the optimal wearable format for the setting. In consultation with industrial customers, the team learned that miners often operate in Tundra-like conditions, requiring them to wear several layers of clothing as well as thick gloves. Accessing a watch under this gear may not always be convenient. Additionally, when a miner is around heavy equipment with names like "cutter", she needs to be mindful about the gear she wears, a misstep or entanglement could be deadly. A cutter looks like a giant drum with sharp teeth located all over it. Given the feedback from customers, one project scope iteration involved exploring other types of wearable technology such as helmets and vests. This exploration confirmed that the watch was the most appropriate device for the setting. The project's initial phase generated a physical demo

---

[1] As background, a cutter or cutting machine, usually used in coal mining, cuts a 10 cm to 15 cm slot in a mine; the slot allows room for expansion of broken coal. Workers who operate these machines also may be referred to as cutters. For additional details, see: http://www.coaleducation.org/glossary.htm and https://www.freepatentsonline.com/5013093.html. Accessed, June 18, 2021.

[2] Illumiti and Vandrico Launch MineSafe Smartwatch Running on SAP HANA Platform, Press Release published by PRNewsWire, November 5, 2015. https://www.prnewswire.com/news-releases/illumiti-and-vandrico-launch-minesafe-smartwatch-running-on-the-sap-hana-platform-300172952.html, accessed June 10, 2021.

designed to model the use of wearables in an industry setting; the demo had the ability to sense and receive data related to employee safety and, when coupled with machine learning, could process edge data in real time to predict risk and reduce harm.

As the project progressed, other questions arose that prompted an additional phase of experimentation and testing. For instance, what type of sensor data was optimal for predicting and analyzing operational risk? To address this question, the team simulated data collection from seismic sensors as well as fire/smoke/gas detection sensors. As a result of this inquiry, a second project phase was planned to examine sensor data from machines and tools in operation. The team thought that expanding the type of sensor data collected would allow a company to categorize levels of risk throughout a mine. For example, sensor data from mine equipment could be correlated with data about an asset such as type, manufacturer, year deployed, and last maintenance performed. Next, the data could be combined with worker information such as age, health status, family status, number of years of experience, and training certifications or other relevant skills. For example, two junior miners might be operating heavy equipment in a shaft where a ripper[3] or cutter had not received regular maintenance. Cutters are notorious for scattering shrapnel when their teeth break loose. The team wondered whether the MineSafe system could be used to assign risk scores for a situation using a combination of data—such as maintenance records and worker experience level. In sum, the iterative nature of the project advanced learning, helped the team refine its original design, and stimulated new project ideas.

Project Details

The platform's operations team provided a multiple node landscape of virtual machines to host SAP HANA and Vandrico's real-time situational awareness platform (RTSA). Using a RESTful API, Vandrico's Canary Platform transmitted information from devices to SAP HANA. Canary's API was then used to send messages to miners' wearable devices. The ops team additionally built a physical model of a mining operation comprising a Raspberry PI system where red and green LEDs were wired to represent communications to and from the watch on a miner's wrist.

---

[3] A ripper is a coal extraction machine that works by tearing coal from the exposed area of a coal bed—where coal is being extracted. A universal ripper includes a cutter head. http://www.coaleducation.org/glossary.htm. Accessed, June 18, 2021.

As noted above, the operations team hosted design thinking sessions with three different miningcustomers to pinpoint the objectives of the project's first phase:

- Demonstrate 2-way communication using 3G/4G and wireless communications between a watch and its Canary RTSA platform.
- Demonstrate RTSA platform acting on IoT sensor data to provide the state of an environment, human wearer, and mine assets to a mine's central office or back office.
- Build a physical demoshowcasing the use of the wearables. Physical watch messages were programmed to correspond with red and green LED lights affixed to figures in a model mine and the demo was designed to simulate scenarios such as seismic activity, smoke, fire, or gas leaks.

Phase One addressed the three goals and ran for approximately ninety days.

Challenges

There were plenty of obstacles in achieving the phase one goals such as the fact that most underground mines had less than 70% wi-fi coverage. As noted above, the project explored other challenges related to the form of wearable device.

Outcome

Partnerships are never what they seem. At the end of phase one, there was a working physical demo illustrating how the MineSafe watch could be used to enhance employee safety. The demo used simulated data sets and communicated sensor data to central monitoring as part of the simulation. Phase one did not include event correlation or prediction.

There was plenty to learn. Unfortunately, Illumiti, the systems integrator, could not convince Vandrico to go to market with them in the mining industry or to make an investment in partnering with the focal firm through its own programs. In the end, Vandrico only used the project as fulfillment for its Canary platform. As a young startup, Vandrico was concerned with becoming too tethered to any single technology such as SAP HANA.

The work spawned other mining projects and brought awarenessto the possibilities of using IoTin mining and other industries. The project occurred in 2015 and yet, in 2020, the platform continued to receive requests from other firms about the demo and the potential to use it for other projects.

Some work was performed to examine phase two requirements with a few subject matter experts who advocated for involving more analytics and data science teams, domain experts from the insurance industry, and global system integrator firms. The subject matter experts also called for additional use case and algorithm development to fine tune risk assessment and measurement.

Glossary

RTSA: Real Time Situational Awareness, the perception of the surrounding environment coupled with a sense of time and space, understanding its meaning as well as a sense of future status.

VLAN: Virtual Local Area Network, a data packet broadcast domain organized at the data link layer. A LAN is a local area network. Virtual indicates a physical object, such as a switch or router, is recreated in software.

IoT Enterprise Bots, January, 2016

Partners

Kore.ai, SAP Partner Management.

Co-innovation Project

U sing bots to interact with SAP systems leveraging IoT Sensor Data.

Project Overview and Details

Kore.ai, an enterprise virtual assistant platform and solutions company, saw an opportunity to bring enterprise bot technology to routine business processes within the SAP ecosystem. The project focused on integrating enterprise bots and IoTwith SAP applications and platforms to serve a variety of SAP customers. In 2016, the topic of "bots" was gaining traction in consumer use cases but the news was not always positive. Reports of bot errors were eroding the reputations of bot producers and creating uncertaintyabout customer adoption rates. An SAP partner management team directed Kore.ai to the co-innovation platform to explore how bots could be used with a variety of SAP applications.

Kore's bots are lightweight programs that could connect directly to SAP HANA and the HANA Cloud Platform, allowing users to send and receive information in SAP systems from within Kore's messaging platform. At the user's direction, the bots can deliver alerts, perform basic tasks, and provide system reports. They offer a way to simplify the execution of tasks within business systems. As an example: Consider the onboarding of new employees. A new employee requires a security badge to enter the building where her office is located; an email could be generated with a badge request or a manager could accomplish the request with multiple phone calls to HR, IT, and security. Once approved, the badge is created and delivered. Instead of this process, what if the manager could send a text to a bot with a message "create badge" and let the bot do the work immediately? These are the types of problems that Kore intended to solve with enterprise bots.

The platform ops team provided Kore an Enterprise Resource Planning (ERP, SAP ECC—an ERP solution referred to as ERP Central Component) landscape and access to an SAP HANA system. The project team built an App Services Java container application using representational state transfer

(Restful) and https protocols. Kore installed its Enterprise BoT messaging platform into the project landscape and built a variety of demos to illustrate use case scenarios such as a maintenance or facilities engineer chatting with the HVAC system of a building to gain status and insight into potential problems. Testing included simulating twenty different user types exchanging about fifty messages per day.

Kore also installed its Natural Language Processing (NLP) engine preprogrammed with tasks and field level synonyms. Bots, using natural language, allows users to receive alerts, access reports, execute direct actions, and complete workflow tasks. The Kore platform provided supervised learning of additional patterns found in transaction data; this capability reduced the deployment and management skills required for building and refining bots. The bots were designed to follow commands as well as make predictions. Different instances of the provisioned landscape allowed for use casedemonstrations featuring APIintegration with SAP ERP, SAP S/4HANA, SuccessFactors, SAP Hybris Cloudfor Customer, Ariba, and Concur.

Challenges

The project's largest challenge was a potential conflict of interest between the project and SAP business group activities related to software solutions using and providing natural language processing. As part of its focus on the intelligent enterprise, SAP development explores and advances use of natural language processing and conversational AI in SAP software tools and products. Co-innovation projects could build on SAP's technology or product development plans or roadmaps but not duplicate activities ongoing at SAP. As part of the project proposal process, the ops team devoted attention to identifying potential overlaps between projects and an SAP business development team's or unit's activities. This internal due diligence can require significant time in large organizations where knowledge and information surrounding early stage product development often is both sparse and diffuse.

Outcomes

The extensive testing resulted in a whitepaper as well as demos and talks at numerous events and the distribution of recorded demos. A leading German IT publication featured a story on the project. The project work also contributed to Kore successfully completing its SAP solution qualification and receiving certification from the SAP Integration and Certification

Center. The public demos showing the effectiveness of Kore's technology in more than half a dozen practical use cases sparked interested and an array press releases and articles in industry news outlets.

Glossary

Bot/Bots: a software application designed to perform simple and repetitive tasks and alleviating human need to process a task. Humans typically interface with bots using natural language processing or text messaging.
OData: open data protocol used to build and consume Restful* APIs.
Restful: an architectural style for an application program interface (API) using HTTP requests to get and consume data.

Moonraker: Improving the Remote Compute Experience, August 2015

Partners

Citrix, Nvidia, SAP 3D Visual Enterprise Product Team.

Co-innovation Project

The Moonraker project explored SAP 3D Visual Enterprise application use cases for manufacturing and asset intensive process industries.

Project Overview

The primary project objective was to test, validate, and illustrate productive use and consumption of simple 3D animation with SAP 3D Visual Enterprise application powered by Citrix XenDesktop and Nvidia GRID. Citrix is a software company that provides server, application and desktop virtualization, networking, software as a service, and cloud computing technologies. Nvidia designs graphics processing units (GPUs) for gaming and professional use and system on a chip units (SOCs) for mobile computing and the automotive market.

The ops team worked with the project team to design, run, and record various demos; the demos were managed and exhibited from the co-innovation platform and accessible to both SAP and the project partners. Product managers from SAP's 3D Visual enterprise applications worked with customers to develop use case scenarios from various sectors (manufacturing, oil & gas, chemicals, etc.) to inform the demos. One project objective was to show how someone such as a field site reliability engineer (SRE) could work with, and manipulate, extremely large CAD drawings from any type of device with any type of connectivity while also interacting with the drawing and its integration with backend Enterprise Resource Planning (ERP) systems. The platform's ops team assisted the project team with integration required for SAP HANA. One of the first demonstrations used a CAD file containing more than 4.2 million vertices built from a CAD drawing of an off-shore oil rig.

A second project objective focused on performance characterization and involved functionality testing across different demo scenarios. The team measured application response time (latency) using a range of large file types and sizes. Each scenario described a specific use case such as a site reliability engineer navigating large CAD drawings of an oil rig while located on a rig with limited internet access and bandwidth. Use performance also was evaluated using a variety of end user devices such as tablets and phones.

By integrating key software architectures and optimizing software configurations, the project team demonstrated that SAP 3D Visual Enterprise could help with viewing and visualizing data when an end user was physically distant in proximity from the applications and data source. The results, replicated across a variety of sectors, demonstrated that worker mobility did not compromise performance.

Project Details

Systems provisioning for the Moonraker project began in early 2015. The co-innovation platform team provided the project a standard ECC 6.x ERP landscape as well as a virtual machine compute (and SAN storage for SAP 3D Visual Enterprise) configured to run using Citrix XenDesktop with an Nvidia GRID GPU server. The partners leveraged hardware that Supermicro contributed to the platform. Using a Supermicro blade server environment, multiple virtual machines operated in the landscape to support the SAP ERP ECC 6.0 × installation. The landscape additionally included an Nvidia Grid Appliance to supply the GPU processors used by SAP 3D Visual Enterprise over Citrix Receiver. The platform operations team collaborated with Citrix on useability testing, data capture, and change management for all provisioned systems. The team also maintained all VPN remote access, bandwidth management, and latency monitoring and ensured demo system readiness when demos were shown at major events.

Challenges

Even longstanding partners can encounter challenges in new projects. The project's core challenge was complexity—integration of multiple technologies and serving multiple use case demos. Complicating the situation, early wins shared within the partner organizations and customers heightened interest in the projects results and contributed to increased demand (we want it yesterday). For Citrix, additional complexity stemmed from overseeing multiple co-innovation projects or multi-phased projects.

Outcomes

A compelling feature of the software was that it allowed the user to fly around an oil rig and explore it. A user could dive into the rig's superstructure to look at a compressor, pump, or some other rig sub-system. A user also could float over a component or part and see a flyout description of the component; right clicking on a component provided useful meta data about the component or element in real time. Imagine a safety engineer or contractor helping to solve a problem; the software enables the engineer to view components or parts and identify which items require replacement. The ability to drill down into this type of meta data and/or other integrated systems and interact with the data while located remotely and using a mobile device such as iPad or iPhone was unexpected.

The project's various demos that were showcased at events such as SAP SAPPHIRE NOW, SAP TechEd, Citrix Synergy, Autodesk University, and executive briefings. Numerous blogs, white papers, solution briefs, and video interviews were co-developed with the platform and provided go-to-market content for Citrix and Nvidia. POC results also were shared broadly with field facing teams of the participating firms. Additionally, subject matter experts—product managers for the SAP Visual Enterprise Application—explored the compute environment to understand the performance improvements achieved with the target use cases.

Co-innovation At 35,000 feet

At the end of Citrix Synergy 2015, the director for the co-innovation platform in Palo Alto, California and the Citrix Alliance Manager were on the same flight back to Silicon Valley from Orange County. The flight offered an additional, although unscheduled, opportunity to replicate the large file demo tests using inflight wi-fi. The flight attendants lacked control over the access point to the network, leaving the tests performed uncontrolled. However, the director and manager successfully connected to the co-innovation platform's F5 VPN gateway in Palo Alto and encountered no challenges in accessing the demo workspace. They began testing with some small files but soon realized that even the oil rig CAD file (4.2 million vertices in total) performed without much delay associated with network latency. They were able to rotate images, and to zoom in and right click to interact with connected asset and inventory data with nearly zero interference. The system performed well enough that the director and manager were able to create a video of the inflight experience. They also replicated the steps it took to connect and the responses recorded were included in future demos.

Glossary

CAD: Computer Aided Design software used in the creation, or optimization of an object, product, or element.

ERP (ECC 6.x): Enterprise Resource Planning. SAP ERP Central Component. SAP offers its ERP suite (SAP S4/HANA Cloud) of which ECC is a component used for managing key business functions (i.e., operations, supply chain, materials management, financials, sales, logistics, product planning, etc.).

F5 (VPN): F5 Network's FirePass SSL VPN is a Secure Socket Layer (SSL) VPN providing broad application support, scalability, installation, and use.

GPU: Graphical Processing Unit. A circuit designed to quickly change memory in order to accelerate output to a display device; ideal for computer graphics and image processing.

Secure Socket Layer (SSL): An encryption-based Internet security protocol.

IoT and AI for Manufacturing, January, 2016

Partners

Telit, Stellium, SAP Analytics, SAP Data Warehouse Product Management.

Co-innovation Project

Telit, an IoT and software solutions provider, and Stellium, a supply chain solutions business, both engaged in co-innovation projects focused on leveraging data from sensors located on physical assets. The two firms had complementary capabilities, common interests and mutual target customers. After connecting at the platform, they began to explore how they might work together on an end-to-end solution set for manufacturers seeking greater automation to support "lights out" manufacturing. This case brief summarizes their projects and the potential novel project intersection that emerged.

Project Overview

Telit. Telit was introduced to the platform by a cloud analytics product team. The team was seeking a partner with the capability to aggregate and flow industry sensor data at scale. The data would be analyzed by predictive analyticssoftware. Telit managed its own physical IoT gateway devices through its DeviseWise platform. The DeviseWise platform could be integrated with a variety of mobile and wide area networks and could aggregate sensor data from any asset with a MAC and IP address.

For example, a deep fryer in a typical fast-food restaurant has a sensor to detect oil temperature. This type of sensor often is equipped with wi-fi capability and can use a wireless network to stream data to a Telit IoT gateway device. The gateway device then uses cloud-based management to ingest and forward the data. While configurable, near continuous transmission of temperature data is cost prohibitive. Imagine not one fryer, but four and not one fast food outlet, but hundreds in a variety of geographic locations. The costs can become significant. As a result, rather than flow temperature data in real time, data might only be sent when temperature has deviated up or down by two degrees. The implication is that the system must be equipped with software that allows a company to precisely manage the flow of sensor data.

Telit worked with the analytics product team to meet specific IoT data analytics end customer requirements including:

- On-premise deployment for SAP Device Management for IoT
- SAP HANA (or SAP application) target with IoT use case requirements
- An ability to connect from hundreds to millions of "things" (devices, sensors, gateways)
- Broad support of devices and device protocols
- Strong capabilities for edge computing
- Edge gateways with pre-installed IoT agents
- Capabilities for remote communication and control of edge devices
- Delivering an end-to-end market-proven IoT platform solution

The bundle of complementary technologies and capabilities supported a go-to-market solution.

Stellium. An SAP product manager for data warehouse and inventory management wanted to pursue a co-innovation project with Stellium and introduced Stellium to the co-innovation platform. The product manager's target audience showed increasing interest in automation using artificial intelligence and machine learning to generate insights from manufacturing asset sensor data.

The project scope included integrating Stellium's software with SAP HANA to augment SAP's data warehouse capabilities. Doing so enabled the team to build a physical model of a lights out automated manufacturing environment. The goal was to demonstrate that a data warehouse automated system could yield an intelligent end to end solution. The demo testing generated proof points to support a broad partner-based solution. The project work was used by the product manager to influence internal stakeholders. Stellium was able to share the working demo and project results with potential customers using youtube videos and other events.

Project Details

Telit and Stellium each had a project system landscape provided by the co-innovation platform. Both system landscapes included a variety of two gigabyte virtual machines and small instances of virtual SAP HANA. These resources were used to provision the required SAP landscapes to support each project's use cases. Both organizations also used the co-innovation platform to test integration capabilities, functionality, and performance.

While the analytics software used by a customer could be cloud-based, the ops team installed the software locally to facilitate integration and testing. The ops team also provided a secure network channel to access Telit's managed service provider (MSP) services located in Telit's private cloud. Telit provided several of its gateway devices to support not only its project and was willing to share its gateway devices with other projects.

In addition to its provisioned landscape, the Stellium project included a 3' × 4' physical model of a manufacturing plant using a Fischertechnik kit (Fig. A.1). The demo simulated the movement of materials and products on a manufacturing shop floor. It had the ability to pick and place raw material or finished goods in inventory and to move items to different manufacturing

Fig. A.1 Stellium Demo displayed at the SAP co-innovation platform

stations such as robot arm-based assembly, spot weld, inspection or shipping and receiving. The demo is a working model of an integrated digital manufacturing prototype used to demonstrate digitization, auto data capturing, auto routing, and a lights-off factory concept. The digital factory setup shows the networking of people, machines, and data that enables clients to improve efficiencies in their manufacturing operations.

Project Intersect

Telit and Stellium both were interested in showcasing their solutions as a complementary end to end IoT-driven solution set. They met at the platform and discussed exploring how Telit's IoT gateway could be physically integrated with Stellium's manufacturing demonstrator. Additionally, both firms along with Kore.ai, an enterprise virtual assistant platform and solutions company, participated in a symposium held by the platform that focused on novel intersections among co-innovation projects. As part of their panel, each firm identified areas of complementary intersection. The event was live streamed and included a panel of CTOs discussing future directions of IoT. While Telit and Stellium were interested in collaborating on a net new project (integrating their demos), the new project had a lower priority relative to the firms' other project work. As a result, it was not always easy for the two co-innovation project managers to find the time to finalize and execute the new project.

Challenges

Stellium's challenges were related to staffing; the original product manager for the data warehouse left the company during the project. As noted above, although the two firms identified an opportunity to capitalize on their unique complementarities, they lacked sufficient staff to support the new initiative.

Outcomes

The project teams each completed their existing projects to satisfaction and generated desired proof points for solution architectures in the form of live demonstrations, video interviews, blogs, and whitepapers. Telit's project began with a go-to-market trajectory and the project results supported its plans. Stellium's project demonstrated the automation of a manufacturing process with pull based material flow, from distribution and production of finished goods to procurement of raw material. Using the demo, customers could experience the solution and make an informed decision.

Despite lacking time to storyboard and design a fully integrated solution demo (the new project), the project managers continued to collaborate. They shared an exhibit station at SAP SAPPHIRE NOW and identified mutual customers for joint selling. And while they did not integrate the Telit IoT gateway device into the Stellium demo, whenever the manufacturing demo was run, the story line described the complementary Telit solution, and a demonstrator gateway device was kept on hand to show an audience.

Glossary

IoT or Asset Gateway: Embedded software running upon Telit certified hardware.

Expense Management Analytics Integration, August 2014

Partners

Tangoe Systems, Inc. and SAP HANA Product Team.

Co-innovation Project

Tangoe and SAP collaborated on a software integration project using Internet of Thing (IoT) data. The goal was to show how Tangoe's Matrix technology running on SAP HANA could deliver enhanced analytics and online transaction processing (OLTP) capabilities and enable global enterprises to analyze and optimize their IT assets and expenses.

Project Overview

Tangoe is a global technology expense and lifecycle solutions company. The company's Connection Lifecycle Management technology (Matrix) solution is an on-demand suite of software and services designed to turn on, track, manage, secure, and support various connections in an enterprise's connection lifecycle, including mobile, fixed, machine-to-machine, cloud software and services, enterprise social, and IT connections. In this project, Tangoe explored integration with SAP HANA to develop next generation data capture and analytics capabilities to support enterprise IT expense management. They wanted to help customers improve real-time decision making by making it easy to consume spatially aware IoT sensor data for analytics and prediction. At the time of the project, SAP had created a new IoT-focused product and development unit dedicated to developing leading solutions using IoT data.

The platform's ops team provided an SAP landscape for the project. Tangoe used the landscape to demonstrate how their existing on premise solution could be integrated with SAP HANA and its Event Stream Processor (ESP) to form a private or public cloud-based solution with new functionality. The solution was designed to run in conjunction with existing legacy systems and to offer seamless migration. The Proof-of-Concept project focused on demonstrating scalability for 10, 50, and 70 users concurrently consuming Matrix technology on SAP HANA.

The flexibility of the co-innovation project contract framework allowed both SAP and Tangoe to specify how coding knowledge could be exchanged among selected project engineers, without unnecessarily fully exposing a code base or other proprietary methods of interest to both parties. Using a workshop approach, engineers and legal representation from both organizations discussed the project workstreams, how the project engineers worked, and how they needed to communicate and share information to support the partner's integration efforts.

Project Details

The ops team provided both virtual and a small bare-metal instances (64 GB) of SAP HANA for the Tangoe project landscape. It also provided multiple virtual machines to host Event Stream Processing (ESP) and a replication server (RepServer) as well as a VPN for remote access by the team. The project landscape included additional virtual machine images from Tangoe to support its test array. The platform ops team also installed an instance of JMeter (Sixteen gigabytes, eight cores) and Tangoe provided the execution scripts for queries as well as configuration parameters to generate the loads for performance characterization. Once tests were executed, the ops team performed SAP HANA runtime monitoring and captured the response time results. Analysis of all non-conformant results was completed by Tangoe and SAP HANA performance engineers. The ops team also provided Tangoe's team with Oracle 12.1.0.2.0 with in-memory option allowing the team to use JMeter to compare the performance of queries to either the Oracle or SAP HANA in-memory database.

Challenges

The project had a variety of challenges, some stemmed from building out a landscape capable of supporting multiple proof of concept objectives. The RepServer was local to the landscape but there also was a Tangoe IT asset that the landscape needed to connect with remotely over open internet. The latter raised concerns about bandwidth requirements and the potential for excess latency to impact the query performance within specific concurrent use ranges.

Some security processes also required attention. The co-innovation platform is designed to operate within a network demilitarized zone (DMZ) and not behind a corporate firewall. As a result, it was possible for the team to address bandwidth constraints with WAN acceleration technology. The ops team also advised security colleagues of the LAN-to-LAN connection between the labs supporting the project.

For the Tangoe project team, the challenges stemmed from how to measure performance running queries against SAP HANA. The team had to learn about SAP HANA's administrative and configuration features to tailor its software to optimize when using JDBC to flow OLTP data between systems. The platform's knowledge broker provided connections to SAP HANA experts who offered insights to support development of the desired solution.

An additional challenge was establishing the appropriate engagement model that would allow Tangoe access to the content it needs to integrate its Matrix software with SAP HANA when no standard application programming interface (api) is available.

Outcomes

Project results documented the comparison of Tangoe on SAP HANA versus Tangoe configured to use an Oracle-based in-memory database. The comparison illustrated better overall performance for concurrent users of Tangoe Matrix running over SAP HANA. The ops team generated a white paper and several blogs and also showcased the results using live demos. The demos showed that using Tangoe Matrix on SAP HANA provided a company the ability to view every asset and expense and in turn, conduct analytics for real-time decision making. The solution generated results in seconds without custom reports or developer intervention.

Glossary

DMZ: Demilitarized Zone, used for information security, a physical or logical subnetwork that contains and exposes an organization's external-facing services to an untrusted, usually larger, network such as the internet.
ESP: SAP Event Stream Processor is a stream processing engine for analyzing and acting upon event streams in real time. This technology provides several different tools and interfaces used to integrate ESP with systems and applications that produce data and/or consume data.
JDBC: Java Database Connectivity is an application programming interface (API) for the programming language Java, which defines how a client may access a database.

JMeter- Apache JMeter: open source software which is a Java application designed to load test functional behavior and measure performance.

LAN to LAN: A LAN (local area network) is a group of computers and network devices connected together, usually within the same building. LAN to LAN is discrete connectivity between two local area networks.

OLTP: Online transaction processing is a category of data processing that is focused on transaction-oriented tasks.

VPN Virtual Private Network: secure connection between a user and the internet where the user's data traffic is routed through an encrypted virtual tunnel.

Edge Computing and IIoT, August 2017

Partners

Dell EMC, Pixel Velocity, Mtell, SAP Industry Business Unit (IBU), SAP Asset Management, SAP Partner Management, and SAP Data Science.

Co-Innovation Project

Addressing real-time situational awareness requirements, this project explored edge computing solutions for the Oil and Gas industry.

Project Overview

The SAP Oil and Gas IBU was a champion of the co-innovation platform. Together, the IBU and the platform collaborated with external partners and internal product and partner teams to show how co-innovation could bring solutions of immediate interest and value to the oil and gas industry. Their target audience included oil and gas reliability engineers, lease operators, and/or field technicians. This audience recognized that industry sensor data would grow to about 40% to 50% of all the data generated by a business's operations. For example, a single oil rig could deploy tens of thousands of sensors to support real-time decision making.

The IBU's objective is, in part, to influence and persuade product managers to figure out how to bring requested innovation to large customers fast. In this project, the IBU wanted to validate that compute activity is performed as close as possible to a data's origination location. This was achieved through edge computing and local processing of the data that matters most. In this context, accessing real-time data is critical to operational integrity. Items, such as reduced network performance, can be disruptive to the business or harmful to both assets and workers.

Regarding the partners: Dell EMC sells data storage, information security, virtualization, analytics, cloud computing, as well as other products and services; Pixel Velocity develops, manufactures, and markets system-level video surveillance and threat detection solutions; and Mtell offers the ability to obtain early and accurate warning of when an asset will fail and how.

Project Details

The project plan and scope evolved over time. As a result, the project involved multiple project landscapes supporting partner solutions and discrete use cases as they emerged. The landscapes featured various configurations of relevant SAP software including its business data warehousing, asset management, and Enterprise Resource Planning (ERP) systems. The landscape also featured virtual and bare metal instances of SAP HANA that were used by Mtell in its use cases, testing, and demo creation. The project team integrated edge computing and IIoT sensor data capture and aggregation technologies with SAP HANA; the team's capabilities augmented core SAP applications. The project team also designed and built two physical IIoT simulators or demos to explore a variety of use case scenarios. The IBU provided use cases and access to customers.

Mtell's machine learning was used to analyze IIoT sensor data from pumps and motors. This data included information such as temperature, vibration, and RPMs. The machine learning performed on sensor data generated prescriptive analytics that distinguished between false positives and false negatives, a common outcome when searching for anti-patterns in edge data flows. Mtell could validate if a false positive or negative was a problem or simply a measure of a new normal.

Additional virtual machines hosted Pixel's software which was used to make sense of real-time video feeds coming from two cameras trained on the two different IIoT simulators. The simulators used both cameras to give the remote users a multi-angle view of the simulators; the cameras also kept the simulators' pressure gauges in view. Pixel's expertise also informed how the cameras were used including helping to identify the optimal mounting points for the simulators' cameras. The project's first objective was to leverage Pixel's software to read the video streams of the simulators' analog pressure gauges (two located on each simulator) and to send an alert when a gauge needle reached redline status. The Pixel team worked with the project team to tailor Pixel's software to use case scenarios. As background, Pixel's software was designed to read and scan image data from everything in a camera lens' field of view; as a result, the software could identify changes in image data, such as a needle moving from green to red, and in turn, send an alert or notification. The video data was flowed back to the edge gateway where SAP machine learning algorithms output correlations. The correlations contributed to real-time situational awareness for site reliability engineers and other operations experts.

The Dell EMC team sponsored compute, storage capacity, and appliance-based IIoT and edge gateways capable of feeding data to SAP analytics systems. Dell EMC also provided subject matter experts to work with the platform ops team to install and configure various software applications and tools within the virtual landscapes.

Testing or demonstration scenarios used both simulators. One of the physical simulators was located at the co-innovation platform location; the other was located at a remote sales office. The simulator in the sales office represented a misbehaving system located on an offshore rig. The simulator at the co-innovation platform location served in the demo story as a back office IT lab for the oil and gas company and was used to reproduce the encountered problem and capture data representing the problem. The simulator's machine learning was applied to the data in order to craft an algorithm that could be applied to the system in the field. A key system field requirement was the ability to access and control the simulators remotely. As a result, the project team needed to ensure that both systems were accessible for testing at any time and from any remote user. For instance, an account manager in Florida could use a mobile app running on a phone or tablet to login to the simulator environment and manipulate controls to open and close valves or start/stop the motor of either simulator. Similarly, an oil and gas reliability engineer located on an oil rig could interact with the simulator to simulate events such as pump cavitation (cavitation in pumps is the rapid creation and subsequent collapse of air bubbles in a fluid). The person running a test could manipulate either simulator as the simulator landscape provided network connectivity between the two simulator locations. Additionally, the app allowed a user to turn on, pan, tilt and zoom the cameras on each simulator.

The simulators were used to explore a variety of real use case problems. For example, data generated from the simulators was used to train the edge gateway's algorithm to send an alert when a data pattern changed. Second, using one of the simulators, the team performed multiple simulations, capturing sensor data while running in a state where all valves controlling water flow through the simulator were open and several runs where the valves were closed off 25%, 50%, 75%, and 100%. Similar tests were conducted under different conditions such as reduced power available to the simulator's motor. Other tests were used to generate abnormal data detection and flow such as simulating a structural impairment that prevented a pump from being level.

Challenge

This project encountered a variety of challenges. Demonstrating machine learning from live sensor data at scale, capturing simulator data to train an algorithm to find anti-patterns, and providing real-time situational awareness required significant time and effort from both developers and IT ops experts. An additional challenge was managing collaboration with IT employees located in the remote sales office. Third, finding stakeholders willing to fund the hands-on project work also took more time than anticipated. As time slipped away awaiting funding for the project, key experts moved to other projects.

Outcome

This was the first time the ops team produced, managed and operated a real-time simulator. The project's proof of concept provided the IBU with a new narrative that it could use to describe edge computing solutions to their customers. Through knowledge sharing and collaborative work, relationships among the project participants strengthened and expanded. The project also gained visibility through executive briefings and marketing events hosted by the platform ops team. The simulators continue to draw interest for testing and exploration.

Glossary

Edge Computing: a distributed computing paradigm which brings computation and data storage closer to the location where it is needed, leading to faster response times and bandwidth preservation.
Industrial Internet of Things (IIoT): the use of the internet of things (IoT) in industrial sectors and applications.
Restful: an architectural style for an application program interface (API) using HTTP requests to get and consume data.

Accelerating Financial Analytics Performance, August 2013

Partners

Vendavo, SAP HANA Product Management, SAP Partner Management.

Co-innovation Project

The purpose of the project was to improve the performance of Vendavo's product Price and Margin Management (PMM) by porting it to run on the SAP HANA columnar in-memory database.

Project Overview

Vendavo helps businesses optimize pricing by applying artificial intelligence(AI) and machine learning (ML) to analyze spreadsheet data. The project proposed running Vendavo's Price and Margin Management (PMM) software on an SAP HANA columnar in-memory database using an SAP landscape. Vendavo already was using another columnar in-memory database. The project results would inform its decision regarding whether to migrate its software to SAP HANA. Vendavo used a phased testing approach beginning with the PPM's Profit Analyzer and a potential phase two of the project would focus on testing the remainder of the software suite. A baseline project objective was to demonstrate the software's capacity to improve beyond the existing performance benchmark. Additionally, and in response to customer needs, Vendavo wanted to demonstrate the system's scalability—for instance, by showing the system could process as much as a billion or more rows of data. The project's goals aligned with the firm's strategic goals of developing a new fifteen million dollar revenue stream from improved application performance.

Project Details

The platform's ops team worked with the vendor's development team to establish the software architecture (virtual, bare-metal) and to obtain and deploy the required SAP configuration items including the SAP HANA database. The sophisticated landscape required the capacity for additional databases for performance benchmarking. The team initially focused on porting the Vendavo software (PPM) to the SAP landscape. PMM is a Java Enterprise Edition (EE) application requiring a relational database to operate. The PMM's analytics module, Profit Analyzer, used another element called Pricemart as an online analytical processing (OLAP) engine; Pricemart is an in-memory database built by Vendavo. A successful port to SAP HANA would demonstrate three outcomes: (1) the Profit Analyzer could benefit from using SAP HANA Capabilities; (2) PPM could yield improved performance with SAP HANA using a JDBC adapter; and (3) the ability to simplify the Extract/Transport/Load (ETL) to load SAP ECC data to the Profit Analyzer.

The ops team supported the project's focus on performance and scalability by provisioning a one hundred and sixty core SAP HANA bare-metal server with at least one terabyte of RAM. The SAP landscape also included SAP Netweaver and SAP Data Services. Adding complexity, the team also provisioned several virtual machines running windows and Linux; theses resources were part of the Vendavo test harness which included Vendavo's Automation Framework Tests designed to measure the timing of actions by specific web browsers. An Apache J Server was added to generate loads used for testing. Vendavo engineering managed the testing. They collaborated with platform's ops team to monitor testing and to be prepared for possible change management required to refine configurations or tests. The ops team also provided collaboration space where project data, documentation and other notes were stored and shared within the project.

Challenges

An initial and notable challenge was sourcing and scheduling high demand assets such as the compute hardware needed to run and test Vendavo's software within SAP HANA. The ops team was responsible for ensuring the project received the necessary shared resources (from a multi-tenant private cloud) and dedicated resources to achieve the project objectives. Given the complexity, additional time was spent developing the project's statement of work (SOW) to clarify resource needs and to ensure that the partner's hardware and software requests mapped to an executable plan. During these discussions, the project team was able to spell out the project's optimal compute, storage and network requirements, develop a plan for testing sprints, and specify objectives and key milestones. The ops team worked with the project team to keep the project on schedule.

During the SOW and frame agreement development process, the Vendavo team sought adjustments to the platform's standard contract framework. The Vendavo project managers introduced Vendavo-specific contract clauses aimed at protecting their firm's intellectual property. Although the project work involved close collaboration among the partner and the ops team to build the desired work landscape, the Vendavo-specific clauses stated that only the partner's assigned project team members had permission to access its application layer, even for debugging purposes. While non-standard contract clauses were uncommon among co-innovation projects, the ops team coordinated with the legal team to accommodate the request. However, the request also meant that platform ops team engineers could not access the application tier assets in the landscape without permission. As a result, the ops team was somewhat constrained in their abilities to assist with project work on the fly.

Outcomes

The project was a success. Vendavo's software achieved superior performance by porting it to operate on SAP HANA. The project leveraged the platform's demand side services—results were shared in a whitepaper, a recorded demo with voice over, and event presentations. The Profit Analyzer demo showing the systems responsiveness was well designed, making it easy for non-subject matter experts to share the demo with others.

Glossary

Columnar store in-memory database: A database management system that keeps the entirety of the data that it manages in memory at all times. SAP HANA features such an in-memory database as part of its platform.
Apache J Server: A popular web server.
JDBC: Java Database Connectivity is an application programming interface for the programming language Java, which defines how a client may access a database.
Java EE (Java Enterprise Edition): a set of specifications, extending Java standard edition with specifications for enterprise features such as distributed computing and web services.
SAP Netweaver: a software stack used by many SAP applications. The stack can be used for custom development and integration with other applications and systems, and is built primarily using the SAP ABAP as well as Java, C, and C ++ programming languages.

Unified Computing for Big Data Analytics, October 2013

Partners

Cisco, Intel, SAP HANA Development.

Co-innovation Project

Integrating Hardware and Software to Simplify Architecture and Improve Big Data Analytics Performance.

Project Overview and Details

Cisco, a network solutions company, viewed the co-innovation platform as an ideal context for promoting its Unified Computing Systems (UCS) as a platform for SAP big data analytics work. The co-innovation platform had the capacity to provide an SAP analytics systems landscape to support any projects focused on big data analytics, including the ability to host or generate large data sets for test and demo. In collaboration with Intel, Cisco planned to integrate its common platform architecture (CPA) for big data with SAP HANA. Cisco wanted to generate more UCS development by extending its reach in serving organizations associated with SAP's ecosystem.

Intel, a semiconductor company, provided its Apache Hadoop Distribution to the project. Intel wanted to explore whether and how customers took advantage of big data using Intel's Apache Hadoop Distribution integrated with SAP HANA. The technology solution stack had several layers. The stack's lowest layer included the Cisco Unifed Computing System. Next in the stack was the Intel Manager and Intel distribution for Apache Hadoop followed by SAP Data Services providing information management featuring federated access, open APIs and protocols. Applications and SAP Business Objects Business Intelligence was installed and configured at the top of the stack.

SAP Data Services software and SAP HANA Smart Data Access technology was used to enable SAP HANA to work in concert with Intel's Apache Hadoop Distribution. The latter provided SAP HANA new capabilities—specifically, the ability to move high value data from Hadoop storage into memory and to federate queries to the Intel Distribution. SAP HANA operating on Cisco UCS with Intel Distribution was designed to take advantage of hardware-enhanced software to address performance, capacity, and security matters specific to big data analytics. The project team deployed six Cisco UCS C240 servers; UCS C240 servers are two-way platforms based on the Intel Xeon processor E5 family the team used for Hadoop cluster testing. Cisco also deployed 4 UCS C460 servers, its four-way platforms based on the Intel Xeon processor E7 family, for SAP HANA development and testing. SAP developers installed SAP HANA on these machines. Intel developers installed the Intel Distribution on the servers using virtual machines provisioned by the co-innovation platform.

The platform's ops team provided multiple virtual machines to build the necessary Hadoop clusters and to support SAP analytics applications and SAP HANA. The project team worked with several large data sets and varied load generation to create real-world big data scenarios that were large enough to demonstrate how Cisco and Intel's integrations could reduce the total cost of ownership.

Challenges

Big Data deployments using native open source software can be complex, time consuming, and expensive to set up and manage. One challenge was using various big data use cases to demonstrate the system's integrated features, functionality and reduced complexity. The ops team worked with Cisco, Intel, and SAP's big data product team experts to identify the appropriate use cases. The selected use cases provided the opportunity to illustrate which big data architect tasks were reduced or eliminated by the solution.

Outcomes

The project achieved its goals and more. Cisco and Intel worked together to optimize deployment of the Intel Distribution technology on the Cisco UCS CPA for Big Data. The result was an enterprise-class solution that delivered performance and capacity while reducing operational risk and accelerating deployment. The ability to replicate running the UCS at scale for SAP Big Data Analytics work streams resulted in a validated, certified solution of real-time big data analytics on Cisco's UCS infrastructure.

The co-innovation platform also benefitted from the project results. The platform hosts multiple clusters of production capable landscapes with virtual machines and other software. The deployment and validation of UCS verified that the team could now reliably use UCS and make changes across the cluster from a single orchestration console.

Lastly, co-innovating with the platform allowed the team to accelerate solution development. By deploying Cisco UCS CPA for big data in a co-innovation project with the platform, SAP and Intel were able to quickly to configure, optimize, and certify an innovative solution featuring a unified architecture and management using UCS.

Glossary

Big Data: Data that is described in volume, velocity, variety or veracity. Big data also is described as a field that involves methods to analyze and systematically extract and leverage information from large, complex datasets.
Hadoop: Distributed machine learning comprised of a multi-node architect used to segment distribute data compute.
Intel Apache Distribution: Intel's own distribution of Hadoop featuring near real-time analytics w/ HBase & Hive enhancements, Access control, encryption, secure data movement, Job throughput efficiency for HDFS, Dynamic replication for HDFS & HBase.

Creating Automated Workflows to Accelerate Development of High-Powered Database Applications, October, 2014

Partners

RedHat, SAP Sybase Product Development, and SAP Partner Management.

Co-innovation Project

The project proposed developing a database testing environment featuring SAP ASE SAP IQ and SAP SQL Anywhere. The team planned to use a multi-database environment to create a database cartridge that would make it easier for RedHat OpenShift applications developers to gain access to key SAP enterprise database technologies.

Project Overview

RedHat is an enterprise open source solutions provider. The project supported a RedHat and SAP Partner Management group goal of adding ten thousand new customers deploying SAP on Red Hat. The intent was to access additional customers by tapping into the ecosystem and developer communities through Red Hat's OpenShift interface. As background, in 2013, RedHat had completed development of its OpenShift Cartridge for Sybase Adaptive Server Enterprise (ASE) to provide a platform as a service (PaaS) environment. Customers could use the easy to access, on-demand PaaS to build applications on an ASE database. The project scope included building cartridges for Sybase IQ and Sybase SQL Anywhere. Deploying a cartridge for SAP SQL Anywhere on OpenShift would provide developers automated workflows and tooling and facilitate rapid development of database-powered, high performing applications.

Project Details

The project took advantage of a co-innovation platform provisioned system landscape. The platform's operations team worked with RedHat and SAP Sybase engineers to build an SAP systems landscape including SAP ASE, SAP IQ, and SAP SQL Anywhere. The database cartridges developed within this collaboration were used to make it easier for developers creating applications on OpenShift to gain access to key SAP enterprise database technologies.

The project environment also was designed to allow developers to develop, host, and scale applications rapidly in both public cloud (OpenShift Online) and on-premise private cloud (OpenShift Enterprise) environments. OpenShift Online and OpenShift Enterprise are built from the OpenShift Origin open source project. The latter leverages RedHat Enterprise Linux and the SE Linux subsystem for a secure, multi-tenant architecture. The partner managers, either through events hosted by the ops team or webinars and workshops hosted by RedHat, could obtain hands-on access to the cartridges in different database environments.

Challenges

A challenge was building awarenesss and demand. At the time, mobility and cloud strategies were in flux and so too were the markets and emerging PaaS development communities. It was not always an easy sell to drive a developer community to a specific PaaS. The project team worked tirelessly to introduce the capabilities to developers and gain their support.

Outcomes

Many developers learned of Openshift's capabilities for SAP database environments through the project. White papers, hands on interactive demos, live events, and press releases were produced and shared, building awareness and demand. The SAP Data Hub employed Kubernetes clusters with services built into the RedHat OpenShift Container Platform. The RedHat OpenShift Container Platform brings Linux containers and Kubernetes to the enterprise. The platform helps organizations build, deploy, and manage new and existing applications across physical, virtual, or public cloud infrastructures. It is recognized to be a proven, reliable container platform for SAP Data Hub. Additionally, the project contributed to building an Openshift developer community and this activity persisted years beyond the project.

The project results were broadcast in various ways. The project's story also was shared via: Press releases; a white paper; platform hosted events, partner workshops, and business development sessions; SAP SAPPHIRE NOW and Tech Ed; and project catalog (web) content. The project work also was shared with multiple visitors to SAP's executive briefing center. Additionally, the ops team provided demonstrations of the project at SAP and

RedHat marketing events and built awareness with PaaS/SaaS developers. These activities boosted developer confidence in the value of the offering. The storytelling capacity of the co-innovation platform benefitted the project team by elevating the visibility of OpenShift on SAP solution.

SAP Hana Intelligent Data Fusion, October 2009

Partners

Axon AI, SAP National Security Service (NS2).

Co-Innovation Project

Create an Intelligent Data Fusion (IDF) solution on the SAP HANA platform.

Project Overview

Axon AI (formerly Convergent AI) applies artificial intelligence technologies to develop complex reasoning products and solutions. NS2 is focused on national security and is a wholly owned subsidiary of SAP. The project focused on managing the complexity encountered by a data analyst managing data foraging and ingest manually. The team also wanted to demonstrate the value of publicly available information and data and how it could be merged or paired with private data to generate a more intelligent understanding of all data. The project integrated Axon AI's artificial and swarm intelligence capabilities with the SAP HANA Intelligent Data Fusion solution. The goal was to provide a data analyst with more robust accuracy in risk forecasting.

The SAPNS2 HANA IDF Platform is based on a closed loop data-to-information process that is used to create knowledge domains where information can be explored and discovered using a variety of tools and techniques. Figure A.2 depicts the data-to-information process.

Project Details

SAPNS2 began the project by specifying the data fusion architecture. The architecture was designed to integrate and correlate data to create a knowledge base within SAP HANA (via its graph engine) for information exploration and discovery and to serve as the data source for other applications. The SAPNS2 HANA IDF platform includes four tools, a graph search engine, a Smart Content Navigator, a 3rd party tool to provide Link Analysis capability, and a risk forecasting tool from Axon AI. The risk forecasting tool is designed to reduce uncertainty by using a process model that connects

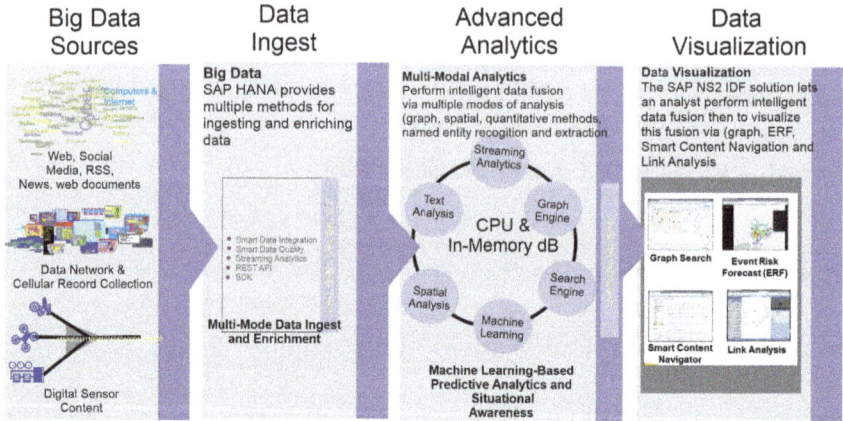

Fig. A.2 SAPNS2 HANA Intelligent Data Fusion (IDF) Platform

past events with their possible origins to analyze and predict future events. Axon AI's risk forecasting tool is delivered through its swarm intelligence and informs SAP's event risk forecasting (ERF) in the IDF platform. The tool's general reasoning and learning approach can be applied to a wide range of domains. One of the tool's key attributes of is the ability to ingest, exploit, make sense of, and create a knowledge base of information that can be used as the source for event risk forecasting. Axon AI's event risk forecasting software required conditioned information in order for the application's swarming model to forecast future events.

Figures A.3 and A.4 illustrate the fusion process that melds structured and unstructured data such as formatted message data, observable events (image/fmv entity extraction), social media, news, RSS feeds, and documents.

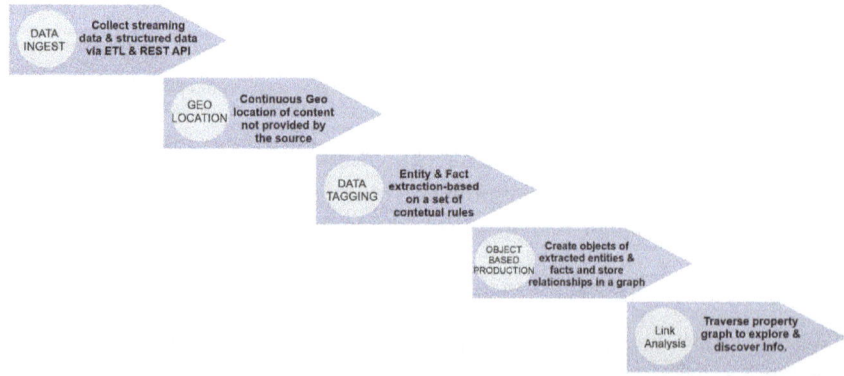

Fig. A.3 SAPNS2 HANA IDF process

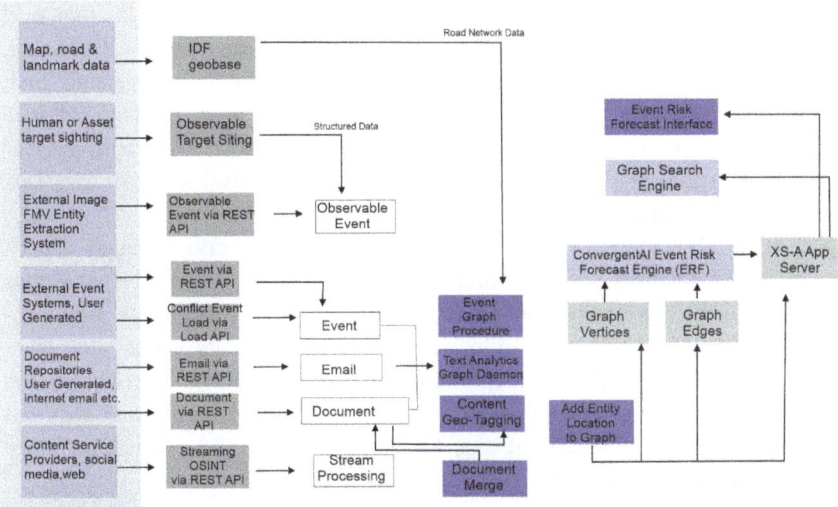

Fig. A.4 SAPNS2 HANA IDF—data sources and flows

The figures provide a high level view of how the fused data is persisted within SAP HANA. Figure A.3 depicts the general data flow and Fig. A.4 shows the flow relative to IDF software system API events and processes.

Event risk forecasting (ERF) requires conditioned information to inform a swarming model to forecast future events. Equally important, the ERF model is implemented as an SAP HANA application. As background:

- ERF depends on the ability to make millions of geospatial calculations when performing risk calculations. The SAP HANA in-memory geospatial engine provides extreme performance without having to move data from an internal data store to an external geospatial engine and back again.
- The ERF engine does not have to perform the function of data ingest and event correlation or establish the spatial and temporal relationships among people, organizations, locations and events and their attributes. SAP HANA performs this function through the integrated use of text analysis and the graph engine.
- SAP HANA has an embedded application server reducing the number of external components required to develop, maintain, deploy, provision, and execute custom analytic applications.
- The integrated use of an in-memory columnar database provides extreme performance due to parallelization across multiple cores/CPUs and advanced data compression techniques. It also simplifies the ERF software design by taking advantage of high speed table scans in lieu of complicated search/query techniques.

- Using ERF on SAP HANA enables it to engage multiple analytical processing functions which include: Text Analysis, Graph Processing, Geospatial Processing, complex, and high speed sql query processing. SAP HANA provides these features in a single integrated analytic software package. The package uses one database where text analysis, graph, geospatial, and quantitative methods can be applied via sql/sql script or Java/Java Script programs.
- SAP HANA computer algorithms improve automatically through experience and data use. This eliminates the need to have multiple external servers provide the aforementioned analytic functions. Tight integration also eliminates the need for application designs to replicate data across processing functions. As a result, the integration significantly reduces the network traffic required to communicate between the analytic functions (none required since they are in the same server) while also increasing overall security since sensitive information can remain in a single database.

The SAPNS2 team built demos using a variety of sample news feeds that aggregated data from service platforms such as Babel-X. The aggregated data was used to derive insights from publicly and commercially available information sources (what SAPNS2 calls OpenINT or open Intelligence, which can be filtered using geospatial, temporal, link analysis, public records search, sentiment, etc.). The project made use of various data sets such as the armed conflict data maintained by the University of Colorado. The landscape supported live and recorded demonstrations using SAP HANA's ability to fuse different data sets. Additionally, the landscape provided an analyst with a variety of analytics reporting and visualization capabilities.

SAPNS2 began its first project landscape with a rack full of Cisco Unified Computing Servers (USC) and network switches. The ops team worked with Cisco and SAPNS2 to obtain the gear permanently to support future projects with SAPNS2. The ops team provided SAPNS2 access to and support for other SAP software systems to enable NS2's own solution work. The SAPNS2 CTO's engineering team led all solutions development from the assets and landscapes deployed to its own project vlan on the co-innovation platform. The ops team also coordinated the daily operations of the SAPNS2 and partner assets and managed project change requests. Lastly, the team also provided an array of virtual machines running Linux and Windows to support the installation and configuration requirements for Axon AI software to perform event risk analysis.

Challenges

SAPNS2's challenge was persuading its customers or clients to engage with them outside of the Washington D.C. beltway. The customers were comfortable with legacy approaches to procurement and often reluctant to consider solutions that were not custom built and used commercial off the shelf (COTS) software. SAPNS2 focused on using SAP technologies wherever and whenever possible to meet a customer's requirements and selectively used partnerships to fill technology gaps.

Another challenge was associated with integrating new AI capabilities that did not overlap with SAP's existing (or planned) core software functionality. Typically, these types of challenges were addressed by sharing executable software architecture and configuration details to support interoperability without involving specific integration details.

Outcomes

SAPNS2's customers valued the solution. The solution provided customers with the ability to ingest open source intelligence into the IDF in a reliable way. As a result, an analyst could stay focused on sense-making rather than be distracted by all of the tasks associated with trying to forage for data. IDF takes advantage of SAP HANA as a platform by avidly using its in-memory data and its geospatial and graph engines. Another outcome from this project was a co-developed research report and white paper on the topics of swarm intelligence and machine learning.

Glossary

Artificial Intelligence (AI): machine-based or machine born intelligence.
Babel X: a platform offered by Babel Street comprised of AI linguistics technology allowing filterable search and analysis of publicly available and commercially available information.
Machine Learning (ML): computer algorithms designed to produce improvement automatically through use of data.
Swarm Intelligence: model and application of some collective behavior of decentralized, self-organized systems, natural or artificial. The concept is often employed in AI work.

Software-Defined Data Centers and Managing Hot, Warm and Cold Data, May 2016

Partners

Vmware (VMW), Hitachi Data Systems (HDS), and SAP Product and Partner Management.

Co-innovation Project

The project focused on Software-defined Data Centers (SDDC) and explored the use of SAP Business Warehouse applications running virtual volumes to address the entire data life cycle of SAP HANA—in-memory component, dynamic tiering, near-line storage, and archiving—as well as any supported combination when creating an SAP HANA landscape.

Project Overview

The project team included Vmware, a virtualization and cloud computing software provider, and SAP partner management with support from an SAP data warehouse product manager. Vmware invited Hitachi Data Systems (HDS) to join the project; the two firms had collaborated on another project using HDS's Unified Compute Platform to formulate SDDC. The organizations collaborated to build a software landscape that simulated an enterprise deployment using SDDC. The purpose was to optimize running and managing an SAP Business Warehouse solution.

Vmware provided the virtual machine technology and capabilities. HDS provided: 1) its Unified Compute Platform (UCP) (which integrated multiple technologies—vSphere, vRealize, and SAP HANA hot/warm/cold dynamic data tiering) and 2) a 42U half populated rack containing its UCP. The ops team brought the system online with HDS and assigned the asset to the project's virtual LAN in the co-innovation platform's environment. SAP provided its business warehouse software to support the project. HDS, Vmware,and the platform's ops team collaborated to integrate the various technologies and systems.

The project provided an opportunity for Vmware to demonstrate its NSX micro-segmentation capabilities for mission critical architectures and to show its scale up and scale out capacity using HDS'sUPC. HDS's UPC was configured to run NSX efficiently. The project created a demanding environment for HDS to readily capture, showcase, and validate its unified compute platform's performance metrics and capabilities. In 2016, HDS also announced support for the Vmware NSX network virtualization platform on its high-performance converged and hyperconverged infrastructure systems.

HDS was interested in delivering the benefits of NSX to its UCP customers to help them automate deployment of applications with complete networking services and advanced network virtualization capabilities. The HDS platform allowed Vmware to create software defined storage using Vmware virtual volumes and storage containers. The software defined storage enabled a system administrator or operator to cast virtual data stores based on the HDS platform's mapping to application and dB requirements of an SAP business warehouse. These data stores address requirements spanning the data lifecycle of SAP HANA where data can be classified as hot (in-memory) to warm as an extension of on disk storage as well as archival cold data.

Project Details

The platform's operations team and the project team created a virtual network design for the SAP Business Warehouse powered by SAP HANA. HDS provided the necessary compute and storage hardware and worked with the ops team's infrastructure engineer to install and operate the HDS system inside the co-innovation platform's computing center. The ops team provided redundant 30 amp breaker boxes to power the 42U half rack and integrated the rack into the project's assigned virtual local area network (vlan) and local computing center resources. The UCP is a software driven architecture that manages chassis or blade compute, Brocade switching fabric for its network interface, and an array of SSD, SAS, and SATA drive storage. The HDS engineers worked closely with Vmware and SAP to configure the SAP Business Warehouse on SAP HANA using HDS's UCP and Vmware's vSphere APIs for storage awareness.

Hitachi's hardware platform covered three categories of storage capabilities:

- Auto-generated capabilities (e.g. RAID type, encryption),
- Managed storage capabilities (e.g. performance class, availability class, cost class)
- Custom capabilities (e.g. availability zone)

Vmware wanted to demonstrate its micro-segmentation capabilities and viewed the SAP Business warehouse as an ideal case given its multiple tiers

(or network zones as SAP calls them). The platform's ops team prepared the HDS hardware, and configured, integrated, and managed all project compute and storage resources to create three zones:
- Client Zone where:
  - access is granted to different clients, such as SQL clients on SAP application servers
  - Features include: browser applications using HTTP/S to communicate with the SAP HANA server; data sources (such as BI) which require a network communication channel to access the SAP HANA database
- Internal Zone which provides:
  - communication between hosts in a distributed SAP HANA system
  - communication replication between two SAP HANA sites
- Storage Zone which allows:
  - data to persist in storage
  - storage to be accessed via a network to provide protection against power or host event failures

The co-innovation platform's ops team and its SAP Basis engineers supported Vmware with the SAP Business Warehouse, installation, and its configuration as well as all project change management activities during validation testing.

Challenges

The project did not encounter any extraordinary technical or execution challenges in part because the partners were veterans of co-innovation work. Veteran co-innovation partners come to the platform prepared to collaborate and with a plan that has executive sponsorship and key stakeholder support. They are familiar with the platform's co-innovation processes; this makes on-boarding easier for the platform's ops team. At the time of the project, market challenges, such as enterprise data centers shifting rapidly to using public cloud, were beginning to emerge. Yet, as late as 2020, the project lead described continued and growing interest in SDDC for on premise enterprise deployments seeking micro-segmentation capability.

Outcome

By decomposing the SAP HANA network specifications and creating a virtual network design, the project:

- Put a face to software defined networks and micro-segmentation
- Made micro-segmentation relevant to application owners and database architects
- Demonstrated that SDDC can be tangible

Value Creation and Seeding Growth: The project's outcome was demonstrated to customers and provided validity for a software-defined storage solution for the SAP Business Warehouse. Customers attending co-innovation events were impressed by what could be accomplished from a centrally located administrator's desktop. The resources demonstrated the functionality and value of using Virtual Volumes as a fundamental model centered around provisioning storage based on application needs rather than on underlying infrastructure. The project also illustrated an additional benefit—how using an application centric model significantly reduces storage design complexity.

Expanding the Opportunity Set: Vmware used the project results to demonstrate software-defined networking via Vmware NSX, including showing how it provides the networking and security foundation for a software defined data center (SDDC). The HDS team delivered the necessary compute and storage resources to a demanding, productive, and scalable SAP Business Warehouse deployment. The testing and validation with Vmware resulted in additional complementary marketing content describing the unified computing platform and its ability to optimize use of Vmware to run SAP via SDDC.

Glossary

Business Warehouse: a model-driven data warehousing product which collects, transforms, and stores data generated in SAP and non-SAP applications and makes it accessible through built-in reporting and business intelligence.

Micro-segmentation: a method of creating zones in data centers and cloud environments to isolate workloads from one another and secure them individually.

NSX: VMware NSX is a network virtualization and security platform that enables the virtual cloud network, a software-defined approach to networking that extends across data centers, clouds, and application frameworks.

RAID: Redundant Array of Inexpensive Disks, combines multiple physical disk drive components into one or more logical units for the purposes of improving performance, efficiency, or redundancy.

SAP Basis: Basis (Business Application Software Integrated solution) is a set of programs and tools from SAP that act as an interface with databases, operating systems, communication protocols, and business applications.

Software Defined Data Center (SDDC): is a data storage facility in which all infrastructure elements—networking, storage, CPU and security—are virtualized and delivered as a service. Deployment, operation, provisioning, and configuration are abstracted from hardware.

Index

A
accelerate 1, 12, 27, 28, 45, 52, 62, 86, 96, 99, 100, 110, 113, 119, 126, 128, 137, 141, 147, 181
Accenture 2, 131
access 2, 6, 8, 11, 13, 23, 24, 26, 27, 29–36, 40, 41, 43, 45, 46, 49, 52, 54, 57, 61, 64, 67, 73, 79, 94, 100, 103–105, 107, 119–121, 126, 127, 130, 137, 138, 140, 148, 149, 156, 157, 160, 161, 165, 169, 170, 173, 174, 178, 179, 182, 183, 188, 192
actors 1–3, 5–7, 10, 13, 18, 21, 22, 25, 27–31, 37, 39, 41, 45, 46, 54, 57, 62–67, 70, 76, 77, 80, 83, 86, 88, 91, 94, 96, 97, 100, 102, 106, 113, 114, 116, 119–121, 123, 129
Adner, Ron 5, 16–18, 49
Airbnb 22, 23, 47
Allen, Scott 11
Alliance Manager 74, 161
Althoff, J. 125, 132
Amazon Web Services (AWS) 23, 125, 126
ambiguity 100
analytics 38, 62, 67, 68, 81, 88, 94, 136, 137, 145–148, 151, 155, 163, 164, 168, 170, 172–174, 177, 179, 180, 187, 188
Anand, B.N. 131
app developers 7, 21, 23, 31, 32, 34
Apple 5, 7, 31, 32, 34
Apple commission rate 31
Apple iOS 7, 23
Apple-tax 31
application program interface (APIs) 35, 78, 101, 112, 128, 132, 153, 157, 179, 187, 191
artificial intelligence (AI) 33, 63, 67, 68, 70, 103, 107, 125, 128, 136, 137, 157, 164, 176, 185, 189
augmented reality (AR) 27, 63, 106, 123, 130
automotive ecosystem 5

awareness 2, 14, 26, 43, 65, 83, 86, 92, 96, 97, 109, 120, 121, 126, 136, 137, 147, 151, 152, 154, 172, 173, 175, 183, 184, 191

B

Barboza, Kathy 12, 19, 73, 75
Barney, J.B. 49
Barry, D. 97
Bartel, C.A. 97, 98
BCG Institute 16
Bellavitis, C. 47
big data 33, 63, 67, 70, 136, 137, 179–181
blockchain 26, 40, 69, 88, 103
blogs 3, 54, 65, 86, 89, 93, 96–98, 139, 161, 166, 170
Bluecoat Systems 39, 43, 62, 124, 136, 145
BMC Innovation Labs 11, 71
BMC Software 11, 71
Boudreau, K. 48
Britehouse 86, 87, 124
Brown, J.S. 98
building 1, 5, 7, 8, 13, 25–27, 35–38, 41, 45, 51, 54, 55, 64, 65, 69, 72–75, 77, 83–86, 88, 89, 93, 97, 105, 111, 120, 122, 123, 127, 128, 142, 145, 147–149, 156, 157, 169, 182, 183
buyin 60, 110, 120, 139

C

capabilities 1, 2, 5–10, 12–14, 18, 19, 21, 23, 26, 27, 29, 30, 34–38, 42, 45, 47, 51–55, 59, 61–64, 66, 67, 69, 70, 74, 76, 77, 79, 81, 87–89, 92–94, 99, 100, 102–104, 107, 121, 123–126, 128, 129, 133, 136, 139, 142, 146, 148, 152, 157, 163, 164, 168, 173, 177, 179, 183, 185, 188–192
Capability Development 10, 13, 29, 122, 124
cases 3, 17, 18, 31, 35, 36, 48, 57–60, 63, 65, 67–69, 72, 84, 87–90, 93, 96–98, 106–108, 110, 112, 123, 126, 129–131, 136, 142, 155–161, 163, 164, 173, 174, 180, 191
Ceccagnoli, M. 48
Cennamo, C. 16, 17, 19, 78
change management 41, 58, 141, 160, 177, 192
Chat bots 36
Chesbrough, Henry 59, 72, 78, 80, 116
CIO 11, 71, 127
Cisco 17, 34, 78, 137, 179–181, 188
Citrix 74, 136, 159–161
cloud 5, 6, 28, 30, 31, 35, 49, 51, 61, 63, 67, 71, 78, 104, 107, 112, 125–129, 132, 138, 157, 163, 165, 168, 177, 183
cloud-based business transformation 15, 125, 126, 129
cloud computing 70, 127, 159, 172, 190
cloud strategy 125, 126, 183
cloud technology 126, 132
coach 15, 58, 59, 86, 101, 120
Coalition for App Fairness 31
co-innovation 1–3, 7–16, 19, 24, 25, 27–30, 32–46, 49, 51–54, 56–64, 66–79, 81, 83–86, 88, 90–94, 96, 97, 99–117, 119–126, 128–132, 139, 140, 145, 147, 149, 150, 157, 160, 163, 164, 166, 169, 172, 178, 181, 192, 193
co-innovation as behavior 8, 15, 40, 86, 99

co-innovation enablement 13, 122, 123
co-innovation platform 1–4, 6–15, 19, 21, 22, 24–40, 42, 44–46, 49, 51–54, 56, 57, 60, 61, 63, 64, 66, 68–72, 74–78, 80, 81, 83, 87, 89, 94, 95, 97, 99, 100, 102, 105, 107, 110–114, 119–122, 124, 128–131, 138, 142, 145, 147–149, 156, 159–161, 164, 169, 172, 174, 179, 180, 182, 184, 188, 190–192
co-innovation platform strategy 16, 22, 27, 120
co-innovation project origins 120
co-innovation project process 57
co-innovation strategy 15, 112, 125
collaboration 2, 6, 8, 9, 12, 13, 16, 26–28, 31, 36, 37, 39, 42, 43, 46, 59, 64, 72–74, 80, 84, 86, 95, 97, 99, 100, 104–106, 113, 116, 123, 125, 129, 130, 140, 175, 178, 179, 183
collaboration space 38, 177
communication 72, 89–91, 101, 106, 108, 151, 153, 154, 164, 192
complementary 1, 2, 5–9, 12, 18, 21, 23, 24, 26–30, 32, 33, 36, 38, 39, 44, 46, 52, 56, 57, 61, 66, 78, 86, 87, 89, 99, 100, 104, 106, 107, 121, 128, 152, 163, 164, 166, 167, 193
complementors 1, 5, 7–9, 12, 13, 18, 19, 23–25, 27, 29–34, 36, 37, 42, 54, 55, 57–59, 65, 66, 76, 114, 121, 128
Continuum of Resource openness 33
contract 8, 29, 33, 34, 39–41, 54, 56–60, 86, 100–102, 110–114, 121, 169, 178
contract development 58, 100, 112, 113, 121

contract formation 3, 12, 13, 15, 29, 34, 40, 54, 56, 59, 60, 71, 77, 84, 86, 100, 101, 106, 110, 111, 113, 117, 120–123, 130, 139
control 1, 6, 31, 32, 48, 64, 100, 103, 108, 114, 141, 151, 161, 164, 174
coordination 101, 102, 122
core offering 23, 24, 29, 30, 43, 44, 77, 112, 114
core product 6, 9, 56, 69
core service 7, 51, 53–55, 67, 120
Critigen 1, 11, 40, 102
cross-side network effects 25
Cruise 5
CTO 1, 40, 74, 102, 127, 166, 188
customer 1, 5, 7, 11, 13, 18, 21, 23, 25, 30, 35–39, 42–44, 46, 49, 51, 54, 55, 60, 62, 67, 69–71, 74, 78, 87–89, 94–96, 99, 102–106, 109, 112, 114, 115, 123, 125, 127–130, 132, 139–141, 145–147, 149, 152, 154, 156, 157, 159, 160, 163, 164, 167, 168, 172, 173, 175, 176, 179, 182, 189, 191, 193
Cusumano, M.A. 17, 18, 26, 46–48

D

dairy cooperative 40, 43, 99, 104, 106, 129
degree of openness 29, 31, 46
Delios, A. 131
Dell EMC 92, 137, 172, 174
Deloitte Insights 131
demand 14, 22, 23, 83, 86, 88, 93, 96, 97, 105, 121, 142, 145, 160, 177, 183
demand-side services 2, 13, 14, 24, 26, 29, 33, 34, 36, 41, 45, 51, 53–55, 57, 58, 66, 76, 83, 84,

88, 89, 93, 96, 97, 120, 121, 130, 139, 178
demand-side users 22
De Meyer, A. 17
Demo & Showcase 10, 24, 45, 53, 54, 56, 83, 88, 97, 120, 139, 147
demo development 15, 29, 54, 71, 89, 97, 120
demo recording 91
demos 14, 34–36, 38, 54, 62, 65, 66, 73, 75, 76, 79, 81, 83, 84, 89–96, 109, 124, 139, 145–147, 150, 152, 154, 157–162, 164–167, 170, 173, 174, 178, 179, 183, 188
development 10, 11, 14, 23, 25, 27, 30, 32, 34, 37, 39, 41, 43, 46, 52, 61–63, 70, 72, 73, 78, 79, 84–87, 89, 93, 96, 97, 100, 107–109, 111, 115, 116, 121, 125, 126, 128, 130, 133, 136–138, 140, 143, 155, 157, 168, 170, 178–183, 188
devOps 126, 128, 133
diagnosing 9, 27, 119
diagnosis 9, 28, 119
Didi Chuxing 22
digital-based business transformation 15, 125, 126, 129
digital tool kits 8, 23
digital twin technology 104, 105, 123, 129, 130
Dignan, L. 132
direct network effects 22
diseconomies of scope 32
DNA 52
drone 107
Duguid, P. 98
Dunbar, R.L.M. 98
Dyer, J.H. 19, 114
dynamic capability 8, 17, 18

E

early stage 3, 27, 32, 39, 43, 70, 113, 157
eBay 22, 136, 138, 139
economies of innovation 25, 28, 32, 46, 119
ecosystem 1–9, 11, 12, 14–18, 21, 27–30, 32, 34, 36–39, 41–46, 48, 54, 56–58, 61–63, 67, 69, 70, 74, 76, 77, 79, 83, 85, 88, 91, 94, 96, 97, 113, 119, 120, 122–124, 128–131, 141, 156, 179, 182
ecosystem generativity 28, 78, 84, 119, 129
ecosystem strategy 2, 5, 6, 16, 27, 131
ecosystem trajectory 6, 8, 57, 76, 121
edge computing 92, 93, 103, 125, 136, 137, 164, 172, 173, 175
efficiency 25, 87, 125, 136, 166, 193
Eisenmann, T.R. 47
Elephants, Rhinos and People (ERP) 107
Elmes, M. 97
enabling co-innovation 9, 13, 54, 66, 122
Enterprise Resource Planning (ERP) 35, 156, 159, 173
equitable value distribution 15, 45, 106, 113, 119, 120, 122, 130
Ericsson 5, 6
event hosting 89, 97
events 14, 15, 26, 36, 38, 39, 54, 63, 68–71, 73, 77, 80, 81, 84, 86, 88, 89, 91, 93–96, 116, 120, 124, 139, 147, 150, 154, 157, 160, 161, 164, 166, 174, 178, 183, 184, 186, 187, 192, 193
exchange hazards 100, 111, 113, 115, 122, 123

experiences 3, 7, 11, 18, 27, 36, 37, 39, 40, 67, 71, 73, 77, 78, 83, 84, 86, 89, 93, 96, 97, 104–106, 109, 110, 121–123, 125, 130, 131, 136, 139, 144–146, 153, 162, 167, 188
experiential learning 10, 37, 124
experimental 102, 106, 122
exposure 8, 10, 34, 36–38, 49, 62, 94, 124
externalities 38

F
F5 Networks 73
feedback processes 108
Fiat-Chrysler 5
Fleming, Lee 65
flexibility 59, 103, 108, 169
food transparency 43, 104
Ford 5, 6, 17
foreground IP 111, 112
for the platform 7, 13, 15, 23, 39, 56, 59, 93, 100, 108, 113, 120, 122, 123, 192
frame agreement 29, 33, 41, 54, 59, 60, 86, 100–103, 110, 111, 113, 178
Fuller, J. 17

G
Garud, Raghu 49, 97, 98
Gawer, Annabelle 16–18, 26, 46–48
General Motors (GM) 5
generativity 13, 19, 57, 58, 64, 66, 72, 74, 77, 78, 122, 123
Gerolsteiner Brunnen GmGH & Co. 30
Google 2, 5, 83
Google Android 7, 21, 23
Google Cloud 12, 73

governance 12–14, 22, 23, 29–31, 37, 45, 46, 114, 119, 121, 122, 130
growth 1, 4, 5, 8, 12–14, 22, 25, 27, 29, 30, 32, 33, 36, 42, 45, 52, 57, 68, 97, 99, 113, 119, 123–125, 128, 129, 131, 142
growth paths 13, 122
GS1 26, 88, 124, 129
Gugnani, Vidya 99

H
Hagedorn, Pascal 102
hands-off 7, 8, 33, 34, 76
hands-on 2, 7, 8, 34, 35, 45, 57, 76, 119–121, 130, 175, 183
Harnessing complexity 29, 39, 41, 46, 120
Held, Rudi 21, 52
Helfat, C.E. 18, 47, 48
Henderson, Rebecca 65, 80
Henisz, W.J. 131
hierarchical 1, 6, 64, 100, 103
Hitachi Data Systems (HDS) 78, 94, 137, 190–193
Hoopes, D. 49
house rules 60, 73, 103
hybrid cloud 49, 126
hyperscalers 49, 126–128

I
Iansiti, M. 17
Illumiti 90, 108, 117, 124, 129, 136, 151, 152, 154
Incentivizing 30
Industrial Internet of Things (IIoT)/Internet of Things (IoT) 5, 12, 28, 33, 35, 37, 38, 63, 67–70, 87, 90, 92, 93, 103, 108, 125, 136–138, 151, 152, 154, 156, 163, 164, 166, 168, 173, 174

informal interactions 24, 25, 72, 77
information asymmetries 100
infrastructure-as-a-service 126
innovation ecosystems 7
innovation platforms 7, 21, 23, 24, 32, 45, 76, 121, 124
integrated services 25, 27
integration 11, 16, 23, 35, 36, 43, 51, 60, 65, 67, 69, 76, 90, 92, 107, 108, 111, 112, 127, 128, 133, 136, 148, 151, 157, 159, 160, 164, 168, 169, 178, 180, 188, 189
Intel 5, 11, 64, 66, 73–75, 136, 137, 140, 142, 179–181
intellectual property (IP) 15, 30, 31, 52, 59, 60, 101, 111, 112, 120, 163, 178
INTENSE AG 30, 31, 107, 124
interactions 2, 5, 6, 11, 17, 21, 22, 25, 27, 29, 31, 36, 38, 40, 41, 52, 57, 65, 73, 74, 80, 101, 102, 106, 108, 111, 120, 121, 129
interdependencies 5, 18, 102
intersects 13, 166
IoT and the mining industry 90, 91
iterative development 10, 41, 59, 71, 101, 108, 124, 143
iterative learning 108, 120, 122, 143
IT Systems Landscape 3, 34, 120

J

Jacobides, M.G. 16, 17
Joint learning 6, 17, 27, 57, 69, 120

K

Kale, P. 19, 114–116
Kaplan, Sarah 65, 79, 80
Karnøe, P. 98
key performance indicators (KPIs) 61, 70, 142

Khanna, T. 131
Klein, C. 125
knowledge broker 27, 29, 41, 54, 58, 61, 62, 65–67, 77, 106, 130, 142, 143, 147, 170
knowledge broker capabilities 62, 63, 66, 144
knowledge brokering 13, 34, 54, 62, 120–122, 144
knowledge building 58
knowledge flows 62
knowledge gaps 63
knowledge sharing 10, 25, 62, 77, 106, 120, 124, 175
Kore.ai 11, 35, 71, 124, 136, 156, 166

L

Lakkundi, Sam 11, 12, 35, 39, 71
Lampel, J. 98
launch 6, 10, 34, 77, 139
legitimacy 3, 34, 38, 39
Leiblein, M. 47
Levien, R. 17
Lieberman, M. 47
limited liability clauses 59, 101
Lyft 5, 6, 17, 23
Lyman, M. 16, 131

M

machine learning (ML) 28, 33, 38, 68, 70, 92, 109, 125, 128, 137, 153, 164, 173–176, 189
Madsen, T.L. 49
managed service provider (MSP) 128, 132, 165
Mapleleaf Foods 39, 43
marketing 52, 67, 76, 86–89, 93, 95, 96, 175, 184, 193
marketing content creation 89
Markman, G.D. 47
matchmaking 22, 25, 46

material artifacts 83, 97
Meggiorin, K. 47, 48
Michelin PAX run flat 18
Microsoft 5, 6, 17, 125, 128, 132
Microsoft Azure 6, 125
milk 43, 104, 105, 116, 123
mineral water 30, 31, 98, 107, 129
MineSafe Smartwatch 90, 108, 151, 152
mining 35, 65, 70, 83, 90, 91, 99, 108, 117, 124, 129, 136, 151–154
mission 52, 94, 139, 190
mobility ecosystem 5
mobilizing participation 29, 36, 46, 120
Monsta project 64, 66, 87, 124, 142
Mtell 92, 137, 172, 173
multi-cloud 125–128, 140
multi-cloud by accident 125
multilateral 1, 2, 59, 114
multi-purpose space 80, 95
mutual understanding 15, 86, 101–104, 121, 142

N

narratives 41, 45, 54, 83–85, 87, 94, 97, 98, 121, 175
NetApp 12, 51, 78
network 5, 8, 10, 12, 13, 21, 22, 24, 27, 34, 36, 54, 61–63, 65, 71, 80, 94, 104, 121–124, 132, 137, 138, 140, 142, 145–147, 161, 163, 165, 169, 172, 174, 177, 179, 188, 191–193
network effects 22
network relationships 24, 120
Nissan 5
non-generic complements 23
non-linear 40, 41, 108, 113
novel intersections 10, 25, 69, 124, 166
Nvidia 136, 159–161

O

objectives 9, 14, 21, 24, 26, 29–32, 34, 45, 51–53, 56, 59, 61, 62, 67, 68, 70, 71, 78, 87, 88, 99, 100, 102, 108, 110–115, 120, 129, 130, 139, 140, 142, 143, 154, 159, 169, 172, 173, 176, 177
oil and gas 27, 35, 68, 92, 103, 124, 137, 172, 174
operations management team (ops team) 26, 32–36, 40, 41, 53–72, 75–78, 83–90, 93–97, 100–103, 105–107, 110–113, 121, 123, 130, 139, 141, 144, 146, 147, 149, 152, 153, 156, 157, 159, 164, 165, 168–170, 174–178, 180, 183, 188, 190–192
orchestrating 6, 76, 130
orchestration 13, 28, 46, 48, 121–123, 181
orchestrator 28, 46, 53, 120, 123
organizational benefits 10, 13, 120, 122–124
organizational memory 13, 41, 65, 66, 77, 85, 122
OSIsoft 67, 68, 124, 136, 148, 149
outcome story development 84, 97

P

Palo Alto, California 3, 19, 38, 68, 69, 71, 73, 75, 80, 89, 94, 95, 147, 161
Parker, G.G. 48
partner 1, 3, 8–15, 25, 27, 29, 30, 33–42, 44, 47, 49, 56–67, 69–72, 74, 75, 77–79, 83, 86–89, 91, 93, 94, 96, 99–104, 106, 107, 109–116, 120–125, 128, 130, 136, 137, 139–145, 149, 151, 156, 159,

160, 163, 169, 172, 173, 177, 178, 182, 183, 188, 190, 192
partner identification 13, 122
partnership failure 8
Peteraf, M. 18
Pidun, U. 16
Pisano, G. 18
Pixel Velocity 92, 137, 172
plan of the book 14, 15
platform as stage 94, 120
platform-based ecosystem 7, 9, 12, 18, 27, 28, 46–48, 64, 77, 78, 120, 121
platform benefits 22, 29, 65, 71
platform builder 59
platform governance 13, 28, 29, 32, 119, 122
platform memory management 85, 97
platform owner 7, 14, 28, 31, 38, 39, 42, 46, 100, 101
podcasts 54, 86, 89, 93, 96, 97, 139, 150
portfolio management 69
practices 1, 6, 9, 12, 14, 15, 29, 37, 42, 45, 58, 59, 86, 88, 99, 100, 103, 107, 110, 112–114, 116, 123, 141
problem-solving 10, 12, 37, 54, 57, 77, 84, 86, 103, 124, 130, 143
process story development 84, 97
productive collaboration 15, 45, 52, 101, 121
project management 10, 41, 54, 71, 108, 124, 139, 144
project opportunities 10, 29, 36, 69, 77, 124
project plan 56, 59, 101, 173
project portfolio 13, 29, 32, 45, 54, 58, 61, 67, 68, 72, 122
project proposal 14, 29, 32, 33, 41, 56, 57, 59, 68, 100, 108, 113, 139, 145, 157
project risk 100, 110
project team 24, 25, 30, 34–36, 38, 40, 51, 55–57, 59, 61, 63, 64, 66, 69–71, 73, 77–79, 84–87, 89, 91, 92, 94–97, 100, 101, 110, 112, 113, 115, 122, 139, 140, 142–144, 146–149, 156, 159, 160, 166, 170, 173, 174, 177, 178, 180, 183, 184, 190, 191
proof of concept (POC) 30, 39, 43, 71, 87, 109, 143, 147, 152, 161, 169, 175
proposal 56, 59, 78, 84, 86, 100–102, 111, 121
protect and manage 3, 34, 39, 54, 58
provisioning 12, 52, 54, 57, 58, 68, 76, 120, 160, 177, 193, 194
publications 34, 54, 69, 70, 157
public cloud 125–128, 183, 192
Puccio, Christine 73

Q

QR code 43, 104, 105, 123
quality 23, 24, 29, 39, 46, 140, 143, 162

R

Raubitschek, R.S. 18, 47, 48
reciprocal interactions 6
recombination 5, 6, 11, 41, 42, 65, 72
recombinatory learning 10, 11, 124
Red Hat 74, 182, 183
Reeves, Martin 16, 17
Ref, R. 16, 131
relational complexity 29, 41, 111
relational governance 13, 100, 102, 113, 120, 122, 123
resource openness 24, 29, 31, 33, 35, 45, 46

Index

resources 1–3, 7–10, 12–14, 21, 23, 26, 27, 29, 30, 33–37, 40–43, 45–47, 49, 51, 53, 54, 56–62, 64–66, 68, 69, 71, 72, 76–79, 93, 100, 101, 103, 104, 107, 110, 111, 113, 119, 121, 127, 130, 132, 138, 142–145, 148, 152, 164, 177, 191, 193

results 2, 3, 10, 11, 23, 24, 26–28, 30, 32, 34–36, 38, 39, 41, 43, 45, 52–55, 57–62, 64–66, 71, 74–76, 83, 84, 87–89, 92, 94, 103, 104, 109–112, 121, 123, 126, 127, 131, 139, 142, 143, 147, 148, 153, 160, 161, 163, 164, 166, 169, 170, 173, 174, 176, 178, 180, 183, 188, 189, 193

RFID 26, 88, 103

Rietveld, J. 47, 48

risk 28, 32, 69, 70, 108–111, 114, 116, 120, 122, 126, 151–153, 155, 180, 187, 188

roadmap 3, 10, 13, 56, 67, 68, 124, 157

Rochet, J.C. 46

Rohr, J. 47, 48, 114, 116, 117

Royal Swaziland Sugar Corporation (RSSC) 86, 87, 124

S

SAP 1, 3, 11, 19, 26, 30, 34–36, 38–40, 43, 44, 49, 52, 62–64, 67–71, 73–75, 79, 81, 87, 90, 92, 94, 98, 102, 107, 108, 125, 128, 136–143, 145–149, 151, 152, 156, 157, 159–164, 168, 169, 172, 173, 176, 177, 179–183, 185, 186, 188–193

SAP Ariba 136, 138

SAP Co-innovation lab (COIL) 3, 11, 35, 37, 51, 52, 74, 75, 99, 165

SAP HANA 23, 30, 67, 68, 74, 81, 94, 107, 136, 137, 147, 149, 151–154, 156, 159, 164, 168–170, 173, 176–180, 185, 187–192

SAP Industry Business Unit (IBU) 92, 137, 172, 173, 175

SAP National Security Service (NS2) 74, 94, 124, 137, 185–189

SAP SAPPHIRE NOW 139, 145, 161

Schilling, Melissa 47

Schneider, Andreas 105

Schussler, M. 16

Schwarzwaldmilch, Dairy Cooperative in the Black Forest, Germany 104, 105, 123, 124

scope 2, 5, 13, 27–29, 33, 35, 41, 51, 52, 54, 56, 60, 66, 67, 69, 71, 72, 77, 87, 101, 107–109, 111, 113, 114, 116, 122, 123, 130, 140–143, 147, 152, 164, 173, 182

Seamans, R. 47, 48

seeding 13, 122, 149, 193

services 1, 6–9, 12, 18, 19, 21–24, 26, 27, 29–31, 33, 34, 36, 38–42, 52, 54–63, 68, 69, 71–73, 76, 77, 87–89, 93, 96, 100, 102, 106, 112, 113, 120, 121, 123, 126–128, 130, 133, 136, 139–141, 147, 148, 159, 168, 172, 177, 179, 183, 188, 191, 194

shaping innovation 3, 6, 8, 121

shared vision 101, 104, 108, 120

Shiplov, A. 18

showcase 15, 36, 38, 52, 54, 57, 69, 76, 86, 87, 89, 93, 95, 96, 124, 146, 191

showcasing 13, 34, 54, 55, 58, 70, 73, 75, 76, 85, 94, 97, 120, 122, 154, 166

Shuen, A. 18
Silicon Valley 53, 63, 75, 95, 161
simplicity 7, 28, 59
sine qua non 104, 105, 123, 124
Singh, H. 18, 19, 114–116
smart packaging 104–106, 116
SOASTA 136, 140–142
solution briefs 15, 54, 89, 93, 96, 97, 130, 161
solutions 2, 3, 6, 7, 9–11, 26, 30, 35–37, 39, 42, 43, 51, 52, 54, 62, 67, 70, 71, 74, 77, 83, 86, 87, 89, 90, 93, 94, 96, 103–105, 107, 108, 112, 114, 125, 128–130, 136–142, 145, 146, 148–152, 156, 157, 163, 164, 166–168, 170, 172, 173, 175, 179–181, 184, 185, 188, 189, 193, 194
solution validation 123
Sorenson, Olav 65, 79, 80
spillovers 10, 25, 27, 37, 73, 74, 124
statement of work (SOW) 27, 29, 33, 40, 41, 56, 59–61, 71, 72, 86, 100–103, 110, 111, 113, 177, 178
Stellium 38, 124, 136, 163–167
stories 16, 45, 46, 60, 77, 83–87, 89, 93, 95–97, 113, 114, 116, 121, 124, 157, 167, 174, 183
storytelling 14, 15, 54, 58, 66, 83–89, 93, 95–97, 120, 121, 130, 184
storytelling opportunities 87
storytelling process 93
strategic alliances 51
strategic benefits 10, 13, 122
strategy 1, 2, 5, 6, 8, 9, 14, 16, 17, 45, 68, 71, 120, 125, 128, 129
subject matter experts 26, 29, 30, 41, 57, 64, 66, 68, 70, 89, 107, 142, 146, 149, 155, 161, 174, 178
sugar mills 87

Supermicro 64, 66, 136, 140–142, 160
suppliers 1, 5, 22, 23, 54, 103, 114, 128
supply-side services 2, 14, 24, 27, 34, 36, 45, 53–55, 57, 58, 76, 77, 112, 121
sustaining participation 29, 36, 46, 120
symbiosis 65
synthesis 65

T

talent 63, 107, 127, 128
Tangoe 136, 168–170
technology 1, 3, 5, 7, 11, 13, 16, 19, 21, 23, 26–29, 31, 35, 36, 39, 40, 42, 44, 51, 54, 61–67, 70–75, 78, 79, 81, 85, 87, 88, 94, 96, 102, 104–107, 109, 116, 122, 123, 125, 127–132, 137, 140, 143, 146, 151, 152, 154, 156–159, 164, 168, 170, 173, 179, 180, 182, 183, 189, 190
Teece, D.J. 16–18, 47, 48
Telit 37, 38, 124, 136, 163–167
temporal complexity 40
tire treads 26
Tirole, J. 46
transaction platforms 21–23, 25, 32, 45
trends 28, 63, 67
trust-building 15, 102, 103, 111, 121
Tuertscher, P. 49
Turchoie, Tom 1, 40

U

Uber 2, 5, 6, 17, 22, 23, 32, 47
uncertainty 19, 27, 100, 103, 106, 156, 185

use value 6, 7, 13, 18, 23, 24, 29, 30, 43, 44, 56, 65, 69, 77, 122
utility 21, 24, 26, 27, 42, 44

V

Vakili, Keyvan 65, 79, 80
Value capture 10, 23, 29, 42, 77, 122, 139
value creation 1, 2, 6, 9–14, 24, 33, 42–44, 56, 58, 65, 121–123, 125, 129, 193
value distribution 8, 14, 24, 25, 29, 31, 42, 46, 47
value minus cost 42, 44
Van Alstyne, M. 48
Van de Ven, A. 49
Vandrico Solutions Inc. 90, 108
Vendavo 137, 176–178
Vicarious learning 10, 37, 124
Virtual Power Systems (VPS) 44, 124, 127
Vmware (VMW) 137, 190–193
Vodafone 5

W

Walker, G. 49, 115
Wang, Y. 47

Wareham, J. 19, 78
Wartenberg, Roland 51
Waymo 5
Wei, L. 47
West, J. 48
wide lens 5
Williamson, P.J. 17, 47
willingness to pay 23, 42
Winter, S.G. 18
with the platform 11, 14, 15, 21, 22, 24–27, 29–31, 34, 36–39, 41–43, 45, 51, 56, 57, 59, 62, 64, 71, 74, 77, 83, 86, 87, 100, 105, 110, 112, 113, 120, 122, 123, 147, 161, 174, 181, 192
Wright, O. 16, 131

Y

Yamssi, Merlin 83
Yoffie, D.B. 18, 26, 46, 47

Z

zero harm industry 70
Zittrain, J. 19
zoo effect 75, 94, 120

Ingram Content Group UK Ltd.
Milton Keynes UK
UKHW021423150623
423489UK00002B/190